PRAYERS ALLEGED TO BE JEWISH

Printed in the United States of America
on acid-free paper

Program in Judaic Studies
Brown University
BROWN JUDAIC STUDIES

Number 65

PRAYERS ALLEGED TO BE JEWISH
An Examination of the
Constitutiones Apostolorum

by
David A. Fiensy

PRAYERS ALLEGED TO BE JEWISH
An Examination of the *Constitutiones Apostolorum*

by
David A. Fiensy

Scholars Press
Chico, California

PRAYERS ALLEGED TO BE JEWISH
An Examination of the *Constitutiones Apostolorum*

by
David A. Fiensy

Library of Congress Cataloging in Publication Data

Fiensy, David A.
Prayers alleged to be Jewish.

(Brown Judaic studies ; no. 65)
Bibliography: p.
1. Prayers, Early Christian—History and criticism.
2. Apostolic constitutions. I. Apostolic constitutions.
English & Greek. 1985. II. Title. III. Series.
BV236.F53 1985 264'.01201 85-10708
ISBN 0-89130-795-8 (alk. paper)
ISBN 0-89130-796-6 (pbk. : alk. paper)

Printed in the United States of America
on acid-free paper

TABLE OF CONTENTS

LIST OF ABBREVIATIONS

AC	*Constitutiones Apostolorum*
ANF	*Ante-Nicene Fathers*, ed. A. Roberts, J. Donaldson, and A. C. Coxe. Volume 7.
Arnim	I. Arnim, *Stoicorum Veterum Fragmenta*
Bunsen	C.K.J. von Bunsen, *Analecta Ante-Nicaena*. Volume 1.
CL	Clementine Liturgy
Darnell	D. R. Darnell, "Hellenistic Synagogal Prayers," *Pseudepigrapha of the Old Testament*, ed. J. H. Charlesworth
HTR	*Harvard Theological Review*
HUCA	*Hebrew Union College Annual*
JBL	*Journal of Biblical Literature*
JE	Jewish Encyclopedia
JJS	*Journal of Jewish Studies*
JQR	*Jewish Quarterly Review*
JTS	*Journal of Theological Studies*
Lampe	G.W.H. Lampe, *A Patristic Greek Lexicon*
LCL	Loeb Classical Library
LSJM	H. G. Liddell, R. Scott, H. S. Jones, and R. McKenzie, *A Greek-English Lexicon*
MGWJ	*Monatschrift für die Geschichte und Wissenschaft des Judentums*
Migne	J.-P. Migne, *Patrologiae: Series Graeca*. Volume 1, cols. 555-1155
NTS	New Testament Studies
REJ	*Revue des études juives*
RSV	Holy Bible: Revised Standard Version
TDNT	*Theological Dictionary of the New Testament*, ed. G. Kittel et al.
ZAW	*Zeitschrift für die alttestamentliche Wissenschaft*
ZNW	*Zeitschrift für die neutestamentliche Wissenschaft und die Kunde der ältern Kirche*

LIST OF CHARTS AND TABLES

ACKNOWLEDGEMENTS

In the summer of 1978, while working as a research assistant to Professor J. H. Charlesworth of Duke University, I was introduced to the notion that a Jewish stratum underlay portions of the liturgy in the AC. The present monograph results from that introduction. I am especially indebted to Professor Charlesworth for his valuable advice in this project. His assistance has been unflagging.

I would also like to thank Kentucky Christian College for the generous subsidy that made this publication possible, and Mr. James McKenzie of the college who kindly spent his time investigating the merits of this publication.

I am also grateful to Professor Jacob Neusner and Brown Judaic Studies for assistance in the publication of my work.

In addition, I wish to thank Professor Carol Phillips for help in proof-reading the English text of the work.

Finally, I want to thank my wife, Molly, *animae dimidium meae*, without whose patience and loving encouragement this work could not have been completed.

CHAPTER I

HISTORY OF THE DISCUSSION OF THE ALLEGED JEWISH PRAYERS

As early as 1893, K. Kohler[1] suggested that the *Constitutiones Apostolorum* (AC) contained prayers that originated in Judaism. He was more concerned at that time to establish the milieu of the prayers than to prove that the prayers were actually Jewish. Since Kohler argued that Essenism was the fountainhead for the prayers of the Synagogue, he referred to the prayers as Christian-Essene liturgy.[2] Kohler understood the Essenes to be the descendants of the ancient Hasideans and the preservers of their thought as found in the synagogal prayers and some of the prayers in AC.[3] Kohler's understanding of the Essene sect must be questioned because of his uncritical use of the Talmud as a source of historical information, his assumption that what was said about the Hasideans applied to the Essenes, and the discovery (since his time) of the Dead Sea scrolls which have greatly expanded the knowledge of the Essenes.[4] The alleged Essene background will be discussed in more detail in a later chapter.

Kohler worked out his thesis about the prayers in AC in three subsequent publications.[5] In book seven of AC is a modified form of the first six of the Jewish Seven Denedictions for Sabbaths and festivals. Kohler asserted that AC 7.33 is parallel to the first benediction, 7.34 to the second, and 7.35 to the third benediction and the Kedusha which is sometimes inserted into the third. AC 7.36 is parallel to the fourth benediction and to Jewish prayers for the Sabbath, and 7.37 is parallel to the fifth benediction. AC 7.38 is an expansion of the sixth benediction.[6] These prayers, according to Kohler, are all pre-Christian and the product of the Jewish Hasideans or Essenes of "Hellenic culture."[7] The church received the prayers in the second century--before Pauline Christianity was predominant--in the Greek form, and inserted the word "Christ" here and there for "Logos" along with similar substitutions. The Jewish Christians who adopted the prayers and incorporated them into the church's worship were probably themselves Essenes.[8]

W. Bousset[9]--apparently without any knowledge of Kohler's publications[10]--subjected the material to a linguistic and source-critical analysis. Bousset began his argument by examining the prayers which most clearly seem Jewish. Thus AC 7.35 quite obviously contains the Kedusha (sanctification of God based on the theophanies of Isa 6:3 and Ezek 3:12) and AC 7.36 which explains the importance of the Sabbath must have been written by a Jew. Since the only mention of Sunday in AC 7.36 comes awkwardly at the very end of the prayer and seems to contradict what has been said before about the Sabbath, that passage must be considered an interpolation. Thus the first two prayers which Bousset examined seemed to him incontestably Jewish.[11]

From this point on, however, the arguments grow weaker and Bousset became increasingly less sure of his results. He used various means to argue for Jewish authorship of the other prayers, often having to rely on a combination of rather weak arguments. Bousset's examination of individual prayers will be evaluated later, but for now his methodology can be summarized. He sought to demonstrate the Jewish authorship of the prayers by: discovering thoughts or expressions which are peculiarly Jewish or which occur in Jewish literature and liturgy;[12] showing that the author(s) of the prayers used a Jewish version of the Greek Old Testament (i.e. Aquila);[13] pointing out inconsistencies between the distinctively Christian sections and the rest of the prayer;[14] citing passages where he would expect a Christian author to speak of Christ or other New Testament characters.[15] To a lesser extent, Bousset also argued that if the Christian elements could be easily slipped out of the text without changing the flow of thought, they were interpolations (and therefore the rest of the prayer was Jewish).[16]

Kohler had only claimed in his later publications that prayers in book seven of AC were Jewish (7.33-38 and 7.26, see Chart A), seven prayers in all, and that though book eight had similar prayers, they had become so thoroughly Christianized that the relationship to the Seven Benedictions of the Synagogue was entirely lost.[17] Bousset concluded that AC had incorporated a Jewish prayer collection (*Gebetssammlung*) from the Synagogue in book seven. Furthermore by comparing these prayers with some of those of book eight which seem Jewish, he asserted that some of the prayers in the eighth book were based on sources common to the Jewish prayers in book seven, while other prayers were based on the very prayers of book seven themselves. Thus, Bousset found seventeen Jewish prayers in all in AC 7 and 8 (see Chart A).

Since there is some evidence that the author(s) of the prayers used Aquila's version, Bousset maintained that the prayers represent late diasporic Judaism, from the second half of the second century A.D. The prayers, then, have preserved the liturgy of the Greek Synagogue from that time.[18]

Kohler's most detailed analysis of the prayers had been only a translation with a few scattered notes, and Bousset, though he took greater pains to prove the Jewish origin of the prayers, scarcely went beyond that effort to examine the milieu or environment which spawned the liturgy. It was E. R. Goodenough who first attempted to establish the milieu of the prayers by detailed evidence.

Goodenough wanted to prove in the final chapters of his *By Light, Light* that Philo's mysticism (i.e. adaptation of the pagan mystery religions, whereby one apprehends "immaterial reality," to Judaism) was not unique among Jews but that the mysticism found in Philo existed independently of him.[19] "Mystic Judaism is the ready-made environment of his (Philo's) writings, not the product of his original genius."[20] Goodenough noted that mystery is spoken of in Philo as if it were commonplace in Judaism, that Philo mentions as his predecessors other Jewish allegorists who had evidently gone to the logical end of the mystic position, and that the mystery is so "developed" by Philo's time[21] that "it may well have lost all localism and been quite as familiar among the Jews of Rome and Tarsus as in Alexandria itself."[22] Goodenough then proceeded to survey the mystical thought in other ancient Jewish works and came at last to the prayers in books seven and eight of AC.

Goodenough followed Bousset's line of argument very closely[3]--he appears also to have no knowledge of Kohler's several works--and, because of his superior knowledge of Philo, was able to suggest several additional parallels between Philo and the prayers.[24] Toward the end of his chapter on the "Mystic Liturgy"[25] he made his original contribution to the study of the prayers. Goodenough divided hellenistic Judaism into two segments: normative literalists and allegorists or mystics.[26] After citing some parallels between Philo the mystic and the prayers--as well as contrasting the prayers with "normative Judaism"[27]--he concluded that the prayers were produced in an environment similar to that in which Philo lived and worked, that is, the environment of the "Mystery." Goodenough believed that the conception of God in the prayers was the decisive proof of his claim. The notion of God "in terms of mystery is not sporadic but is the fundamental approach to God...,"[28] while there is nothing "distinctively normative"[29] in the prayers.

Goodenough went even further in his definition of the milieu of the prayers. While Philo came from a Sadducean mystical thought-world the prayers were composed in a Pharisaic mystical thought-world. Philo avoids angelology, Goodenough argued, but the prayers (AC 8.12.8) speak of angelic hosts ranking just beneath Logos or Sophia in the heavenly order.[30]

Goodenough dated the prayers after the time of Philo since the phrase τὸ μὴ ὄν, "non-being" used in AC 8.12 is, according to him, post-Philonic. But the prayers are probably not much later than the middle of the second century A.D., he maintained, since after that date relations between Jews and Christians were not cordial enough for the prayers to have been appropriated by Christians.[31]

Even ignoring Goodenough's main thesis, that Philo represents mystic Judaism (this has been challenged),[32] we must still wonder if these prayers are as mystic as Philo is supposed to be. A detailed criticism of Goodenough's argument must wait, but for now we ask only the following methodological questions: Since Goodenough used mostly the long prayer in AC 8.12[33] to outline the mystic theology in the prayers as a whole, could not these mystical elements be confined mainly or entirely to that one prayer? Second, since Goodenough argued that there are stages of development in the prayers--in particular that AC 8.12 is later than AC 7.34[34]--could the mystical content be only from the earlier or later stage? Third, are the parallels to Philo peculiarly mystical in content or are they merely philosophical concepts which each author could have obtained from a knowledge of Greek philosophy--especially Stoicism--but which do not require a common mystical theology? Fourth, is it helpful to break diaspora Judaism down into only two categories (normative and mystic), and is it helpful further to define mystic Judaism as Pharisaic or Sadducean simply because mystic Judaism may have one thing, and only one thing, in common with either one of these sects?

Goodenough's work in 1935 had been based on Bousset's work of twenty years earlier, but in between Bousset and Goodenough, W.O.E. Oesterley published his monumental monograph.[35] His stated intention was to devote a whole book to showing "that the Jewish Liturgy has left many marks of its influence, both in thought and word, on early forms of Christian worship, and, therefore, ultimately on the Christian Liturgy itself."[36] As Oesterley stated, this thesis was already admitted by most liturgical scholars, but he wanted to "give definite details and illustrations on a fairly comprehensive scale."[37]

Oesterley first established what elements in the Jewish liturgy are pre-Christian and then compared these elements to

Christian liturgy as we find it in several early Christian documents.[38] Oesterley was convinced that the influence of Jewish liturgy on the early church and its worship could be seen by comparing the prayers of both religions.[39]

After citing parallels of expression in prayers of early Christian texts and Synagogue worship, Oesterley came to his brief discussion of the AC. He named four places in AC where older Jewish prayers are echoed: AC 8.12.8 is based on the Yotzer (יוצר);[40] AC 8.11.5 on the Ahabah (אהבה);[41] AC 8.12.24 on the Geullah (גאולה);[42] and 8.12.27 on the Kedushah (קדושה).[43]

Oesterley's work has received the strongest criticism from C. W. Dugmore[44] and O. S. Rankin.[45] Dugmore followed L. Finkelstein's dating for the individual parts of the Jewish liturgy based on the Geniza fragments.[46] If Finkelstein is correct then, argued Dugmore, the parallels Oesterley had pointed to are improbable since some of the Jewish prayers are too late to have influenced many of Oesterley's Christian prayers.[47] For example, Oesterley asserted that the Liturgy of Serapion appropriated the Jewish Ahabah prayer. But according to Finkelstein, this latter prayer was quite unknown before A.D. 150-200.[48] "It is unlikely that any conscious borrowing of prayers from the Synagogue took place at so late a date." Dugmore affirmed that there is nothing to suggest any "wholesale borrowing from the liturgy of the Synagogue."[49]

However, Dugmore only assumed that no borrowing could take place after A.D. 150-200. This assumption must now be questioned since scholars[50] have found recently that there was much more mutual influence than has been assumed. Second, Dugmore and Rankin based their conclusions on Finkelstein whose methodology is rather dubious in light of the work of J. Heinemann. Finkelstein attempted to date the Jewish liturgy by an analysis of the wording of an "original text." But Heinemann maintained that there was probably no original text, but original texts, composed, transmitted and modified orally. The plurality of versions of the individual prayers makes it difficult to trace their chronology by philological analysis.[51]

The thesis of Kohler, Bousset and Goodenough has received general acceptance among scholars of liturgy. A. Spanier,[52] influenced by both Kohler and Bousset, argued that the original theme and function of the first Benediction can be recovered by comparing it to AC 7.33, the Greek version of the first Benediction. The theme of the first prayer is to be found in those elements which emphasize God as the imminent helper. It was a petitionary prayer as it is in AC and not a prayer of praise as it exists today in the Hebrew first Benediction. This is established by the absence of ברוך אתה, "blessed art thou," the introductory formula for prayers of praise, from the AC 7.33 version. The formula is found first in AC at 7.34 (εὐλογητὸς εἶ). The present Hebrew first Benediction was originally then only an introduction to the Benedictions.

E. Peterson, apparently influenced by Bousset,[53] argued that there were parallels to the synagogal morning prayers in AC 7.33. Of special interest was the latter part of paragraph three where Peterson affirmed that there is a veiled reference to Enoch's journey through the heavens (διὰ μέσων οὐρανῶν)[54] and the regeneration (παλιγγενεσία) in the time of Noah. The latter word is used in 1 Clement 9:4 in reference to Noah where again Enoch and Noah are juxtaposed. Other references were cited by Peterson in which Enoch and Noah occur side by side (Jubilees 4, Heb 11:5f, Sir 44:16f). What stands in the text now is an allegory of faith based on the stories of Enoch and Noah.[55]

Peterson states concerning the prayers in general (I take it, 7.33-38?) that they were not composed for the synagogue but were private prayers at first, since they are similar in content to prayers used in the modern synagogue which according to I. Elbogen[56] originated as private prayers. Second, Peterson dates the prayers, without giving any reason, in the time of Hadrian, just after the Bar Cocheba revolt.[57]

H. Lietzmann devoted some attention in his work *Messe und Herrenmahl* to the prayer in AC 8.12. He was convinced that Bousset had proven that AC 8.12.9-27 was from a Jewish original. However, Lietzmann maintained that AC 8.12.6-8 also belonged to the Jewish original and thus--except for some Christian interpolations--the prayer is a unity. The whole prayer is based on Psalms 104 and 105, as is the Jewish Yotzer prayer, the prayer parallel to AC 8.12.[58] Lietzmann's analysis was followed by F. Gavin who concluded that the influence of Jewish liturgy on AC 8.12 developed after the second century (since the elements in this prayer are not in the Egyptian Church Order). After this period there was a supplementing of the Christian rite during which prayers from Judaism were incorporated.[59]

The affirmation that behind AC 7.33-38 were originally Jewish prayers was accepted by no less a scholar of comparative liturgy than A. Baumstark in 1923. Influenced by Bousset's article, Baumstark claimed that the basis of AC 7.33-38 was the Jewish liturgy of the morning service of the Synagogue with special additions for sabbaths, festival days and fast days, parallel to the Benedictions accompanying the Shema and the nucleus of the Shemoneh Esreh (= Seven Benedictions?).[60]

Baumstark stated in 1939 that under "the light veneer of a somewhat superficial Christian revision" in AC book seven there is "a complete Greco-Jewish ritual for the Morning Service of the Sabbath and feast days."[61] Baumstark emphasized the parallels between the Shema Benedictions and AC 7.33-38 and not merely the parallels with the Shemoneh Esreh. Baumstark offered no suggestion for the date or provenance of the prayers but was intrigued with the "curious resemblance with the Samaritan liturgy" the prayers bear.[62]

Another scholar of comparative liturgy, E. Werner, agreed that there are Jewish elements in AC seven and eight. Werner found what he termed "post-biblical Hebraisms"--by which he must have meant parallels to the Jewish Hebrew prayer book and other Hebrew literature and not necessarily grammatical semitisms--in several parts of the AC seven and eight as well as other sources of Christian liturgy.[63] According to Werner, the "Hebraisms" in the Christian prayer books:

> could have been borrowed only by Jews, well conversant with these texts and their liturgical functions in the service; nor were they accessible in translated form. Such Jews were the intermediaries between the liturgies of church and Synagogue. In their mouths the very same words and tunes were alive which still resound in the churches, demonstrating the Hebrew origin of some of the loftiest prayers of Christianity.[64]

Werner's parallels are sometimes unconvincing. They may only contain similar themes such as praise of God for creation and for the resurrection (Werner's parallels 11 and 12)[65] themes which obviously require no dependence of one source upon another. Other parallels are somewhat more convincing.

M. Simon in his work of 1948, *Verus Israel*, made use of Bousset's article to establish his claim that diaspora Judaism continued after A.D. 70 much the same as it had previously. Since Bousset proved--to Simon--that the prayers were composed after the middle of the second century A.D., they furnish one with an example of diaspora Jewish thought and piety after the destruction of Jerusalem. Polemicizing against A. Harnack and others, Simon pointed out parallels between the prayers and pre-70 Jewish literature of the dispersion. The same employment of Greek thought is found in both periods; e.g. man as λόγικος (AC 8.12.17) possessed the natural means of determining right from wrong (AC 7.33.3). Furthermore, there is still a universalistic attitude in the prayers. The two hymns of creation (AC 7.34, 8.12.9-20) represent all of humanity as disobeying God and incurring death, but having the hope of resurrection. Thus, argued Simon, diaspora Judaism after the destruction of Jerusalem, even after the Bar Cocheba war, did not withdraw into intself, reject Greek thought, and abandon its universalistic attitude toward the Gentiles.[66]

The last author to discuss the prayers at length has been L. Bouyer who included a translation and brief introduction to them in his book *Eucharistie* in 1966. Bouyer is convinced by Bousset's claim that the prayers are Jewish, but critical of Goodenough's contention that the prayers were produced in mystic Jewish circles. The prayers owe nothing more than their language to Hellenism, and this language has little trace of the mystery *jargon* used by Philo.[67]

Bouyer asserts that AC 7.33, 34 and 35 are simply more wordy equivalents of the first three Benedictions of the Shemoneh Esreh. AC 7.36 is a prayer for the Sabbath while 7.37 is a synthesis of Benedictions 14-17 and AC 7.38 an expansion of Benediction 18.[68]

Bouyer appears to have condluded that the prayers were composed by Alexandrian Jews.[69] He makes the startling claim that even though the prayers were composed in Greek the hellenized Jews who worked on them were working with Hebrew sources. He concludes this simply because in AC 7.35 appears φέλμουνι, a transliteration of פלמוני.[70] But this transliteration is found in LXX, Aquila, and Theodotion.

According to Bouyer, the long prayer before the *sanctus* (i.e. AC 8.12.6-27) combines the three prayers in AC 7.33-35. It is still very Jewish but with much more hellenic thought added.[71]

As we saw above, Dugmore challenged Oesterley's assertion that Christians borrowed prayers from the Synagogue, but affirmed that the general outline of the worship service was borrowed. Dugmore did not speak about the alleged Jewish prayers in AC seven and eight, though he knew about the thesis.[72] The most serious challenge to the theory has come from the revisor of Baumstark's work on liturgy, D. B. Botte.[73]

Botte argued that one should not expect the church to have borrowed anything more from the Synagogue than the music and scripture readings. That Christianity borrowed the prayers is unlikely because Christianity and Judaism were at odds with one another from the very beginning (recall the parable of new wine in the old wineskins).[74] This breach between the two led to a polemical or hostile relationship. Second, earliest Christianity was more charismatic and thus less inclined to employ ritual in the worship service.[75] This is of course arguing a priori. We must insist that the texts themselves be examined to determine such points without bringing these assumptions to the text. We have already pointed out that the alleged breach between Judaism and Christianity, at least in some geographical areas, is now being questioned. Furthermore, why could not charismatics have employed ritual?

In reference specifically to Bousset's thesis, Botte stated that the idea that a Christian of the fourth century (i.e. the compiler of AC) could easily obtain a Jewish document but that the Jews allowed the text to perish is, though not impossible, rather troubling (*un peu inquietant*).[76]

Bousset's most formidable argument, said Botte, was that there is nothing specifically Christian in the prayers. But, observed Botte, there are some passages which are peculiarly Christian. However, when Bousset encountered such passages, he claimed that they were interpolations. Such reasoning, maintained Botte, is to argue in circles.[77] One first must ignore the Christian elements to argue that the prayers are Jewish, then explain the Christian elements, as interpolations, based upon that argument.

Botte's last two points are very important for this endeavor. What do Bousset's parallels prove? Further, can we argue for Jewish authorship of the prayers without employing circular reasoning?

Such questions and the details of analysis will be handled at the appropriate time. For now we may summarize the material which this chapter has surveyed. It has been alleged that certain prayers in AC seven and eight were composed by Jews. The number of prayers supposed to be Jewish has varied (see Chart A). It has usually been suggested that the prayers were composed sometime in the second century (Kohler, Bousset, Goodenough, Peterson). It has also been suggested that the milieu which produced the prayers was Essenism (Kohler) or mystical Judaism (Goodenough).

The most detailed works on this subject, and those to which we shall refer most often in our analysis of the prayers are the publications by Kohler, Bousset and Goodenough. Though the thesis was first suggested at the turn of the century, and apparently by two scholars working independently (Kohler and Bousset), and advanced by Goodenough in 1935, no one since then--except perhaps Bouyer--has analyzed the prayers in AC books seven and eight in great detail. The thesis has met with relatively little opposition. As a matter of fact several of the more recent scholars of the liturgy have given their endorsement to the hypothesis.[78] It would appear that the hypothesis has won broad acceptance.

The first chapter has set up the questions for us to consider: (1) Are any of these prayers Jewish? (2) Have Kohler, Bousset and others proven the thesis? (3) When and where were they composed and in what circles? (4) If some or all of these prayers are Jewish, what are the implications for the history of Christian-Jewish relations?

CHART A

The Alleged Jewish Prayers in AC Seven and Eight

Kohler's List	Bousset's List	Goodenough's List
7.26.3		7.26.1-3
7.33	7.33	7.33
7.34	7.34	7.34
7.35	7.35	7.35
7.36	7.36	7.36
7.37	7.37	7.37
7.38	7.38	7.38
	7.39.2-4	7.39.2-4
	8.5.1-4	8.5.1-4
	8.6.5	8.6.5-8
	8.9.8f	8.9.8f
	8.12.6-27	8.12.6-27
	8.15.7-9	8.15.7-9
		8.16.3
	8.37.1-4	8.37.1-4
	8.37.5-7	8.37.5-7
	8.38.4f	8.38.4f
	8.39.3f	8.39.3f
		8.40.2-4
	8.41.4f	8.41.2-5

NOTES

CHAPTER I

[1]K. Kohler, "Ueber die Ursprünge und Grundformen der synagogalen Liturgie," *MGWJ* 37 (1893) 441-51, 489-97. Kohler only mentioned AC 7.35, 8.12 and 8.41 at that time.

[2]Ibid., 497: "...so kommen wir zu dem Schluss, dass alle unsere Gebete, auch die späteren poetanischen Alphabetarien, bis auf den Mystiker Eliëser ha-Kalir, aus dem Kreis der Essäer, resp. der Chassidim in directer Traditionskette stammen."

[3]But Kohler is a little confusing in his use of the term Essene. In his article "Ueber die Ursprunge" (497), he seemed to equate Essenes with Hasideans. But elsewhere (443) the Hasideans are the predecessors of the Essenes. Kohler is also unclear about the distinction between Essenes and Pharisees (497) and even maintained in his later article, "Essenes" (*Jewish Encyclopedia*, ed. I. Singer [New York: Funk and Wagnals, 1903] vol. 5, 224f.), that the Essenes were a branch of the Pharisees, then later that the Pharisees "were scarcely different from those elsewhere called 'Essenes'" (225).

[4]See ibid., 224-31. I. Elbogen was critical of Kohler's handling of the sources because Kohler equated the Hasideans and the Essenes without proof. See Elbogen, *Der jüdische Gottesdienst in seiner geschichtlichen Entwicklung* (Frankfurt: Kauffmann, 1931) 538.

[5]K. Kohler, "Didascalia," *Jewish Encyclopedia*, ed. I. Singer (New York: Funk and Wagnals, 1903) vol. 4, 592-94; idem, "The Essene Version of the Seven Benedictions as Preserved in the vii Book of the Apostolic Constitutions," *HUCA* 1 (1924) 410-25; idem, *The Origins of the Synagogue and the Church* (New York: MacMillan, 1927) 257-59.

[6]Kohler, "Didascalia," 593 and "The Essene Version," 410-22. Kohler claimed in *JE* that the seventh benediction could be found in AC 8.37, but in *HUCA* that it had merely dropped out.

[7]Kohler, "The Essene Version," 418; *Origins*, 257; "Didascalia," vol. 4, 593.

[8]Kohler, *Origins*, 259. See L. O'Leary (*The Apostolical Constitutions* [London: Society for Promoting Christian Knowledge, 1906] 71-73), who dispensed with Kohler's parallels for AC 7.34,35, 37 and 38 and the Jewish prayer book as merely common use of the OT. However he was convinced that the other chapters (e.g. AC 7.36) did derive from Judaism.

[9]W. Bousset, "Eine jüdische Gebetssammlung im siebenten Buch der apostolischen Konstitutionen," *Nachrichten von der Königlichen Gesellschaft der Wissenschaften zu Göttingen; Philologische-historische Klasse, 1915* (1916) 438-85; reprinted in A. F. Verheule, *Religionsgeschichtliche Studien* (Leiden: Brill, 1979) 231-86.

[10]But E. Werner (*The Sacred Bridge* [London: Dobson, 1959] 47 n. 95) implies that Bousset did know of Kohler's article. See also p. 283.

[11]Bousset, *Nachrichten*, 435-45.

[12]Ibid., 435-38, 443, 448, 450, 462.

[13]Ibid., 465f.

[14]Ibid., 445, 447.

[15]Ibid., 446, 447.

[16]Ibid., 461.

[17]Kohler, "Essene Version," 418.

[18]E.g. the word ὁραματισμός is used in AC 7.33 which is only found in Aquila; see Bousset, *Nachrichten*, 465.

[19]E. R. Goodenough, *By Light, Light* (New Haven: Yale University, 1935). The definition of mysticism is from his *Introduction to Philo Judaeus* (New Haven: Yale, 1940) 182f.

[20]Ibid., 236.

[21]Ibid., 237. "In Philo the Mystery is not only fully developed but ripe with the ripeness of very many years." We must ask here what "developed" mysticism is and by what standards it can be judged developed?

[22]Ibid. In the very next line the "may well" description of this state of affairs becomes "quite likely," from possibility to probability in one bold stroke but with no new evidence.

[23]Ibid., 306 and passim.

[24]Ibid., e.g., 317, 337, 339, 340.

[25]Ibid., 306-58.

[26]Ibid., 336, 340.

[27]Ibid., 339f.

[28]Ibid., 340; see also 337 where God according to Goodenough is represented in "philosophical conceptions of space" as is the hellenistic deity of Philo.

[29]Ibid., 340.

[30]Ibid., 344f.

[31]Ibid., 357. But the idea that Judaism and Christianity had fewer and fewer contacts after the Bar Cocheba war is being questioned today. See the work by W. A. Meeks and R. L. Wilken, *Jews and Christians in Antioch in the First Four Centuries of the Common Era* (Missoula, MT: Scholars Press, 1978), the whole thrust of which is to show the influence of Judaism upon the church during the first four centuries.

[32]See H. A. Wolfson, *Philo* (Cambridge, MA: Harvard, 1948) vol. 1, 44-55. Goodenough continued to develop his thesis of a widespread mystical Judaism in his *Jewish Symbols* of thirteen volumes. The reaction to this publication has been mostly critical. See M. Smith, "Goodenough's Jewish Symbols in Retrospect," *JBL* 86 (1967) 53-68, who summarizes the criticism and gives an extensive list of reviews.

[33]Goodenough, *By Light, Light*, 348, "Fragment vii (i.e. AC 8.12) which is proving our best guide to the theology and philosophy of the Fragments...."

[34]Ibid.

[35]W.O.E. Oesterley, *The Jewish Background of the Christian Liturgy* (Oxford: Clarendon, 1925).

[36]Ibid., 5.

[37]Ibid.

[38]In addition to our text, the AC, Oesterley looked at 1 Clement, Didache, Justin Martyr, and the Liturgy of Serapion.

[39]Oesterley, *Jewish Background*, 125.

[40]P. Birnbaum, *Daily Prayer Book* (New York: Hebrew Publishing, 1977) 71f.

[41]Ibid., 73f. That this is based on a Jewish prayer has been suggested by no one else. Bousset and Goodenough were convinced that 8.12 was Jewish, but did not cite these parallels except for the last one, the Kedusha.

[42]Ibid., 195.

[43]Ibid., 73, 83.

[44]C. W. Dugmore, *The Influence of the Synagogue upon the Divine Office* (London: Humphrey Milford, 1944).

[45]O. S. Rankin, "The Extent of the Influence of the Synagogue Service upon Christian Worship," *JJS* 1 (1948) 27-32.

[46]L. Finkelstein, "The Development of the 'Amidah,'" *JQR* N.S. 16 (1925/26) 1-43, 127-70; idem, "La Kedouscha et les Bénédictions du Schema," *REJ* 93 (1932) 1-26.

[47]Dugmore, *Influence*, 75-77.

[48]Finkelstein, "La Kedouscha," 26.

[49]Dugmore, *Influence*, 113.

[50]Among others, Meeks and Wilken, *Jews and Christians in Antioch*; L. Bouyer, *Eucharist*, trans. E. U. Quinn (Notre Dame: Notre Dame Press, 1968) 91-119.

[51]J. Heinemann, *Prayer in the Talmud*, trans. R. S. Sarason (Berlin: Gruyter, 1977) 37-64.

[52]A. Spanier, "Die erst Benedicktion des Achtzehngebetes," *MGWJ* 81 (1937) 71-76.

[53]E. Peterson, "Henoch im jüdischen Gebet und in jüdischer Kunst," *Miscellanea Liturgica in honorem L. C. Mohlberg* (Roma: Liturgiche, 1948) vol. 1, 413-17. He cited no previous work but used Bousset's word *Gebetssammlung* to describe the prayers in AC 7, and later on he polemicized against the view that these prayers originated in the Synagogue (ibid., 413f.).

[54]F. X. Funk, *Didascalia et Constitutiones Apostolorum* (Paderborn: Schoeningh, 1905) 424.

[55]Peterson, *Miscellanea*, vol. 1, 414-17. This suggestion is criticized in Chapter III in the notes on AC 7.33.

[56]Elbogen, *Der jüdische Gottesdienst*, 15, 89.

[57]Peterson, *Miscellanea*, vol. 1, 414, 417.

[58]H. Lietzman, *Mass and the Lord's Supper*, trans. D.H.G. Reeve (Leiden: Brill, 1953) 102-105.

[59]F. Gavin, *The Jewish Antecedents of the Christian Sacraments* (New York: KTAV, 1969) 88-90.

[60]A. Baumstark, "Trishagion und Qeduscha," *Jahrbuch für Liturgiewissenschaft* 3 (1923) 18-32.

[61]A. Baumstark and B. Botte, *Comparative Liturgy*, trans. F. L. Cross (Westminster, MD: Newman, 1958; first printed, 1939) 11.

[62]Ibid., 12. See also Baumstark's last article which touched on this subject ("Zur Herkunft der monotheistischen Bekenntnisformeln im Koran," *Oriens Christianus* 37 [1953] 6-22) in which he suggested that AC 7.37.2-4 is based on the prayer for the day of Purim while AC 7.38.2 is based upon the Temple consecration feast (17).

[63]Werner, *Sacred Bridge*, 31-36. He is only interested with those parts of the liturgy which were rendered musically (31). See also his article, "The Doxology in Synagogue and Church, a Liturgico-Musical Study," *HUCA* 19 (1945/46) 276-328. Another interesting confirmation of the close relationship between church and Synagogue is the music itself which was shared by each. See E. Wellesz, *A History of Byzantine Music and Hymnography* (Oxford: Clarendon, 1949) 35: "It is obvious that the oldest versions of both Byzantine and Gregorian melodies go back to a common source, the music of the churches of Antioch and Jerusalem, which in their turn derived from the music of the Jews." In addition, see K. G. Kuhn (*Achtzengebet und Vaterunser und der Reim* [Tübingen: Mohr, 1950] 26) who asserts that rhyme in Christian liturgy has its antecedent in rhyme in Jewish liturgy: "Der Reim ist aus der jüdischen Synagogue in die Kirche der jungen Christenheit herübergenommen worden." He finds several examples of rhyme in AC 7 and 8 (pp. 48-50).

[64]Werner, *Sacred Bridge*, 30.

[65]Ibid., 32.

[66]M. Simon, *Verus Israel* (Bibliotèque de écoles françaises d'Athènes et de Rome; Paris: Boccard, 1948) 8, 52, 74-82 (esp. 78). See A. Harnack, *Die Mission und Ausbreitung des Christentums* (Leipzig: Hinrichs'sche, 1915) 15 n. 3.

[67]L. Bouyer, *Eucharist*, 120f (French edition in 1966).

[68]Ibid., 121.

[69]Ibid., 125f.

[70]Ibid., 121.

[71]Ibid., 259.

[72]Dugmore, *Influence*, 134 cites Kohler's article in *HUCA* in his bibliography.

[73]D. B. Botte, "Liturgie chrétienne et liturgie juive," *Cahier Sioniens* 3 (1949) 215-23.

[74]Ibid., 216: "la forme la plus agissante du judaïsme, le pharisaïsme, et son esprit prophétique est nettement opposé à un ritualisme étrait."

[75]Ibid., 217: "plus charismatique que rituelles, et il est probable que ce vin nouveau de l'Esprit a fait éclater les vieilles outres des formulaires juifs."

[76]Ibid., 220.

[77]Ibid.

[78]See also J. Daniélou (*Theology of Jewish Christianity*, trans. J. A. Baker [London: Longman and Todd, 1964] 44f) who states that AC 8.5-14 has prayers which are "connected beyond dispute with Jewish sources"; L. Ligier ("The Origins of the Eucharistic Prayer: From the Last Supper to the Eucharist," *Studia Liturgica* 9 [1973] 161-85) who claims that AC 7.38 is a Hoda'ah; F. Perles,("Notes critique sur Le Text de la Liturgie Juive," *REJ* 80 [1925] 101f) who said that AC 7.38 is a Nishmath; E. R. Hardy ("Kedusha and Sanctus," *Studia Liturgica* 6 [1969] 183-88) who states that the prayers in AC 7.33-38 are "clearly of Jewish origin"; and C. P. Price ("Jewish Morning Prayers and Early Christian Anaphoras," *Anglican Theological Review* 43 [1961] 153-68) who says that the prayers in AC 7.33-38 and 8.12 are from Jewish morning prayers; A. Z. Idelsohn (*Jewish Liturgy* [New York: Henry Holt, 1932] 305-307) who followed Kohler's analysis of the prayers; E. J. Bickerman ("The Civic Prayer for Jerusalem," *HTR* 15 [1962] 169 n. 29) who followed Kohler; M. Liber ("Structure and History of the Tefilah," *JQR* 40 [1950] 336) who followed Bousset; and J. Heinemann (*Prayer in the Talmud*, 223, 231) who affirmed that AC 7. 35 contained the Kedusha and 8.12 was originally a Yotzer prayer. All of the above mention the alleged Jewish prayers in passing.

CHAPTER II

THE NATURE OF THE *CONSTITUTIONES APOSTOLORUM*

Before we translate the prayers and analyze the claim that there are prayers in the Christian *Constitutiones Apostolorum* which were originally composed by Jews we must have in mind the nature of the AC. We want to know not only if Jews composed some prayers in the AC, but if so, where and when they were composed and to what extent the prayers were edited later. To answer these questions it is helpful to know the date, provenance and sources of the AC and to understand their compiler.

The AC claims (1.1, 6.18)[1] to be regulations for the church delivered by the apostles and published by Clement of Rome. As a manual of ecclesiastical life, it contains instruction, exhortation and examples for proper Christian living.[2] It also has preserved in book eight one of the oldest examples of Christian liturgy.[3] Nearly all scholars agree today that the AC was compiled around A.D. 380 in Syria.[4]

Not only is the AC a compilation of older material, but the sources of the AC are themselves compilations, and seem originally to have been written also as a manual of church life.

Didascalia

Books one through six of AC are based on the Didascalia, a church order which professes to have been written shortly after the events in Acts 15.[5] The author wrote about such subjects as bishops' duties, penance, worship, persecution, widows, deaconnesses and disputes within the church. He is alleged to have drawn material from the Didache, the Epistles of Ignatius, Justin's works, the Shepherd of Hermas, Irenaeus and other works.[6] The original Greek is no longer extant, but is represented by translations into Syriac, Latin, Ethiopic and Arabic.[7]

Most scholars agree that the Didascalia was composed sometime in the third century A.D.[8] Nevertheless, there has remained for over a century disagreement as to a more precise date. The pivotal events for determining the date are the Decian persecution and the Novatian controversy, both about the middle of the century. A later date depends on one's ability to discern references in the Didascalia to these events. Thus A. Harnack[9] and others have regarded chapters six and seven of the Didascalia as directed against Novatian and as a consequence, the Didascalia must have originated in the latter part of the century. Chapter nineteen "breathes an atmosphere of persecution" as R. H. Connolly[10] observed and may indicate that the Didascalia was written after the Decian persecution. However, chapter thirteen seems to imply that Christian assemblies were unmolested and therefore Connolly concluded that there seems to be no organized persecution against Christians implied in the Didascalia. Connolly's early third century date has been accepted by most scholars.[11] For our purpose it matters little precisely when the Didascalia was composed. It is only important to know that the compiler of the AC in incorporating a writing from the third century into his work has used a source and did not compose his work originally.

It is also generally agreed that the work sprang from Syria. The parallels with Syrian literature and Syrian rites, and the fact that a Syrian sect called the "Audiani" are supposed to have used the work (Epiphanius, *Haer*. 70.10) lead to no other conclusion.[12] Further, most would point to Northern Syria or Coele-Syria as the place of composition.[13]

Of special interest to us is the redaction-interpolation of the Didascalia by the compiler of the AC. Connolly observed:

> ...in some passages, and chiefly in the earlier part, the editorial process is comparatively slight, but in others, and notably towards the end, it becomes so destructive that hardly anything is left of the original work.[14]

H. Leclercq described the editorial activity of the compiler of AC books one through six as follows: Books one and two of AC incorporate material from Didascalia virtually untouched. In book three the modifications increase. Chapters 10, 11, 17, 18 and 20 are added; chapters 8 and 9 are recast;[15] everything except chapter 13 is more or less retouched. In book four of AC chapters 12, 13 and 14 are added; chapters 6 and 10 are lengthened; all others are recast. In book five chapters 8 and 9 are new; chapters 7, 13 and 20 are recast; the rest are retouched. In book six, chapters 2, 6, 11, 15-18 and 23-27 are almost entirely new; all chapters without exception are changed somewhat.[16]

These observations are significant since they demonstrate that the compiler at times became an editor, at other times an author. If there are prayers in AC books seven and eight which originated from Judaism they might be so heavily edited as to be useless for determining what the original text of the prayers was, and nearly useless for determining the theology of the Judaism that produced them.

Nevertheless, the nature of the added material and the editorial recasting must be kept in mind. In AC book three, for instance, the new material concerns changing functions and rites. Thus chapters 10 and 11 deal with the priestly functions while chapters 17-20 deal with the rites of baptism and ordination. Other new chapters concern heresies which are contemporaneous with the compiler (6.6, 18, 23-27), and there is at least one chapter which is devoted to making a christological statement (6.11). These examples are typical of all the new material listed by Leclercq as well as the recast material.

From this evidence alone we would expect editorial alterations in a prayer when it handles a new practice or custom, or when a theological statement must be changed or added. Therefore the editorial activity which is seen in AC books one through six indicates that one must look for the hand of the editor in any alleged Jewish prayer, especially where there might be any evidence of theological polemic.

Didache

The Didache was used by the compiler of AC as the basis of AC 7.1-32. The Didache itself is a composite of varying material: Chapters 1-6 consist of general ethical teaching; chapters 7-10 contain liturgical material; chapters 11-15 relate disciplinary instruction; chapter 16 is an eschatological conclusion.[17]

Unlike the Didascalia, the Didache is extant in the original Greek in the eleventh century manuscript found by Bryennius in 1873 and Greek fragments of an Oxyrhynchus papyrus. In addition, there are a Latin manuscript of the first six chapters and a fragment of a Coptic version.[18]

The Didache is generally said to have been composed in its final form in the early to middle second century A.D.[19] The notable exception to this consensus is J.-P. Audet who maintained that the work was completed A.D. 50-70.[20] Perhaps the best suggestion for dating the Didache is made by R. A. Kraft[21] who maintains that although the Didache contains material from the first or early second century, in its present form it is no earlier than mid-second century A.D.

Syria is usually suggested as the home of the Didache.[22] However, Kraft,[23] although he inclines toward assigning a Syrian provenance to the liturgical sections, wants to allow for Egypt as a possible place of composition for the rest of the work.

L. O'Leary has analyzed the redaction of the Didache in AC 7.1-32. The compiler has: (1) inserted scriptural (especially OT) quotations and illustrations; (2) used more contemporary liturgical formulae and practices; (3) softened difficulties. There is no doubt that the same hand was at work here as in AC books one through six.[24]

Thus where the Didache begins with "There are two ways..." (ὁδοὶ δύο εἰσί) the AC 7.1 presents a series of biblical quotations as embellishments of this idea. The baptismal rite of the Didache 7, where running water is preferred and unction is not mentioned, is changed in AC 7.22 to requiring an unction; reference to running water is absent. An example of the third type of change is found in AC 7.9 which alters the exhortation of Didache 4 to honor the one speaking the word of God "as the Lord" (τιμήσεις δὲ αὐτὸν ὡς κύριον) to "honour him not as the cause of your birth but as the occasion of your well-being" (τιμήσεις δὲ αὐτὸν οὐχ ὡς γενέσεως αἴτιον, ἀλλ᾽ ὡς τοῦ εὖ εἶναί σοι πρόξενον γινόμενον).[25]

The most interesting chapters of AC 7.1-32 for our purposes are 25f, the sections parallel to Didache 9f. Here we have the first opportunity to examine the compiler's handling of prayers.[26] A comparison of the Greek texts of both can prove instructive for our later study of the alleged Jewish prayers (see Chart B). The compiler deletes phrases from the Didache, adds phrases and substitutions for them: (1) He eliminates the refrain "to you be the glory forever" (σοὶ ἡ δόξα εἰς τοὺς αἰῶνας) and phrases similar to it (Didache 9:1,3,4, 10:2,4,5). (2) He also omits some words in the prayer after participation about the spiritual food of creation (10:3). He inserts: (3) in AC 7.25.2 an account of the life of Jesus where the name "Jesus" is mentioned in the text of the Didache; (4) in AC 7.26.2 the phrase "God of the universe" (ὁ θεὸς τῶν ὅλων); (5) the phrase "through him" (δι᾽ αὐτοῦ) (7.26.2) after a reference to God as creator to emphasize that God created through Christ; (6) the notion of an implanted law (νόμον κατεφύτευσας) (AC 7.26.3) which is prompted by mention of the creation; (7) the section in 7.26.3 "God of our holy and blameless fathers..." which becomes a christological statement (i.e. Christ was both man and the Word); (8) the reference to purchasing the church with "the precious blood" of Christ (τῷ τιμίῳ αἵματι) which is a combination of Acts 20:28 and 1 Pet 1:19; (9) and the quotation from Matt 21:9 ("Blessed is he who comes in the name of the Lord") which completes the phrase "Hosanna to the Son of David." (10) The compiler of AC did not leave in the thanksgiving for the "holy vine" (ὑπὲρ τῆς ἁγίας ἀμπέλου) or the "broken bread" (περὶ τοῦ κλάσματος, Didache 9:2f), but substituted a later thanksgiving for the "precious blood" and "precious body" (AC 7.25.1). (11) The words "O holy Father" (πάτερ ἅγιε) become "God and Father of Jesus our Saviour" (ὁ θεὸς καὶ πατὴρ Ἰησοῦ τοῦ σωτῆρος ἡμῶν

To summarize, the compiler has once added a narrative about Jesus where his name has appeared in the Didache (no. 3 above), he has added what may be favorite phrases and themes to any mention of creation (nos. 4, 5 and 6), and he has added scriptural embellishments (nos. 8 and 9). The puzzling addition is number 7 which sounds very Jewish ("God of our fathers Abraham, Isaac and Jacob") but becomes a christological statement ("who sent upon earth Jesus your Christ to live with men as a man, when he was God the Word"). There seems to be no reason why this section was inserted.[27] The compiler preferred to use the more scriptural language "precious" blood and body instead of the reference to the vine and bread in the eucharistic prayer (no. 10). He also substituted "Father of Jesus our Saviour" for "Holy Father," by merely inserting a reference to Jesus through a genitival relationship with the word "Father" already in the text (no. 11). Although the additions and substitutions are interesting, the omissions seem uninstructive.[28]

These prayers offer us the most solid ground for determining the editorial tendencies of the compiler. We must inquire whether these tendencies are present in the alleged Jewish prayers when we examine them in detail.

Book seven of the AC continues with prayers and instructions, the source of which is unknown.[29] Here, among other places, Jewish prayers were allegedly incorporated (i.e. AC 7.33-38).

The Apostolic Tradition

In 1916 Connolly[30] proved what E. Schwarz had claimed in 1910: that the "Egyptian Church Order" (so called because it first became known in its Ethiopic and Coptic versions) is in the main the genuine work of Hippolytus of Rome and is listed as one of his works on his statue found in Rome. Since Connolly's publication, this view has gained general acceptance.[31] Aside from the Ethiopic and Coptic versions, the work is also extant in Arabic and, partly, in Latin.[32] The Apostolic Tradition is a church manual with much the same kind of instruction as found in the Didascalia.

There is some debate about the date of the work. B. S. Easton dated it to A.D. 217 right after the schism in Rome, but G. Dix preferred A.D. 215, toward the end of Zephyrinus's rather than the beginning of Callistus's episcopate. C. C. Richardson attempted to push the date back even further to A.D. 197.[33] For our purposes this debate matters little since it is generally agreed that the work was produced sometime around the beginning of the third century. Since Hippolytus lived in Rome at this time, the provenance is, of course, Rome. It appears that although the work had no great influence in the West it has had considerable influence in the East, especially Egypt.[34]

The distribution of the Apostolic Tradition in the AC must be indicated to show the method of the compiler in the eighth book. AC 8.1f may be based on a lost work of Hippolytus, "On Spiritual Gifts."[35] At AC 8.3f the compiler incorporates the Apostolic Tradition, chapters 1 and 2. The compiler then substituted in AC 8.5-15 a completely different liturgy (the Clementine Liturgy) for the one in Apostolic Tradition 3-6. At AC 8.16 the compiler resumed his use of Apostolic Tradition, continuing through AC 8.25 (Apostolic Tradition 8-15). AC 8.26-31 is inserted, then 8.32 continues with Apostolic Tradition 16 and 17. The material in AC 8.33-39 is foreign to the Apostolic Tradition. It appears that the compiler has constructed a prayer in AC 8.40 modeled on Apostolic Tradition 28. The rest of AC 8 (41-46) is drawn from material other than the Apostolic Tradition. Thus the compiler became very selective when he came to the last book of his work. He has used only about thirteen of the thirty-eight chapters in Apostolic Tradition, and much of this material had been recast.

The compiler's handling of the prayers in book eight is somewhat different from what we saw in book seven. In AC 8.16, after he supplied a preface he followed the text of the Apostolic Tradition 8 almost verbatim except for three interpolations. The compiler inserted into the beginning of the prayer for the ordination of presbyters a section praising God as creator and provider (AC 8.16.3).[36] The second interpolation comes after the request (8.16.4) "look down now on this your servant" (νῦν ἔπιδε ἐπὶ τὸν δοῦλόν σου τοῦτον). This clause is followed by the interpolated clause which explains that the servant was elected to the presbytery. The third interpolation comes after the request to "keep in us the Spirit of your grace" (τηρῶν ἐν ἡμῖν τὸ πνεῦμα τοῦ χάριτος σου, 8.16.5) which explains the function of the presbyter using a scriptural embellishment (2 Macc 1:3). These last two interpolations would seem to have been prompted by the desire for contemporaneity which we can see behind so many of the compiler's interpolations.

The prayer in AC 8.18, except for a few faint echoes, is completely different from the corresponding prayer in Apostolic Tradition 9, as is the prayer in AC 8.40 (= Apostolic Tradition 28).

Thus we see that the compiler can remold prayers adding numerous scriptural embellishments and favorite themes and phrases; he can quote a prayer almost verbatim except for the necessary interpolations for the sake of contemporaneity; finally, he may freely compose a prayer which only faintly echoes the original.

The Clementine Liturgy

Since we do not possess the Clementine Liturgy[37] (= CL AC 8. 5-15) as a separate source, and most scholars agree that the liturgy bears strong traces of the compiler's hand it is difficult to maintain that the compiler has utilized a source.[38] Thus one might conclude that the compiler had merely composed the CL. Nevertheless, there is some evidence that the compiler has merely edited a text. First, it appears that there are at least two sources represented in the CL. The notion of multiple sources goes back at least as far as F. Probst[40] who held that there were two sources used for the CL with the second source beginning at AC 8.13. Others[41] subsequently have posited two or more sources. The evidence for multiple sources is: useless repetitions (cf. AC 8.12.40-50 with 8.13.1-9 where prayers are offered for the same things) and use of different terms for the same idea ("bishop" is termed both ἐπίσκοπος and ἀρχιερεύς).[42] Although R. E. Brightman[43] warned against relying too heavily on the results of such evidence--since some inconsistencies in the text may be the result of inconsistencies of liturgical practice--this warning does not seem to destroy the conclusion that, however the sources have been distributed and whatever their number, a source--or sources--*has* been used. Brightman himself in spite of his conclusion that the prayers are largely the work of the compiler seemed convinced that the compiler had used a source.[44]

In addition to repetitions and multiple terminology, H. Leclercq, Probst and R. E. Warren[45] have listed several other reasons for concluding that the CL is older than the fourth century compilation of the AC. (1) The long prayers in the CL contrast sharply with the shorter prayers of the fourth century rites. By the fourth century, through the influence of Chrysostom, the tendency was to abbreviate prayers. (2) The creed is absent. (3) There is no mention of incense. (4) The Lord's Prayer is omitted. Although these things were sometimes omitted in the earlier liturgies, they were used in fourth century Syrian rites. (5) The theological language is imprecise and contrasts with the neat expressions of the post-Nicene liturgies.[46] But we must be cautious with this argument since the imprecise language may be due to the compiler's christological ambiguity (see below). (6) There are several references to the persecution of Christians which would be inappropriate after the Edict of Milan (A.D. 313; see AC 8.10.15f, 12.46, but cf. AC 6.24) as well as imprecations for tolerance on the part of the "king" (βασιλεύς) and the army (AC 8.12.42). Leclercq[47] believed that the CL was composed in the third century. Whatever the precise date, there is enough evidence to conclude that the compiler of the AC did not entirely compose the CL, but had at least one source which he edited. Thus there could be prayers in the CL which have come from Jewish circles. Nevertheless, Brightman[48] again, though allowing that the compiler used a source for the CL, asserts that the prayers are largely his free compositions. The examination of his linguistic evidence must await a detailed analysis of the alleged Jewish prayers.

There is general agreement as to the provenance of the CL. It is so similar in structure to other Syrian rites that it was probably composed on Syrian soil.[49]

The Compiler of the *Constitutiones Apostolorum*

The compiler of our work has been labeled as either an Arian[50] or a semi-Arian.[51] It is partly for these theological reasons and partly for linguistic reasons that he has been identified with Pseudo-Ignatius the fourth century interpolator of the Ignatian letters, who also had Arian inclinations. In spite of protestations from such scholars as J. B. Lightfoot[52]--who thought that Pseudo-Ignatius had simply quoted from AC--this identification prevails today. To decide this issue is beyond the scope of this work. However, if there are strong resemblances in language and thought to Pseudo-Ignatius in any of the phrases of alleged Jewish prayers, it should cause us to doubt that at least that particular phrase has come from the pen of a Jew, especially if the phrase appears elsewhere in the AC. Thus any claim that there is an authentic Jewish text in the AC must be analyzed in light of the linguistic and theological tendencies of both the compiler of the AC and Pseudo-Ignatius.

We have already gained valuable insight toward examining the affirmation of Jewish authorship of some of the prayers in the AC. First, we have seen that the AC is a compilation of older material. Could some of this older material, which is as yet unidentified, have come from Jewish circles? Second, the sources about which we know, except for the Apostolic Tradition of Hippolytus, appear to have come from Syria. Might there be sources from Syrian Judaism among them? Third, the known sources date from approximately the mid-second century to the mid-third century A.D. If there are Jewish sources, may we not expect at first view a similar period of time for composition? Fourth, the compiler was not a slavish collector of sources but an editor as well, and at times it seems, an author. If there were Jewish prayers among his sources can we now retrieve their original wording? This last question, which is so important, virtually everyone has failed to ask.

CHART B

The Compiler's Redaction of Didache Nine and Ten

Didache	*AC*
	25.1 γίνεσθε δὲ πάντοτε εὐχάριστοι ὡς πιστοὶ καὶ εὐγνώμονες δοῦλοι
9.1. περὶ δὲ τῆς εὐχαριστίας	περὶ μὲν τῆς εὐχαριστίας
οὕτως εὐχαριστήσατε	οὕτω λέγοντες
2. πρῶτον περὶ τοῦ ποτηρίου	
εὐχαριστοῦμέν σοι, πάτερ ἡμῶν	2. εὐχαριστοῦμέν σοι, πάτερ ἡμῶν
ὑπὲρ τῆς ἁγίας ἀμπέλου Δαυὶδ τοῦ παιδός σου	ὑπὲρ τῆς ζωῆς
ἧς ἐγνώρισας ἡμῖν διὰ Ἰησοῦ τοῦ παιδός σου	ἧς ἐγνώρισας ἡμῖν διὰ Ἰησοῦ τοῦ παιδός σου
σοὶ ἡ δόξα εἰς τοὺς αἰῶνας. 3. περὶ δὲ τοῦ κλάσματος· εὐχαριστοῦμέν σοι, πάτερ ἡμῶν, ὑπὲρ τῆς ζωῆς καὶ γνώσεως ἧς ἐγνώρισας ἡμῖν διὰ Ἰησοῦ τοῦ παιδός σου· σοὶ ἡ δόξα εἰς τοὺς αἰῶνας.	
	δι' οὗ καὶ τὰ πάντα ἐποίησας καὶ τῶν ὅλων προνοεῖς, ὃν καὶ ἀπεστείλας ἐπὶ σωτηρίᾳ τῇ ἡμετέρᾳ γενέσθαι ἄνθρωπον, ὃν καὶ συνεχωρήσας παθεῖν καὶ ἀποθανεῖν, ὃν καὶ ἀναστήσας εὐδόκησας δοξάσαι καὶ ἐκάθισας ἐκ δεξιῶν σου, δι' οὗ καὶ ἐπηγγείλω ἡμῖν τὴν ἀνάστασιν τῶν νεκρῶν. 3. σὺ δέσποτα παντοκράτορ, θεὲ αἰώνιε
4. ὥσπερ ἦν τοῦτο	ὥσπερ ἦν τοῦτο
τὸ κλάσμα	
διεσκορπισμένον	διεσκορπισμένον
ἐπάνω τῶν ὀρέων	
καὶ συναχθὲν ἐγένετο	καὶ συναχθὲν ἐγένετο
ἕν	εἷς ἄρτος
οὕτω συναχθήτω σου ἡ ἐκκλησία ἀπὸ τῶν περάτων τῆς γῆς εἰς τὴν σὴν βασιλείαν	οὕτως συνάγαγέ σου τὴν ἐκκλησίαν ἀπὸ τῶν περάτων τῆς γῆς εἰς τὴν σὴν βασιλείαν
ὅτι σοῦ ἐστιν ἡ δόξα καὶ ἡ δύναμις διὰ Ἰησοῦ Χριστοῦ· εἰς τοὺς αἰῶνας	

CHART B

The Compiler's Redaction
of Didache Nine and Ten

Didache	*AC*
	7.25.1. Be thankful always as faithful and honest servants
9.1. And concerning the thanksgiving (of the eucharist) thus	and concerning the thanksgiving (of the eucharist) thus
give thanks:	say:
2. First concerning the cup, we give thanks to you, our Father,	We give thanks to you, our Father,
for the holy vine of David your child	
	for the life
which you made known to us through Jesus your child.	which you made known to us through Jesus your child,
To you be glory forever. 3. And concerning the fragment (of bread) we give thanks to you our Father, for the life and knowledge which you made known to us through Jesus your child. To you be glory forever.	
	through whom also you made all things and you provde for the universe, whom also you sent to become a man for our salvation, whom also you permitted to suffer and to die, whom also you raised up and were well-pleased to glorify and you seated him on your right hand, through whom also you promised us resurrection from the dead. 3. You, Master almighty, eternal God
4. As this	as this
fragment (of bread)	
was scattered	was scattered
upon the mountains	
and gathered	and gathered
into one	into one loaf
thus let your church be gathered	thus gather your church
from the corners of the earth into your kingdom	from the corners of the earth into your kingdom.
because to you is the glory and the power through Jesus Christ forever.	

Didache	*AC*
	4. ἔτι εὐχαριστοῦμεν, πάτερ ἡμῶν ὑπὲρ τοῦ τιμίου αἵματος Ἰησοῦ Χριστοῦ τοῦ ἐκχυθέντος ὑπὲρ ἡμῶν καὶ τοῦ τιμίου σώματος, οὗ καὶ ἀντίτυπα ταῦτα ἐπιτελοῦμεν, αὐτοῦ διαταξαμένου ἡμῖν καταγγέλλειν τὸν αὐτοῦ θάνατον· δι᾽ αὐτοῦ γάρ σοι καὶ ἡ δόξα εἰς τοὺς αἰῶνας ἀμήν.
5. μηδεὶς δὲ φαγέτω	5. μηδεὶς δὲ ἐσθιέτω
μηδὲ πιέτω ἀπὸ τῆς εὐχαριστίας ὑμῶν	
	ἐξ αὐτῶν τῶν ἀμυήτων
ἀλλ᾽	ἀλλὰ
	μόνοι
οἱ βαπτισθέντες εἰς	οἱ βεβαπτισμένοι εἰς
ὄνομα κυρίου	
	τὸν τοῦ κυρίου θάνατον.
καὶ γὰρ περὶ τούτου εἴρηκεν ὁ κύριος μὴ δῶτε τὸ ἅγιον τοῖς κυσί.	
	6. εἰ δέ τις ἀμύητος κρύψας ἑαυτὸν μεταλάβοι, κρίμα αἰώνιον φάγεται, ὅτι μὴ ὢν τῆς εἰς Χριστὸν πίστεως μετέλαβεν ὧν οὐ θέμις, εἰς τιμωρίαν ἑαυτοῦ. 7. εἰ δὲ τις κατὰ ἄγνοιαν μεταλάβοι, τοῦτον τάχιον στοιχειώσαντες μυήσατε, ὅπως μὴ καταφρονητὴς ἐξέλθοι.
10.1. μετὰ δὲ	26.1. μετὰ δὲ
τὸ ἐμπλησθῆναι	
	τὴν μετάληψιν
οὕτως εὐχαριστήσατε	οὕτως εὐχαριστήσατε
εὐχαριστοῦμέν σοι	εὐχαριστοῦμέν σοι
	ὁ θεὸς καὶ
πάτερ	πατὴρ
	Ἰησοῦ τοῦ σωτῆρος ἡμῶν
ἅγιε	
ὑπὲρ τοῦ ἁγίου ὀνόματός σου	ὑπὲρ τοῦ ἁγίου ὀνόματός σου
οὗ κατεσκήνωσας ἐν	οὗ κατεσκήνωσας ἐν
ταῖς καρδίαις ἡμῶν	
	ἡμῖν
καὶ ὑπὲρ τῆς γνώσεως καὶ	καὶ ὑπὲρ τῆς γνώσεως καὶ
πίστεως	πίστεως
	καὶ ἀγάπης
καὶ ἀθανασίας ἧς	καὶ ἀθανασίας ἧς
ἐγνώρισας	
	ἔδωκας
ἡμῖν διὰ Ἰησοῦ τοῦ παιδός σου	ἡμῖν διὰ Ἰησοῦ τοῦ παιδός σου
σοὶ ἡ δόξα εἰς τοὺς αἰῶνας	
σὺ δέσποτα παντοκράτορ	σὺ δέσποτα παντοκράτορ
	ὁ θεὸς τῶν ὅλων
ἔκτισας	ἔκτισας
τὰ πάντα	

Didache	*AC*
	4. We further give thanks, our Father, for the precious blood of Jesus Christ which was poured out for us and the precious body, the representation of which we celebrate, since he himself commanded us to show forth his death. Amen.
5. And let no one eat	5. And let no one eat
nor anyone drink from your thanksgiving	
	of them who are uninitiated
but	but
	only
they who have been baptized	they who have been baptized
into	into
the name of the Lord,	
	the Lord's death.
for also concerning this the Lord has said, "Do not give dogs what is holy."	
	6. And if any uninitiate should participate by hiding himself, he will eat eternal condemnation, because though he was not a believer in Christ he participated in those things which are not lawful, for his punishment. 7. And if anyone partakes in ignorance, quickly instruct him and initiate him, that he might not depart a despiser.
10.1. And after	7.26.1. And after
you are filled up with food	
	the participation
thus give thanks:	thus give thanks:
2. We give thanks to you	2. We give thanks to you
	God and
holy	
Father	Father
	of Jesus our Savior
for your holy name which you made to dwell in	for your holy name which you made to dwell in
our hearts	
	us
and for the knowledge and faith	and for the knowledge and faith
	and love
and immortality which	and immortality which
you made known	
	you gave
to us through Jesus your child.	to us through Jesus your child.
To you be glory forever.	
3. You, Master almighty,	3. You, Master almighty,
	God of the universe
created	created
all things	

Didache	*AC*
	τὸν κόσμον καὶ τὰ ἐν αὐτῷ δι' αὐτοῦ, καὶ νόμον κατεφύτευσας ἐν ταῖς ψυχαῖς ἡμῶν καὶ τὰ πρὸς μετάλυψιν προευτρέπισας ἀνθρώποις· ὁ θεὸς τῶν ἁγίων καὶ ἀμέμπτων πατέρων ἡμῶν Ἀβραὰμ καὶ Ἰσαὰκ καὶ Ἰακώβ, τῶν πιστῶν δούλων σου, ὁ δύνατὸς θεός, ὁ πιστὸς καὶ ἀληθινὸς καὶ ἀψευδὴς ἐν ταῖς ἐπαγγελίαις· ὁ ἀποστείλας ἐπι γῆς Ἰησοῦν τὸν Χριστόν σου ἀνθρώποις συναναστραφῆναι ὡς ἄνθρωπον, θεὸν ὄντα λόγον καὶ ἄνθρωπον, καὶ τὴν πλάνην πρόρριζον ἀνελεῖν.
ἕνεκεν τοῦ ὀνόματός σου, τροφήν τε καὶ ποτὸν ἔδωκας τοῖς ἀνθρώποις εἰς ἀπόλαυσιν, ἵνα σοι εὐχαριστησωσιν, ἡμῖν δὲ ἐχαρίσω πνευματικὴν τροφὴν καὶ ποτὸν καὶ ζωὴν αἰώνιον διὰ τοῦ παιδός σου. 4. πρὸ πάντων εὐχαριστοῦμέν σοι ὅτι δυνατὸς εἶ· σοὶ ἡ δόξα εἰς τοὺς αἰῶνας.	
	4. αὐτὸς καὶ νῦν δι' αὐτοῦ
5. μνήσθητι	μνήσθητι
κύριε	
τῆς	τῆς ἁγίας
ἐκκλησίας σου	σου ἐκκλησίας
	ταύτης, ἣν περιεποιήσω τῷ τιμίῳ αἵματι τοῦ Χριστοῦ σου
	καὶ
τοῦ ῥύσασθαι αὐτῆν ἀπὸ παντὸς πονηροῦ καὶ τελειῶσαι αὐτὴν ἐν τῇ ἀγάπῃ σου	ῥῦσαι αὐτὴν ἀπὸ παντὸς πονηροῦ καὶ τελείωσον αὐτὴν ἐν τῇ ἀγάπῃ σου
	καὶ τῇ ἀληθείᾳ σου
καὶ σύναξον	καὶ συνάγαγε
αὐτὴν ἀπὸ τῶν τεσσάρων ἀνέμων	
τὴν ἁγιασθεῖσαν	
	πάντας ἡμᾶς
εἰς τὴν σὴν βασιλείαν ἣν ἡτοίμασας αὐτῇ	εἰς τὴν σὴν βασιλείαν ἣν ἡτοίμασας αὐτῇ
ὅτι σοῦ ἐστιν ἡ δύναμις καὶ ἡ δόξα εἰς τοὺς αἰῶνας.	
6. ἐλθέτω χάρις καὶ παρεθέτω ὁ κόσμος οὗτος.	
	5. μαραναθά
ὡσαννὰ τῷ θεῷ Δαυίδ	ὡσαννὰ τῷ υἱῷ Δαυίδ
	εὐλογημένος ὁ ἐρχόμενος ἐν ὀνόματι κυρίου, θεὸς κύριος ὁ ἐπιφάνεις ἡμῖν ἐν σαρκί

Didache	*AC*
	the world and the things in it through him, and you implanted a law in our souls and prepared beforehand the things for the participation of men. God of our holy and blameless fathers, Abraham, Isaac, and Jacob, your faithful servants, the powerful God, faithful and true and without falsehood in promises, who sent upon the earth Jesus your Christ to live with men as a man, being God the Word and man, and to utterly remove error.
for the sake of your name. Both food and drink you gave to men for enjoyment, that they might give thanks to you, and you graciously gave us spiritual food and drink and eternal life through your child. 4. For all things we give you thanks because you are powerful. To you be glory forever.	
	4. You yourself also now through him
5. Remember	remember
Lord	
	this
your	your
	holy
church	church
	which you have obtained by the precious blood of your Christ
to	and
deliver it from all evil	deliver it from all evil
and perfect it in your love	and perfect it in your love
	and in your truth
and gather it together	and gather together
from the four winds when it is made holy	
	all of us
into your kingdom	into your kingdom
which you prepared for it	which you prepared for it
because yours is the power and the glory forever and ever.	
6. Let grace come and let this world pass away.	
	5. Maranatha
Hosanna to the	Hosanna to the
God	son
of David.	of David.
	Blessed be the one who comes in the name of the Lord, God the Lord who was manifest in the flesh.

Didache	*AC*
εἴ τις ἅγιός ἐστιν ἐρχέσθω	εἴ τις ἅγιος προσερχέσθω
εἴ τις οὐκ ἔστι	εἴ τις οὐκ ἔστιν
μετανοείτω	γινέσθω διὰ μετανοίας
μαρὰν ἀθα· ἀμήν	[μαραναθά]
τοῖς δὲ προφήταις ἐπιτρέπετε εὐχαριστεῖν, ὅσα θέλουσιν.	ἐπιτρέπετε δὲ καὶ τοῖς πρεσβυτέροις ὑμῶν εὐχαριστεῖν.

Didache	*AC*
If anyone is holy, let him come. If anyone is not, let him repent	6. If anyone is holy, let him come. If anyone is not,
	let him become (holy) through repentance.
Maranatha. Amen	
7. And permit	And permit
the prophets to give thanks as they wish.	your presbyters to give thanks also.

NOTES

CHAPTER II

[1]References to the AC are according to the paragraph divisions of Funk (*Didascalia et Constitutiones Apostolorum* (Paderborn: Schoeningh, 1905).

[2]See Brightman's description in *Liturgies, Eastern and Western* (Oxford: Clarendon, 1896) xvii.

[3]See the Clementine Liturgy discussed below.

[4]The early attempts by the eccentric W. Whiston and others to make the AC a first century product appear to have been totally abandoned. See Whiston, *Primitive Christianity Reviv'd* (London: n.p., 1711) vol. 3, 1-28, and the discussion in P. Schaff, *History of the Christian Church* (New York: Scribner's, 1887) vol. 2, 186 n. 1. Among those who accept the late fourth century date and Syrian provenance are: R. H. Cresswell, *The Liturgy of the Eighth Book of the Apostolic Constitutions* (Lond, NY: Young, 1900) 9; L. O'Leary, *The Apostolical Constitutions*, 68f; L. Deiss, *Early Sources of the Liturgy*, trans. B. Weatherhead (New York: Alba House, 1967) 151 (Deiss also offers Constantinople as a possible provenance); W. D. Maxwell, *An Outline of Christian Worship* (Oxford/London: Milford, 1936) 26; R. L. Cross and E. A. Livingstone, eds., *The Oxford Dictionary of the Christian Church* (London: Oxford University, 1974) 75f; A. J. MacLean, *The Ancient Church Orders* (Cambridge: University Press, 1910) 149; Brightman, *Liturgies*, xxviii; H. Achelis, "Apostolic Constitutions and Canons," *The New Schaff-Herzog Encyclopedia of Religious Knowledge*, ed. S. M. Jackson (Grand Rapids, MI: Baker, 1949) vol. 1, 245; B. Altaner, *Patrology*, trans. H. C. Graef (New York: Herder and Herder, 1960) 59 (Altaner also offers Constantinople as an alternative provenance); J. Quasten, *Patrology* (Utrect-Antwerp: Spectrum, 1950-53) vol. 1, 74.

[5]See R. H. Connolly, *Didascalia Apostolorum* (Oxford: Clarendon, 1929) lxxii, 204. References to the Didascalia will be to Connolly's translation of the Syriac text.

[6]See ibid., lxxv-lxxxiii; Quasten, *Patrology*, vol. 2, 149; Cross and Livingstone, *Oxford Dictionary*, 401.

[7]For a discussion of the MSS of the translations of the Didascalia, see Quasten, *Patrology*, vol. 2, 147; O'Leary, *Apostolical Constitutions*, 13f; Connolly, *Didascalia*, xi-xxvi. The most important versions are the Syriac and Latin.

[8]The view of K. Kohler (in "Essenes," 224f) that the Syriac version is an abridgment of AC 1-6 seems to have few supporters. See O'Leary's rebuttal in *Apostolical Constitutions*, 15-19.

[9]A. Harnack, *Geschichte Altchristliche Literature* (Leipzig: Hinrichs, 1904) Th. 2, Bd. 2, p. 490. However, Harnack changed his mind, concluding that this anti-Novatianist polemic was a later addition. See Connolly, *Didascalia*, lxxix. F. X. Funk is said to have at first decided upon the earlier date and then changed

his mind; see *Apostolischen Konstitutionen* (Frankfurt: Minerva, 1970, first published 1891) 50-54, and Connolly, *Didascalia*, lxxxix. Others who have accepted the later date are: O'Leary, *Apostolical Constitutions*, 29f; and most recently, P. Galtier, "La date de la Didascalie des Apôtres," *Aux Origines du Sacrement de Penitence* (Rome: Universitatis Gregorianae, 1951) 190-221. The great scholar H. Achelis could not decide; see *Die Ältesten Quellen des Orientalischen Kirchenrechts: Die Syrische Didaskalia* (Leipzig: Hinrichs, 1904) 266.

[10]Connolly, *Didascalia*, lxxxvii-xci.

[11]See F. C. Burkitt, "The Didascalia," *JTS* 31 (1930) 258-65; Quasten, *Patrology*, vol. 2, 147; Altaner, *Patrology*, 56; Cross and Livingstone, *Oxford Dictionary*, 401; Deiss, *Early Sources*, 77.

[12]Connolly lists the parallels: the baptismal rite is typical of Syria; the order of deaconesses is similar to that of the Syriac Acts of Judas Thomas. For other evidence, see *Didascalia*, lxxxviii.

[13]Connolly (ibid., lxxxix) preferred the area between Antioch and Edessa but allowed for the possibility of lower Syria or Palestine as the provenance; Quasten, *Patrology*, vol. 2, 147; Altaner, *Patrology*, 56; Cross and Livingstone, *Oxford Dictionary*, 401; Deiss, *Early Sources*, 77.

[14]Connolly, *Didascalia*, xxf.

[15]By saying that the chapters have been "recast" (*remaniés*), Leclercq apparently means that the compiler of AC has presented the same general instruction of the Didascalia within a framework more appropriate for his situation. Hence the teaching on widows in Didascalia 15 is brought up to date in AC 3.8f.

[16]H. Leclercq, "Constitutions Apostoliques," *Dictionaire D'Archeologie Chrétiènne et De Liturgie*, ed. F. Cabrol and H. Leclercq (Paris: Letouzey, 1914) T. 3, pt. 2, cols. 2735f. For a general idea of the similar material, see Funk's edition of the AC (*Didascalia et Constitutiones*) where new material is underlined in books one through six.

[17]Altaner, *Patrology*, 52.

[18]See R. A. Kraft, *Barnabas and the Didache*, The Apostolic Fathers, vol. 3; ed. R. M. Grant (Toronto/New York/London: Nelson, 1965) 57-59. The literature for the Didache is vast. See the bibliographic information in Quasten, *Patrology*, vol. 1, 36f; Altaner, *Patrology*, 53f.

[19]So Altaner, *Patrology*, 51 (first half of second century); Quasten, *Patrology*, vol. 1, 37 (100-150); A. Harnack, "Didache," *Schaff-Herzog Encyclopedia*, vol. 3, 420-24 (120-65). See the summary of opinions in F. E. Volkes, "The Didache-Still Debated," *The Church Quarterly* 3 (1979) 57-62. Most of the opinions listed by Volkes range from A.D. 110 to 150.

[20]J.-P. Audet, *La Didache: Instructions des Apotres* (Etudes Biblique; Paris: Gabalda, 1958) 24. Chapters 1-6 of the Didache have since the early time of C. Taylor (*The Teaching of the Twelve Apostles* [Cambridge: D. Bell, 1886] 49) been regarded by many as originally a Jewish manual for proselytes, dating from the first century. This argument was advanced by E. J. Goodspeed (*The*

Apostolic Fathers [New York: Harper, 1950] 285-310) who argued that the Latin translation of 1-6 was not of the Didache but of the source of the Didache.

[21]Kraft, *Barnabas and the Didache*, 76.

[22]Quasten, *Patrology*, vol. 1, 37; Altaner, *Patrology*, 51; Cross and Livingstone, *Oxford Dictionary*, 401.

[23]Kraft, *Barnabas and the Didache*, 77. Harnack (*Schaff-Herzog Encyclopedia*, vol. 3, 420-24) had preferred Egypt. Pella has also been suggested. See the summary of opinions by Volkes, "The Didache-Still Debated," 57-62.

[24]O'Leary, *Apostolical Constitutions*, 31. I know of no one recently who believed that several compilers worked over the material. See Brightman, *Liturgies*, xxv.

[25]See other examples given in O'Leary, *Apostolical Constitutions*, 31-34. The character of the editorial activity is clearly perceived if one reads the footnotes supplied by J. Donaldson to W. Whiston's translation of AC. These notes indicate that, while much of the subject matter of Didache is incorporated into the AC, there is also much addition made to it and that these additions are of the same type as those found in AC books one through six. A general idea of the verbal parallels between the Didache and AC 7.1-32 may be gained by examining F. X. Funk's edition of AC where the verbal parallels are underlined. The editor has used a heavy hand on the Didache as well. See Donaldson, *Ante-Nicene Fathers* (New York: Scribner's, 1899) vol. 7, 465-72, and Funk, *Didascalia et Constitutiones*, 386-422.

[26]The only prayer in Didascalia is the Prayer of Manasseh (Didascalia 7, AC 2.22.12-14). Here the compiler has quoted the prayer almost verbatim. But he may have believed he was quoting scripture.

[27]The compiler may have had another prayer before him which he simply wanted to include (see Kohler's claim in Chapter I, Chart A), or this section may have been in the MS of the Didache which he possessed. At any rate, this is the only addition or substitution for which no rationale can be seen.

[28]It is difficult to know why the compiler did not want something in his AC. At any rate, when later we study the alleged Jewish prayers we can only ask what may the compiler have added to the prayers not what is missing.

[29]Except for a prayer in 7.47f, the *gloria in excelsis* which is also found in codex Alexandrinus (included in Funk's text) and a seventh century Irish prayer book called the Antiphony of Bangor. See R. E. Warren, *The Liturgy and Ritual of the Ante-Nicene Church* (London: Society for Promoting Christian Knowledge, 1912) 236-40. Drawing conclusions from a comparison of the recensions of this prayer is difficult since one can not judge with certainty whether any of the three was the source for the others. However, since the versions of the prayer in the Irish prayer book and codex Alexandrinus are so similar and usually agree against the version in AC, we may assume that the differences are due to additions by the compiler of the AC. According to Warren's English translation of the text in the Irish prayer book and Funk's Greek text of both the AC and codex Alexandrinus prayers, the prayers differ only slightly

until the first "amen" (which is left out of the AC but should come at the end of 7.48.2). After this it appears that all three texts have been expanded at will. The comparison of the texts before the first amen is instructive. They are very similar except 1) AC 7. 47.2 interpolates after "we worship you" the section "through the great high priest, you the one unbegotten God, alone unapproachable" (διὰ τοῦ μεγάλου ἀρχιερέως, σὲ τὸν ὄντα θεὸν ἀγέννητον ἕνα, ἀπρόσιτον μόνον). 2) In addition to this interesting interpolation, a trinitarian formula which should be at the end of paragraph two has been omitted. In the text of Alexandrinus it reads: κύριε, υἱὲ μονογενῆ Ἰησοῦ Χριστὲ, καὶ ἅγιον πνεῦμα. In each case the other two texts agree against the AC. According to Brightman (*Liturgies*, xxv), the emphasis on the pre-eminence of the Father is typical of the compiler. I can see no reason why the compiler omitted the trinitarian formula since he included such formulas elsewhere (e.g. AC 8.40.4, 8.41.5). It should be repeated that, except for these changes, made perhaps for theological reasons, there is almost no difference between the AC and the other texts.

[30] R. H. Connolly, *The So-Called Egyptian Church Order and Derived Documents* (Cambridge: University Press, 1916).

[31] Altaner, *Patrology*, 55; Quasten, *Patrology*, vol. 2, 180; B. S. Easton, *The Apostolic Tradition of Hippolytus* (New York: MacMillan; Cambridge: University Press, 1934); G. Dix, *The Treatise of the Apostolic Tradition* (London: Society for Promoting Christian Knowledge, 1937); Cross and Livingstone (*Oxford Dictionary*, 7) say that the Egyptian Church Order "is now generally held to be the work of Hippolytus." For two exceptions to this conclusion, see the bibliography of Altaner (*Patrology*, 55).

[32] For the Latin text, see Dix, *Treatise*. For the Ethiopic and Coptic texts, see the bibliography in Altaner, *Patrology*, 55. Citations and comparisons are according to Dix's text.

[33] Easton, *The Apostolic Tradition*, 25; Dix, *Treatise*, xxxv-xxxvii; C. C. Richardson, "The Date and Setting of the Apostolic Tradition of Hippolytus," *Anglican Theological Review* 30 (1948) 38-44.

[34] Quasten (*Patrology*, vol. 2, 180) notes this fact. But we must not neglect the influence of this work upon another Eastern area: Syria. The seventh century work Testament of our Lord is a Syriac translation of a Greek adaptation of the Apostolic Tradition.

[35] Cresswell, *Liturgy*, 8.

[36] See Chapter III for a translation of most of AC 8.16.3. This paragraph, Goodenough maintained, is based on a Jewish prayer (*By Light, Light*, 335). See Chapter IV for the discussion of this paragraph.

[37] So called because Clement supposedly published the AC; see above.

[38] Maxwell, *Outline of Christian Worship*, 26; J. H. Strawley, *The Early History of the Liturgy* (Cambridge: University Press, 1947) 87; Brightman, *Liturgies*, xxiv-xxvii.

[39] R. Probst, *Liturgie der drei ersten christliche Jahrhunderte* (Darmstadt: Wissenschaftliche, 1968; first printed, 1870) 278-81.

[40]V. Brückner ("Über die Zusammensetzung der Liturgie im achten Buche der apostolischen Konstitutionen," *Theologische Studien und Kritiken* 56 [1883] 1-32) saw two sources, the second beginning at AC 8.12. P. Kleinert ("Bemerkungen zur Komposition der Clemensliturgie," *Theologische Studien und Kritiken* 56 [1883] 33-59) saw three sources behind the CL: a rubrical scheme, an ἐπίσκοπος document and an ἀρχιερεύς document.

[41]See Cresswell's discussion in *Liturgy of the Eighth Book*, 31-35; also Brightman, *Liturgies*, xlii-xlv.

[42]Brightman, *Liturgies*, xlii-xlv.

[43]See ibid., xliv, where Brightman explains the use of both ἐπίσκοπος and ἀρχιερεύς: ἐπισκοπός was in the source, ἀρχιερεύς is from the compiler's hand. See also p. xxxiii, "Whatever sources the compiler has used, it is plain that he has dealt very freely with them, and that in particular the prayers are substantially his own work."

[44]Leclercq, *Dictionaire*, T. 3, pt. 2, col. 2752; Probst, *Liturgie*, 289-95, where he offers extensive parallels between the CL and Justin Martyr; Warren, *Liturgy and Ritual*, 254-56.

[45]Warren, *Liturgy*, 251: "...much of the language used in these Clementine devotions seems to fall short of the full Catholic doctrine of the co-equality of the Persons in the Trinity." Leclercq (*Dictionaire*, T. 3, pt. 2, col. 2753) and Probst (*Liturgie*, 289-95) think that the Christology of CL finds its best parallel in Justin (mid-second century). See Probst's comparisons, e.g. p. 291 where the Son is described in both CL (AC 8.12.7) and Justin (*Dial*. 128f, *Apology* 2.6) in similar terms (creator, "angel" "begotten before all") but with none of the Nicene language (especially ὁμοούσιος).

[46]Leclercq, *Dictionaire*, T. 3, pt. 2, col. 2753. Warren simply argued for an ante-Nicene date. Probst believed that there were elements in the CL from the first century.

[47]Brightman, *Liturgies*, xxxiii-xliii. Note also that Brightman (xxxiii) claimed that the prayers in AC 7.33-38 are also largely the work of the compiler. These are some of the prayers that have been claimed for Jewish authorship. Leclercq agreed with this analysis of the prayers; see *Dictionaire*, T. 3, pt. 2, col. 2750.

[48]Brightman, *Liturgies*, xlv; Warren, *Liturgy*, 256; Cresswell, *The Liturgy of the Eighth Book*, 10; O'Leary, *Apostolical Constitutions*, 59f.

[49]Deiss, *Early Sources*, 151; Altaner, *Patrology*, 59; Cross and Livingstone, *Oxford Dictionary* , 75f.

[50]Brightman, *Liturgies*, xxv; O'Leary, *Apostolical Constitutions*, 69; Funk, *Apostolischen Konstitutionen*, 97-102, 120-23. Brightman pointed out among other things that the pre-eminence of the Father is emphasized (ὁ εἷς καὶ μόνος ἀληθινὸς θεός 2.6.9, 2.56.1, 5.6.7, 5.16.3) while the subordination of the Son is repeated (2.26.2, 2.30.2, 5.7.12, 5.20.6).

[51]J. B. Lightfoot, *The Apostolic Fathers* (London: MacMillan, 1889) vol. 1, pt. 2, 262-64. Quasten agreed with Lightfoot (*Patrology*, vol. 1, 74). For those who identify the two, see: Cross and Livingstone, *Oxford Dictionary*, 75f; Brightman, *Liturgies*, xxvii; Leclercq, *Dictionaire*, T. 3, pt. 2, col. 2739; Achelis, *Schaff-Herzog Encyclopedia*, vol. 1, 245; Cresswell, *Liturgy*, 9.

CHAPTER III

TEXT AND TRANSLATION OF THE PRAYERS

The reader must have the text of the prayers in front of him before he can understand the material in the subsequent chapters. This chapter presents a fresh translation with notes of all of the prayers alleged to be Jewish, along with the text of Funk. Chapter IV will evaluate the claim that these prayers have originated in Judaism.

Text

The *editio princeps* of the AC was made by F. Turrianus in 1563.[1] Turrianus's text was reprinted with slight changes by J. B. Cotelerius in 1678; by J. Clericus in 1698 and 1724; and by W. Ültzen in 1853.[2] Cotelerius's text may also be found reprinted in J.-P. Migne's *Patrologiae*.[3] C.K.J. von Bunsen's text of 1854 has been called the "first critical edition."[4] This was followed by P. de Lagard's critical edition of 1862.[5] The best edition made to date is F. X. Funk's text, published in 1905, since he both made use of older MSS than any previous edition (MSS from the tenth and eleventh centuries) and he utilized more MSS than any other (twenty-one MSS). In addition, Funk furnished an excellent critical apparatus to enable one to check his editorial decisions. Therefore, Funk's text has been used as the basis of the present translation and has been reproduced in this chapter.[6] Funk's critical apparatus is absent here, since his work is readily available, and since the notes examine the most important variants.

It seemed advisable to make some investigation of Funk's reliability as an editor and collator, and therefore his text has been checked against one of the oldest MSS. Since C. H. Turner's[7] discovery of the Verona fragment of an early Latin version of AC led him to believe in the superiority of Funk's MS d (Vat. Gk. 1506, A.D. 1024)[8] over the others, we decided to use this MS as a check against Funk.[9] It is sufficient to report that Funk has faithfully supplied all the variants from his text of MS d in his apparatus, at least as far as the prayers here translated are concerned. The texts in Migne (essentially that of Turrianus, Cotelerius, Clericus and Ültzen) and Bunsen[10] will serve as additional helps in making decisions about the text.

Translation

The only complete translation of AC in English was made by W. Whiston in 1711 and reprinted "with considerable alterations" in volume seven of the *Ante-Nicene Fathers* (ANF).[11] The main weakness of this version--apart from certain infelicities in translation--is that Whiston used Turrianus' Greek text.[12] An improved translation of the alleged Jewish prayers by D. R. Darnell[13] will appear shortly. These works in addition to other partial renderings of AC books seven and eight have proved useful in the present translation.

The Notes

The intention in this chapter is to explain and annotate the prayers as they now stand in AC, without attempting to establish or differentiate a Jewish stratum. The parallels indicate other ancient sources in which the main ideas appear. Scriptural references generally represent only direct quotations.

To assist the reader, for this chapter only the notes regarding the translation will appear at the bottom of each page, and the notes for this chapter's introductory text will appear on the next page instead of at the end of this chapter.

NOTES

CHAPTER III

[1]See C. H. Turner, "A Primitive Edition of the Apostolic Constitutions and Canons: An Early List of Apostles and Disciples," *JTS* 15 (1913/14) 53.

[2]See Cross and Livingstone, *Oxford Dictionary of the Christian Church*, 76.

[3]According to Achelis, *Schaff-Herzog Encyclopedia*, vol. 1, 246. See Migne, *Patrologiae: Series Graeca* (Paris: Garnier, 1886) vol. 1, cols. 555-1155; and C.K.J. von Bunsen, *Analecta Ante-Nicaena* (Aalen: Scientia, 1968; first published 1854) vol. 1, 35.

[4]Achelis, *Schaff-Herzog Encyclopedia*, vol. 1, 246.

[5]Cross and Livingstone, *Oxford Dictionary*, 76.

[6]Funk, *Didascalia et Constitutiones Apostolorum*, 424-42. See Turner's appraisal of Funk's work: "...no doubt Funk's text has superseded those of all previous editors..." ("A Primitive Edition," 54) and see Turner's discussion of Funk's work (53-62).

[7]See Turner's articles in *JTS*: "A Fragment of an Unknown Latin Version of the Apostolic Constitutions," *JTS* 13 (1911/12) 492-510; "A Primitive Edition of the Apostolic Constitutions and Canons," *JTS* 15 (1913/14) 53-65; "Notes on the Apostolic Constitutions. The Compiler an Arian," *JTS* 16 (1914/15) 54-61; "Notes on the Apostolic Constitutions," *JTS* 31 (1929/30) 128-41. Turner dated the fragment to the sixth century A.D., merely two hundred years after the composition of AC ("Notes on the Apostolic Constitutions," 129). Unfortunately, the fragment only contains one of the prayers under consideration here. It extends from AC 8.41-46. See the notes on 8.41.

[8]Funk, *Constitutiones*, xxv.

[9]I wish to thank the Vatican library and the International Institute for Christian Origins for making the microfilm of Vat. Gk. 1506 accessible to me (books seven and eight of AC are fols. 36-72^{v}).

[10]In addition Lagard's text--which was otherwise inaccessible to me--is used for the prayer of AC 8.12 since it is reprinted in Brightman's *Liturgies*.

[11]Whiston, *Primitive Christianity Reviv'd*, vol. 2; A. Roberts et al., *The Ante-Nicene Fathers* (New York: Scribner's, 1899) vol. 7, 385-508.

[12]Bunsen, *Analecta Ante-Nicaena*, vol. 1, 35.

[13]In J. H. Charlesworth, ed., *Old Testament Pseudepigrapha* (Garden City, NY: Doubleday, in press).

7.26.1-3

Μετὰ δὲ τὴν μετάληψιν οὕτως εὐχαριστήσατε· 2. Εὐχαριστοῦμέν σοι, ὁ θεὸς καὶ πατὴρ Ἰησοῦ τοῦ σωτῆρος ἡμῶν, ὑπὲρ τοῦ ἁγίου ὀνόματός σου οὗ κατεσκήνωσας ἐν ἡμῖν, καὶ ὑπὲρ τῆς γνώσεως καὶ πίστεως καὶ ἀγάπης καὶ ἀθανασίας ἧς ἔδωκας ἡμῖν διὰ Ἰησοῦ τοῦ παιδός σου. 3. σὺ δέσποτα παντοκράτορ, ὁ θεὸς τῶν ὅλων, ἔκτισας τὸν κόσμον καὶ τὰ ἐν αὐτῷ δι' αὐτοῦ, καὶ νόμον κατεφύτευσας ἐν ταῖς ψυχαῖς ἡμῶν καὶ τὰ πρὸς μετάληψιν προευτρέπισας ἀνθρώποις· ὁ θεὸς τῶν ἁγίων καὶ ἀμέμπτων πατέρων ἡμῶν, Ἀβραὰμ καὶ Ἰσαὰκ καὶ Ἰακώβ, τῶν πιστῶν δούλων σου, ὁ δυνατὸς θεός, ὁ πιστὸς καὶ ἀληθινὸς καὶ ἀψευδὴς ἐν ταῖς ἐπαγγελίαις·

7.26.1-3

1. After the participation,[1] thus give thanks: 2. We thank you, God and Father of Jesus our savior for your holy name which you made to dwell among us, and for knowledge and faith and love and immortality which you gave to us through Jesus your child. 3. You, Master almighty, God of the universe, created the world and the things in it through him, and you implanted a law in our souls and prepared before hand the things for the participation of men; God of our holy and blameless fathers, Abraham, Isaac, and Jacob, your faithful servants, the powerful God, faithful and true and without falsehood in promises.

---

[1]The underlined words are those underlined in Funk's Greek text. They indicate where the compiler of AC has incorporated words from his source, the Didache. Occasionally, however, Funk's underlined words represent no more than the general idea of the source. The word μετάληψις, "participation," e.g., is not in the text of the Didache but μετὰ τὸ ἐμπλησθῆναι, "after being filled" (i.e. in eating the eucharistic meal). The compiler has evidently replaced this phrase with a more contemporaneous expression. See Chapter II, Chart B.

7.33.2-7

2. Αἰώνιε σῶτερ ἡμῶν, ὁ βασιλεὺς τῶν θεῶν, ὁ ὢν μόνος παντοκράτωρ καὶ κύριος, ὁ θεὸς πάντων τῶν ὄντων καὶ θεὸς τῶν ἁγίων καὶ ἀμέμπτων πατέρων ἡμῶν τῶν πρὸ ἡμῶν, ὁ θεὸς Ἀβραὰμ καὶ Ἰσαὰκ καὶ Ἰακώβ, ὁ ἐλεήμων καὶ οἰκτίρμων, ὁ μακρόθυμος καὶ πολυέλεος, ᾧ πᾶσα γυμνοφανὴς βλέπεται καρδία καὶ πᾶν κρύφιον ἐνθύμημα ἀποκαλύπτεται· πρὸς σὲ βοῶσιν ψυχαὶ δικαίων, ἐπὶ σοὶ πεποίθασιν ἐλπίδες ὁσίων, ὁ τῶν ἀμέμπτων πατήρ, ὁ τῶν μετ' εὐθύτητος ἐπικαλουμένων σε ἐπήκοος, ὁ καὶ σιωπωμένας ἐπιστάμενος ἐντεύξεις (χωρεῖ γὰρ μέχρι σπλάγχνων ἀνθρωπίνων ἡ σὴ πρόνοια, καὶ διὰ συνειδήσεως ἐρευνᾷς ἑκάστου τὴν γνώμην),

7.33.2-7

2. Our eternal Savior, the King of the gods,[1] the one alone who is almighty and Lord, God of all that is,[2] and God of our holy and blameless fathers and of those before us;[3] God of Abraham, Isaac and Jacob,[4] the merciful and compassionate, the patient and very merciful,[5] the one to whom every heart is seen as naked[6] and (to whom) every hidden thought is revealed; to you the souls of the righteous cry out, upon you the hopes of the pious rely;[7] father of the blameless ones, the one who listens to those with uprightness whom summon you, the one who even knows the petitions which are kept silent--for your providence[8] reaches even to the inward parts of men and you search out the thought[9] of each through

---

[1]Esth 4:17^{r} LXX.

[2]Or as in ANF and Darnell: "God of all beings."

[3]So reads MS d at variance with Funk's and Bunsen's text (which omitted the *καί*) but in agreement with Migne.

[4]Exod 3:16, Prayer of Manasseh 1.

[5]Joel 2:13, Jonah 4:2.

[6]ANF: "to whom every heart is naked and every heart is seen." I have attempted a more literal rendering.

[7]The preceding two clauses could have a relationship of *parallelismus membrorum*. See Chapter VI.

[8]"Providence" is a very common term in Stoicism. See Cicero, *De Nat. De*. 2.22.57f, Epictetus, *Diss*. 1.6, 14, 16, 2.14.11, 3.15. 14, 3.17, Seneca *de Prov*. and Philo's *de Prov*. See also E. V. Arnold, *Roman Stoicism* (Cambridge: University Press, 1911) 203f; and E. Zeller, *Stoics, Epicureans and Sceptics*, trans. O. J. Reichel (New York: Russel, 1962) 171-78.

The term is also commonly used in the church fathers: 1 Clem 24:5, Hermas Vis 1:3.4, Clement, *Strom*. 6.16, Origen, *Prin*. 3.1.17, *Contra Celsum* 8.70; see G.W.H. Lampe, *A Patristic Greek Lexicon* (Oxford: Clarendon, 1961) 1157f; Daniélou, *Gospel Message and Hellenistic Culture* (London: Longman and Todd) 53, 63.

When used of divine providence, πρόνοια includes foreknowledge, foreordination, foresight and provision (J. Behm, "*Pronoia*" *Theological Dictionary of the New Testament*, ed. G. Kittel (Grand Rapids, MI: Eerdmans, 1974) vol. 4, 1011-17. In our text at this point πρόνοια seems to mean "providential care" or "provision." God in his providential care searches out even the unexpressed needs of men.

[9]Or "judgment" or "disposition" (γνώμη). The immanence of providence is a common theme in Stoicism: Seneca, *Nat. Quaest*. 6.16.1f, Diogenes of Babylon in I. Arnim, *Stoicorum Veterum Fragmenta* (Lipsiae: Teubneri, 1921) vol. 3, 210.

καὶ κατὰ πᾶν κλίμα τῆς οἰκουμένης τὸ διὰ προσευχῆς καὶ λόγων ἀναπέμπεταί σοι θυμίαμα. 3. ὁ τὸν παρόντα αἰῶνα στάδιον δικαιοσύνης ἐνστησάμενος, πᾶσι δὲ ἀνοίξας πύλην ἐλεημοσύνης, ὑποδείξας δὲ ἑκάστῳ τῶν ἀνθρώπων διὰ τῆς ἐμφύτου γνώσεως καὶ φυσικῆς κρίσεως καὶ ἐκ τῆς τοῦ νόμου ὑποφωνήσεως, ὡς πλούτου μὲν οὐκ ἀΐδιον τὸ κτῆμα,

the consciousness[10]--and in every region of the inhabited earth incense is sent up to you through prayer and words.[11] 3. The one who began[12] the present world[13] as a race course[14] of righteousness, and opened to all the gate of mercy, and showed to all[15] mankind through implanted knowledge and natural judgment[16] and from the exhortation[17] of the Law, how the possession of wealth is not

---

[10]For use of this term see Arnim 3.43.5, Diogenes Laertius 7.85, Philo *de Dec.* 87, *Conf. Ling.* 24, *de Tranquil.* 476f, Xenophon, *Anabasis* 2.5.7. The term συνείδησις (Latin *conscientia*) was employed in Greek philosophic circles (and not exclusively Stoic circles. See W. D. Davies, "Conscience" *Interpreter's Dictionary of the Bible*, ed. G. A. Butterick [New York: Abingdon, 1962] vol. 1, 671-76) to mean the innate accuser and rebuker of man's wrong deeds, the conscience. See also C. Maurer "*Suneidesis*" *TDNT*, ed. G. Friedrich, vol. 7, 902-19.

The term also meant "consciousness" (M. S. Enslin, *The Ethics of Paul* [New York: Harper, 1930] 99, and H. G. Liddell, R. Scott, H. S. Jones and R. McKenzie, *A Greek-English Lexicon* [Oxford: Clarendon, 1968] 1704) or the "mind" or "disposition" (1 Clem 34:7, Clement, *Strom.* 7.7, Origen, *Celsum* 5.1; see Lampe). Here in AC 7.33 the term appears to mean man's "consciousness," the thought of which God searches out to learn the unexpressed petitions.

[11]More literal than the ANF: "the incense of prayer and supplication (λόγων) is sent up to Thee." Cf. Darnell, "words."

[12]ἐνίστημι in the first aorist middle has the meaning "to put in" which usually requires a preposition (ἐν or εἰς) or "to begin"; see LSHM.

[13]Or "age" (αἰών).

[14]The ANF "place of combat" is misleading. Warren's translation (*Liturgy and Ritual*, 244) "the place where men should run the race of righteousness" is a good paraphrase. This metaphor is reminiscent of 1 Cor 9:24 and Heb 12:1, but the idea that life is a struggle or contest in the stadium is a common place in Stoicism: Epictetus, *Diss.* 4.4.11, 3.6.8, 4.4.30, *Encher.* 19, 51, Cicero, *de officiis* 3.10, 42.

[15]ἑκάστῳ τῶν ἀνθρώπων. Perhaps one should supply γένος: "to each race of mankind." See Bouyer's very literal translation (*Eucharistie* [Tournai, Belgium: Desclee, 1966] 124) "Chacun des hommes."

[16]"Implanted knowledge" and "natural law" are common themes, found in Greek philosophy, in Philo, and in Christian authors. See Arnim 3.17.14 (ἔμφυτος) 2.288.1 (ἔμψυχος). Philo speaks of the ideal king as the incarnate law (ἔμψυχος νόμος) but also reserves the concept for merely exemplary persons (*de Abr.* 4, *de Virt.* 194). Clement speaks of a φύσικος νόμος in *Paid.* 3.3, *Strom.* 1.29. See also Origen, *Comm. Rom.* 7:7, *Contra Cels.* 5.37. Cf. Rom 2:14, Jas 1:21; AC 8.9.8, 8.12.18, 25.

[17]ὑποφώνησις, "answer," "retort," LSJM. ANF, "the admonitions of the law"; Warren, *Liturgy*, 244, "the exhortation of the law"; Bouyer, *Eucharistie*, 124, "d'apres l'expression de (ta) loi"; Darnell, "by their response to the law," (reading it as an objective genitive). The meaning seems clear: God has taught all men by both innate and revealed knowledge. Therefore the "retort of the law" must be viewed as an exhortation.

εὐπρεπείας οὐκ ἀέναον τὸ κάλλος, δυνάμεως εὐδιάλυτος ἡ ἰσχὺς καὶ
ἀτμὸς μὲν καὶ ματαιότης τὰ σύνολα, μόνη δὲ συνείδησις πίστεως
ἀνύπουλος διαμένει διὰ μέσων οὐρανῶν μετὰ ἀληθείας ἀνερχομένη,
τῆς μελλούσης τρυφῆς δεξιὰν ἀπολαμβάνει, ἅμα

eternal, the beauty of comeliness[18] is not everlasting, the strength of power[19] is easily dissolved.[20] And though all is vapor and entirely vain, only the undisguised[21] consciousness of faith traverses[22] through the midst[23] of the heavens (and) returning with truth receives the right hand of impending joy.[24] At the same time

---

[18]ANF "ornament of beauty." Bouyer, *Eucharistie*, 124, "la beaute d'une apparence agreable." Perhaps this is a Semitism for "comely beauty." See Chapter VI for other Semitisms.

[19]ANF "strength and force." Bouyer, *Eucharistie*, 124, "la force physique." Again this is possibly a Semitism for "powerful strength."

[20]The preceding three lines may be in poetic parallelism.

[21]Or "sincere." See Philo, *Quod omn. prob.* 155 for this word. Here Philo defines the term as meaning that thoughts must agree with words and words with thoughts. "Undisguised faith" is also recommended in the Liturgy of James (Brightman, *Liturgies*, 39), and the Apocalypse of Sedrach speaks of "undisguised love" (1:1). Lampe lists only Macarius Magnes (fourth-fifth century) and Nilus Ancyrus (c. 430) as examples of the use of this rare word besides AC 7.33.

[22]Reading with MSS d, e and h, διαβαίνει. The following phrase διὰ μέσων οὐρανῶν would seem to demand movement through the heavens. Migne and Bunsen read διαβαίνει.

[23]MS d omits διά and reads μέσον instead of Funk's μέσων. Migne and Bunsen include διά but read μέσον. If we accept Migne and Bunsen we are forced to translate διά plus the accusative as "through." This meaning, however, is rare outside of poetry (see LSHM). If we accept the reading μέσων (Funk) we should probably translate (see H. W. Smyth, *A Greek Grammar for Colleges* [New York: American, 1920] §1172) "through the middle heavens" a possible reading but not as obvious as MS d "through the midst of the heavens."

[24]This reading is in harmony with Funk and MSS d and v and at variance with Migne and Bunsen (and MSS a, e and h) which read τροφῆς "nourishment" for τρυφῆς "joy."

καὶ πρὸ τοῦ παραστῆναι τὴν ὑπόσχεσιν τῆς παλιγγενεσίας αὐτὴ
ἡ ψυχὴ

also, before the promise of rebirth[25] is fulfilled[26] the soul

---

[25]It is tempting to conclude with Warren (*Liturgy*, 244) that "it is impossible to make any sense of this sentence." Παλιγγενεσία (see F. Büchsel, "*Palingenesia*" *TDNT*, ed. Kittel, vol. 1, 686-89; M. Dibelius and H. Conzelmann, *The Pastoral Epistles*, trans. P. Buttolph and A. Yarbro [Philadelphia: Fortress, 1972] 148-50; J. Dey, *Palingenesia* [Neutestament Abhandlungen; Münster: Aschendorffschen, 1937] 6-14) was used in antiquity mainly for: (1) rebirth of the cosmos. The Stoics are usually said to have first given the word this significance. The world is restored or reborn to begin a new cycle (Arnim 2.596, 598, 625, 630, Philo *de Aet. Mund*. 6.75.13). Both Philo (*Vit. Mos*. 2.65) and 1 Clem (9:4) use the word to refer to the restoration of the world after the Flood. (2) rebirth of the individual. This usage includes pagan reincarnation (Nemesius, *de nat. hom*. 2, Plutarch *Is. et Os*. 72; see Dibelius and Conzelman, *Pastoral Epistles*, 148) the initiation to the pagan mysteries (Apuleius, 11.21.24, *Corpus Herm*. 13.1; see R. Reitzenstein, *Hellenistic Mystery-Religions*, trans. J. E. Steely [Pittsburgh: Pickwick, 1978; German 3rd ed. 1926] 39) which results in rebirth ("transformation of the essence," Reitzenstein; see also S. Angus, *The Mystery-Religions and Christianity* [New York: Scribner's, 1925] 45 "the object of every initiation was *palingenesia*"), the resurrection of the body (Justin Martyr *Frag. in res*., Clement *quis dives salvetum*, Chrysostom *Frag. Job*; see Lampe), to spiritual rebirth in Christian literature (Chrysostom *hom. in Tit*. 5.3, Clement *Prot*. 9; see Lampe). (3) A new creation in the eschatological age to come (Matt 19:28, Origen *Comm. in Matt*., Eusebius, *Demon. evangel*. 1.9). The last meaning would seem to have been used here. This fits the context: before receiving the joys of the eschatological new age, the soul can already rejoice since it has traversed heaven and partaken of the joys in anticipation. This word also is found in several other places in AC: at 5.7.14 it means the same as here; at 7.34.8 and 8.12.20 it means the bodily resurrection; at 7.39.4, 7.43.3, and 8.6.6 it means spiritual rebirth by baptism.

This passage appears to describe a symbolic or mystical ascent of the mind toward God. It reminds one of the mind's (or soul's) ascent in Philo (e.g. of Moses in *Gig*. 54f, *Leg. All*. 2.54-56; see Goodenough, *By Light, Light*, 235-64; but note the rejection of Goodenough's emphasis on the role of the mysteries in Philo by H. A. Wolfson, *Philo* [Cambridge: Harvard, 1948] vol. 1, 43-51) as well as the later Christian authors like Origen the Alexandrian (fl. 230), e.g. *Homily on Numbers* 27 and *On Genesis* 1.7: "the higher and further (our spirit) goes in its approach to Christ, the more nearly it exposes itself to the glory of His light, the more finely and splendidly is it illuminated by His radiance...And if a man be even so advanced as to be able to go up with Him to the mount, as Peter and James and John, he shall have the illumination not only of the light of Christ but even of the very Father's voice"; (quoted in Quasten, *Patrology*, vol. 2, 97f). This element is also found in Gregory of Nyssa the Cappadocian (fl. 380) in e.g. *De orat. dom*. 2 (see Quasten, *Patrology*, vol. 3, 295f) and Pseudo-Dionysius the Syrian (fl. 500) in *Mystical Theology* (see C. E. Rolt, *Dionysius the Areopagite* [London: SPCK, 1940] and I. P. Sheldon-Williams, "The Pseudo-Dionysius" in A. H. Armstrong, ed. *The Cambridge History of Later Greek and Early Medieval Philosophy* [Cambridge: University Press, 1970] 466-72). The prayer continues to describe the experiences of such ascents. Abraham, Jacob and Moses all have special visions about the nature of the world or see Christ.

Peterson's suggestion (*Miscellania*, vol. 1, 413-17) that this passage refers to Enoch's journey through heaven (see Chapter I) is simply too speculative. Enoch is not mentioned here.

τῇ ἐλπίδι γαυρουμένη εὐφραίνεται. 4. ἐξ ὑπαρχῆς γὰρ τοῦ προπάτορος ἡμῶν 'Αβραὰμ μεταποιουμένου τὴν ὁδὸν τῆς ἀληθείας, ὁραματισμῷ ὡδήγησας, διδάξας, ὅ,τι ποτέ ἐστιν ὁ αἰὼν οὗτος· καὶ τῆς μὲν γνώσεως αὐτοῦ προώδευσεν ἡ πίστις, τῆς δὲ πίστεως ἀκόλουθος ἦν ἡ συνθήκη· εἶπας γάρ· "Ποιήσω τὸ σπέρμα σου ὡς τοὺς ἀστέρας τοῦ οὐρανοῦ καὶ ὡς τὴν ἄμμον τὴν παρὰ τὸ χεῖλος τῆς θαλάσσης." 5. ἀλλὰ μὴν καὶ τὸν 'Ισαὰκ αὐτῷ δωρησάμενος καὶ ὅμοιον αὐτὸν εἰδὼς ἐκείνου τῷ τρόπῳ, καὶ αὐτοῦ ἐπεκλήθης θεὸς εἰπών· "Ἔσομαί σου θεὸς καὶ τοῦ σπέρματός σου μετὰ σέ·" καὶ τοῦ πατρὸς ἡμῶν 'Ιακὼβ ἐπὶ Μεσοποταμίαν στελλομένου, δείξας τὸν Χριστόν,

itself exalts in hope and rejoices. 4. For from the beginning[27] when our forefather Abraham laid claim[28] to the way of truth, you guided (him) in a vision,[29] you taught him what this world is.[30] And Faith traveled before his knowledge, and the covenant followed faith.[31] For you said, "I shall make your seed as the stars of heaven and as the sand on the shore of the sea."[32] 5. Yet truly also after you had presented Isaac to him and you knew that he was like him by his manner, and you were called his God saying, "I shall be your God and (the God) of your seed."[33] And when our father Jacob was sent to Mesopotamia, you showed the Christ,[34]

---

[26]Παρίστημι in the second aorist means "to be at hand," hence of a promise "fulfilled." See LSJM.

[27]The reading in MS d ὑπαρχούσης for ὑπαρχῆς does not change the translation. ὑπάρχω in the active voice signifies "to be in the beginning" (LSJM).

[28]MS a, Migne and Bunsen read μεταπονουμένου, a compound not listed in either LSJM or Lampe.

[29]As L. Lütkemann and A. Ralfs first pointed out ("Hexaplarishe Randnoten zu Isaias 1-16," *Nachrichten der Königlichen Gesellschaft der Wissenschaften zu Göttingen. Philologish-historishe Klasse* [1915] 259-61) this word, ὁραματισμός, is almost certainly from Aquila. The LXX word for "vision" is usually ὅρασις. Aquila, however, sought to distinguish between ראה and חזה by translating the former ὁρᾶν and the latter by a word of his own creation, ὁραματίζεσθαι. This verb and its corresponding noun occur no where else outside of Aquila and this place in AC (see LSJM). The Hebrew noun in Gen 15:1 which speaks of Abraham's vision is מחזה (LXX ὅραμα). Whether or not this means a Jewish source used Aquila or the compiler used him here must be determined in Chapters IV and V.

[30]The ποτέ has an intensive force and is untranslatable. We might paraphrase it: "you taught him what this world could possibly be." See LSJM.

[31]Lit., "was the follower of faith." MS a, Migne and Bunsen read from Funk's καὶ τῆς μὲν γνώσεως to συνθήκη as follows: καὶ τῆς μὲν πίστεως αὐτοῦ πρώδευσεν ἡ γνῶσις, τῆς δὲ γνώσεως ἀκόλουθος γέγονεν ἡ πίστις, τῆς δὲ πίστεως ἦν ἐκακολούθημα ἡ συνθήκη.... "And knowledge went before his faith, and faith was the consequence of his knowledge and the covenant did follow after his faith" (ANF). Goodenough argued (*By Light, Light*, 317, 356) that it is best to follow MS a here since this schema fit his notion of the mystic road: gnosis leads to faith. However, it seems unwise to follow only one MS against all the others especially when nothing has been found to commend the superiority of its witness as in the case of MS d.

[32]Gen 13:16, 22:17.

[33]Gen 17:7.

[34]Cf. Justin, *Dial with Trypho* 58 who also speaks of the patriarchs seeing Christ.

δί αὐτοῦ ἐλάλησας εἰπών· "Ἰδοὺ ἐγὼ εἰμι μετὰ σοῦ καὶ αὐξανῶ σε καὶ πληθυνῶ σε σφόδρα." 6. καὶ οὕτως εἶπας πρὸς Μωϋσῆν τὸν πιστὸν καὶ ἅγιόν σου θεράποντα ἐπὶ τῆς ὀπτασίας τῆς βάτου· "Ἐγώ εἰμι ὁ ὤν, τοῦτό μοι ὄνομα αἰώνιον καὶ μνημόσυνον γενεαῖς γενεῶν." 7. ὑπέρμαχε γένους Ἀβραάμ, εὐλογητὸς εἶ εἰς τοὺς αἰῶνας.

through whom you spoke saying, "Behold, I am with you and I will increase you and multiply you exceedingly."[35] 6. And thus you said to Moses, your faithful servant, in the vision of the bush, "I am the one who is. This is my name forever and a memorial for generations and generations."[36] 7. O Defender of the offspring of Abraham, blessed are you forever.

---

[35]Gen 28:15, 48:4.

[36]Exod 3:14f.

7.34.1-8

Εὐλογητὸς εἶ, κύριε βασιλεῦ τῶν αἰώνων, ὁ διὰ Χριστοῦ ποιήσας τὰ ὅλα καὶ δι᾽ αὐτοῦ ἐν ἀρχῇ κοσμήσας τὰ ἀκατασκεύαστα, ὁ διαχωρίσας ὕδατα ὑδάτων στερεώματι καὶ πνεῦμα ζωτικὸν τούτοις ἐμβαλών, ὁ γῆν ἑδράσας καὶ οὐρανὸν ἐκτείνας καὶ τὴν ἑκάστου τῶν κτισμάτων ἀκριβῆ διάταξιν κοσμήσας. 2. σῇ γὰρ ἐνθυμήσει, δέσποτα, κόσμος πεφαίδρυται, οὐρανὸς δὲ ὡς καμάρα πεπηγμένος ἠγλάϊσται ἄστροις ἕνεκεν παραμυθίας τοῦ σκότους, φῶς δὲ καὶ ἥλιος εἰς ἡμέρας καὶ καρπῶν γονὴν γεγένηνται, σελήνη δὲ εἰς καιρῶν τροπὴν αὔξουσα καὶ μειουμένη, καὶ νὺξ ὠνομάζετο καὶ ἡμέρα προσηγορεύετο, στερέωμα δὲ διὰ μέσων τῶν ἀβύσσων ἐδείκνυτο "καὶ εἶπας συναχθῆναι τὰ ὕδατα καὶ ὀφθῆναι τὴν ξηράν." 3. αὐτὴν δὲ τὴν θάλασσαν πῶς ἄν τις ἐκφράσειεν; ἥτις ἔρχεται μὲν ἀπὸ πελάγους μαινομένη, παλινδρομεῖ δὲ ἀπὸ ψάμμου τῇ σῇ προσταγῇ κωλυομένη· εἶπες γὰρ "ἐν αὐτῇ συντριβήσεσθαι αὐτῆς τὰ κύματα, ζώοις" δε "μικροῖς καὶ μεγάλοις καὶ πλοίοις πορευτὴν" αὐτὴν ἐποίησας.

7.34.1-8

1. Blessed are you, O Lord, king of the ages,[1] who through Christ made the universe and through him in the beginning[2] brought order to the unformed (matter); who separated waters from waters by the firmament and put a living spirit in them; who caused the earth to settle and stretched out heaven[3] and precisely arranged the disposition of each of the creatures. 2. By your resolution,[4] O Master, the world has beamed (with joy)[5] and heaven as a vault[6] has been fixed and adorned with the stars for consolation in darkness; and light and sun have been created for the days and for the generation[7] of fruit; and the moon waxing and waning for the change of seasons. Also night was named and day proclaimed[8] and the firmament appeared in the midst of the abyss, and you said, "Let the waters be collected and the dry land appear."[9] 3. And how could anyone tell about even[10] the sea? It comes from the ocean raging, and being hindered by your command runs back from the shore. For you said, "In it its waves are shattered."[11] But "you have made it a thoroughfare for small and large (creatures) and for

---

[1] 1 Tim 1:17

[2] The next two lines are very reminiscent of the LXX language of Gen 1:1f, 6.

[3] Ps 101:26, 103:2.

[4] MS a and Migne read δυνάμει here (thus ANF "by thy power"). Funk, MS d and Bunsen read ἐνθυμήσει. Cf. Darnell "by your conception."

[5] φαιδρύνω "to beam or brighten up with joy" (in med.), LSJM. The translations of ANF ("the world is beautified"), Bouyer ("le mond a été etabli dans sa beauté" *Eucharistie*, 126) and Warren (*Liturgy*, 245) are off the mark and fail to catch this very picturesque description.

[6] Isa 40:22.

[7] The MS variants here do not change the meaning of the text significantly. Funk follows MS d.

[8] Gen 1:5.

[9] Gen 1:9.

[10] Or "the sea itself." For this use of αὐτός as an emphatic see Smyth, *Greek Grammar*, §1209, a.

[11] Job 38:11.

4. εἶτ᾽ ἐχλοαίνετο γῆ, παντοίοις ἄνθεσι καταγραφομένη καὶ ποικιλίᾳ δένδρων διαφόρων· παμφαεῖς τε φωστῆρες τούτων τιθηνοί, ἀπαράβατον σώζοντες τὸν δόλιχον καὶ κατ᾽ οὐδὲν παραλλάσσοντες τῆς σῆς προσταγῆς, ἀλλ᾽ ὅπη ἂν κελεύσῃς, ταύτῃ ἀνίσχουσι καὶ δύουσιν εἰς σημεῖα καιρῶν καὶ ἐνιαυτῶν, ἀμειβόμενοι τὴν τῶν ἀνθροίπων ὑπηρεσίαν. 5. ἔπειτα διαφόρων ζώων κατεσκευάζετο γένη, χερσαίων, ἐνύδρων, ἀεροπόρων, ἀμφιβίων, καὶ τῆς σῆς προνοίας ἡ ἔντεχνος σοφία τὴν κατάλληλον ἑκάστῳ πρόνοιων δωρεῖται· ὥσπερ γὰρ διάφορα γένη οὐκ ἠτόνησεν παραγαγεῖν, οὕτως οὐδὲ διάφορον πρόνοιαν ἑκάστου ποιήσασθαι κατωλιγώρησεν.

boats."[12] 4. Next the earth became green, (and) was painted[13] with all kinds of flowers and with a multicolor[14] of various trees; and the radiant luminaries are their nurses, who preserve the unalterable course and never vacillate from your command; but just as you order, so[15] they rise up and they set, for signs of seasons[16] and years, changing for the service of mankind. 5. Next different kinds of animals were prepared, those on dry land, in the water, traversing the air (and) amphibians, and the artful wisdom of your providence[17] gives graciously the corresponding providence to each; for as he was not too weak to introduce different kinds (of animals) thus he did not neglect to make a different providence for each.[18]

---

[12]Ps 103:25f.

[13]Again very picturesque language which is not represented by most translators: ANF "planted" (a typographical error?); Warren (*Liturgy*, 245) "picked out"; Bouyer (*Eucharistie*, 127) "a fait germer"; but cf. Darnell "engraved" another rendering for καταγράφω.

[14]ποικίλια may mean only "diversity" but means primarily "marked with various colors" (LSJM).

[15]Lit. "in which (way) you order, in this (way) they rise..." ὅπη was usually written with the iota subscript in post-classical Greek (see LSJM). Its appearance here without the iota may be an attempt at Atticizing.

[16]Gen 1:14.

[17]Creation and beautification of the world by divine Providence is a common theme in Stoicism. The function of Providence is to create a universe capable of enduring and endow it with beauty. It was believed that "it is the best world which possibly could be made" (Arnold, *Roman Stoicism*, 204). See Cicero's description of the beauty of the earth put in the mouth of the Stoic Lucilius (*Nat. D.* 2.39f) where striking parallels exist with AC 7.34: the earth is clothed with flowers, various animals are mentioned, the beauty and power of the sea and its marine life are praised, the winds of the atmosphere which produce the weather are marveled at, the stars, moon and sun are praised. See also Philo's admonition to thank God for his creation according to its individual parts, i.e. stars, earth, planets, seas, etc. (*Spec. Leg.* 1.97, 210). For the Stoic character of AC 8.12.9-20, the parallel section of 7.34, see F. Skutsch, "Ein neuer Zeuge der altchristlichen Liturgie," *Archiv für Religionswissenschaft* 13 (1910) 291-305 (esp. 302f) and P. Wendland, "Zwei angeblich christliche liturgische Gebete," *Nachrichten der Königlichen Gesellschaft zu Göttingen. Philogisch-historische Klasse* (1910) 330-34.

[18]This clause probably means as Bouyer has freely rendered it (*Eucharistie*, 129) "car elle ne néglige pas plus de pourvoir à leurs besoins divers qu'elle n'a failli à produire leur diversité." That is, Wisdom provides for each created entity according to its special need. Or we could understand it: "to endow each with a different foresight." This then, might refer to the Stoic doctrine of the different gradations of πνεῦμα in matter. Inanimate objects have the least, plants the next, animals next and rational animals the most. See Philo, *All. Leg.* 2.22.

6. καὶ τέλος τῆς δημιουργίας τὸ λογικὸν ζῶον, τὸν κοσμοπολίτην, τῇ σῇ σοφίᾳ διαταξάμενος κατεσκεύασας εἰπών· "Ποιήσωμεν ἄνθρωπον κατ' εἰκόνα καὶ καθ' ὁμοίωσιν ἡμετέραν", κόσμου κόσμον αὐτὸν ἀναδείξας, ἐκ μὲν τῶν τεσσάρων σωμάτων διαπλάσας αὐτῷ τὸ σῶμα, κατασκευάσας δ' αὐτῷ τὴν ψυχὴν ἐκ τοῦ μὴ ὄντος, αἴσθησιν δὲ πένταθλον αὐτῷ χαρισάμενος καὶ νοῦν τὸν τῆς ψυχῆς ἡνίοχον ταῖς αἰσθήσεσιν ἐπιστήσας. 7. καὶ ἐπὶ πᾶσι τούτοις, δέσποτα κύριε, τίς ἐπαξίως διηγήσεται νεφῶν ὀμβροτόκων φοράν, ἀστραπῆς ἔκλαμψιν, βροντῶν πάταγον, εἰς τροφῆς χορηγίαν καταλλήλου καὶ κρᾶσιν ἀέρων παναρμόνιον; 8. παρακούσαντα δὲ τὸν ἄνθρωπον ἐμμίσθου ζωῆς ἐστέρησας, οὐκ εἰς τὸ παντελὲς ἀφανίσας, ἀλλὰ χρόνῳ πρὸς ὀλίγον κοιμίσας, ὅρκῳ εἰς παλιγγενεσίαν ἐκάλισας ὅρον θανάτου ἔλυσας, ὁ ζωοποιὰς τῶν νεκρῶν διὰ Ἰησοῦ Χριστοῦ τῆς ἐλπίδος ἡμῶν.

6. And the end of the creation, the rational being, the cosmopolitan,[19] you ordained by[20] your wisdom and prepared saying, "Let us make man in our image and our likeness," presenting him an ornament[21] of the world. You formed his body from the four elements[22] but his soul you made from nothing;[23] and you endowed him with fivefold[24] sense perception and you set the mind (as) the helmsman[25] of the soul over the senses.

7. And in all these things, O Lord Master, who will worthily recount the movement of the rain producing clouds, the flash of lightning, the clap of thunder; for the abundance[26] of appropriate nourishment and the harmonious blending[27] of air.

8. And you deprived wayward mankind of the reward of life, not removing it for all time but making (mankind) sleep for a little while; you called (them) into rebirth[28] by an oath, you shattered the bonds of death, O Quickener of the dead through Jesus Christ our hope.

---

[19]Or "world-citizen." It was a Stoic emphasis that man should replace ordinary relations of civil society by a citizenship of the world. See Arnim 1.262, Diogenes Laertius 6.63, Seneca, *Ep.* 95.52, Philo *Op.* 3, *Conf.* 106, Plutarch *Mor.* 32 and the discussion in Zeller, *Stoics*, 326-31. Cf. AC 7.39.2, 8.12.16 and 8.41.4.

[20]ANF reads, "gavest directions to Thy Wisdom." The translator evidently wanted to personify σοφία. This is possible, especially in light of Gen 1:26 which is quoted later ("Let us..."), but difficult grammatically since διατάσσω does not usually take the dative case (see LSJM).

[21]It is tempting to understand this (κόσμου κόσμον) as Goodenough did (*By Light, Light*, 319), as another way of expressing the Greek notion of man as the microcosm of the universe. See Aristotle, *Physics* 8.2.252b, Galenus Medicus *de Usu Partium* 3.10. However, the expression is usually μικρός or βραχύς κόσμος (see LSJM). For the Stoic employment of this concept see Arnold, *Roman Stoicism*, 181, 240 and Seneca *Nat. Quaes.* 6.16, Arnim 3.33. Cf. AC 8.12.16.

[22]This seems an unusual use for σῶμα (LSJM do not list this meaning). Lampe gives "unit" as a meaning for σῶμα. MS a has added στοιχεία as a gloss. Nevertheless the meaning seems clear.

[23]Or "non-being."

[24]An unusual use of πένταθλος, the name for the competitor in the pentathlon of the Olympic games (LSJM). Lampe renders this "operating in five ways" and cites only this passage in AC as an example of this usage. The emphasis on the five senses as characteristic of man is also found in T Reub 2:3-9, T Naph 2:8, 2 En 30:9, Sir 17:4f.

[25]Plato, *Phaedrus* 246.

[26]Migne reads χορηφίαν, an obvious misprint.

[27]Or "temperature" (LSJM).

[28]παλιγγενεσία. See note on 7.33.3.

7.35.1-10

1. Μέγας εἶ, κύριε παντοκράτορ, καὶ μεγάλη ἡ ἰσχύς σου καὶ τῆς συνέσεώς σου οὐκ ἔστιν ἀριθμός· κτίστα, σωτήρ, πλούσιε ἐν χάρισιν, μακρόθυμε καὶ ἐλέους χορηγέ, ὁ μὴ ἀφιστῶν τῶν σῶν κτισμάτων τὴν σωτηρίαν· φύσει γὰρ ἀγαθὸς ὑπάρχεις, φείδῃ δὲ ἁμαρτανόντων, εἰς μετάνοιαν προσκαλούμενος· οἰκτίρμων γὰρ σοῦ ἡ νουθέτησις. πῶς γὰρ ἂν ὑπέστημεν ἐπειγομένην ἀπαιτούμενοι κρίσιν, ὁπότε μακροθυμούμενοι μόλις ἀνανεύομεν τῆς ἀσθενείας;
2. σοῦ τὸ κράτος ἀνήγγειλαν οἱ οὐρανοὶ καὶ γῆ κραδαινομένη τὴν ἀσφάλειαν ἐπ' οὐδενὰς κριμαμένη. θάλασσα κυμαινομένη καὶ μυρίαν βόσκουσα ζώων ἀγέλην πεπέδηται ἄμμῳ, τὴν σὴν βούλησιν πεφρικυῖα, καὶ πάντας ἀναγκάζει βοᾶν· "Ὡς ἐμεγαλύνθη τὰ ἔργα σου, κύριε· πάντα ἐν σοφίᾳ ἐποίησας, ἐπληρώθη ἡ γῆ τῆς κτίσεώς σου".
3. καὶ στρατὸς ἀγγέλων φλεγόμενος καὶ πνεύματα νοερὰ λέγουσιν· "Εἷς ἅγιος τῷ Φελμουνι",

7.35.1-10

1. Great are you O Lord almighty and great is your strength, and of your understanding there is no measure,[1] O Creator, Savior, rich in kindnesses, patient and abundant in mercy, who does not withdraw salvation from your creatures. For you are good by nature; and you spare sinners, calling (them) to repentance; for merciful is your admonition, for how could we subsist if quick judgment were demanded for us when after you are patient with us we can barely control our weakness?[2] 2. The heavens proclaim your power and earth being shaken is hung on nothing secure.[3] The sea swells and feeds a myriad herd of animals and is bound by the beach. (The sea) stands in awe[4] of your will and compels everything to cry out: "How magnified are your works O Lord; you made everything in wisdom, the earth is full of your creation."[5] 3. And the flaming army of angels and the intellectual spirits say to Phelmuni,[6]

---

[1]Ps 147:5. Literally, "of your understanding there is no number." This translation is based on the RSV rendering of the Hebrew.

[2]It is necessary to paraphrase this difficult sentence. Literally it reads: "How could we subsist being demanded of urgent judgment when, being treated patiently we can scarcely pull back from our weakness?"

[3]τὴν ἀσφαλείαν appears to be accusative of respect (Smyth, *Greek Grammar*, §1600f). But is the earth shaken with respect to security or does it hang upon nothing with respect to security? Bouyer (*Eucharistie*, 129) understood the former. The latter makes more sense. It could be either way grammatically, however. ANF understood a verb for "declare" and thus translated "the earth shakes...and, hanging upon nothing declares Thy unshaken stedfastness." This appears to be taking too great a liberty with the text.

[4]φρίσσω, "to bristle or shudder with fear" can also mean "to ripple." We might translate: "the sea ripples at your will" (LSJM).

[5]Ps 103:24.

[6]Dan 8:13, Theodotion. The reason Theodotion's version was quoted and not LXX must wait until a later chapter. Φελμουνί is a transliteration of פלמני ("a certain one" F. Brown, S. R. Driver and C. A. Briggs, *A Hebrew and English Lexicon* [Oxford: Clarendon, 1968] 812) which is found in LXX, Theodotion and Aquila. For the LXX and Theodotion, see A. Ralfs, *Septuaginta* (Stuttgart: Würthembergische, 1935) vol. 2, 918. For Aquila, see J. Reider and N. Turner, *An Index to Aquila* (Leiden: Brill, 1966) 249. Most translators (ANF, Darnell, Warren) assume that the army of angels etc. are speaking to Phelmuni (dative case). It could be translated: "the intellectual spirits say, 'there is one who is holy to Phelmuni.'" Bouyer's (*Eucharistie*, 129) rendering in which he gives the proper translation of the Hebrew phrase is not helpful, since the fact of its transliteration proves that the phrase was not thus understood by the Greek-speaking readers.

καὶ Σεραφὶμ ἅγια ἅμα τοῖς Χερουβὶμ τοῖς ἑξαπτερύγοις σοι τὴν ἐπινίκιον ᾠδὴν ψάλλοντα ἀσιγήτοις φωναῖς βοῶσιν· "Ἅγιος, ἅγιος, ἅγιος κύριος Σαβαώθ, πλήρης ὁ οὐρανὸς καὶ ἡ γῆ τῆς δόξης σου", καὶ τὰ ἕτερα τῶν ταγμάτων πλήθη, ἀρχάγγελοι, θρόνοι, κυριότητες, ἀρχαί, ἐξουσίαι, δυνάμεις, ἐπιβοῶντα λέγουσιν· "Εὐλογημένη ἡ δόξα κυρίου ἐκ τοῦ τόπου αὐτοῦ". 4. Ἰσραὴλ δέ, ἡ ἐπίγειός σου ἐκκλησία ἡ ἐξ ἐθνῶν, ταῖς κατ᾽ οὐρανὸν δυνάμεσιν ἁμιλλωμένη νυκτὶ καὶ ἡμέρᾳ ἐν καρδίᾳ πλήρει καὶ ψυχῇ θελούσῃ ψάλλει· "Τὸ ἅρμα τοῦ θεοῦ μυριοπλάσιον, χιλιάδες εὐθηνούντων, κύριος ἐν αὐτοῖς ἐν Σιναΐ, ἐν τῷ ἁγίῳ". 5. οἶδεν οὐρανὰς τὸν ἐπὶ μηδενὸς αὐτὸν καμαρώσαντα ὡς λιθόκυβον, καὶ γῆν καὶ ὕδωρ ἑαυτοῖς ἑνώσαντα, καὶ ἀέρα διαχέαντα ζωοτρόφον, καὶ τούτῳ πῦρ συμπλέξαντα εἰς θάλπος καὶ σκότους παραμυθίαν· ἐκπλήσσει χορὸς ἀστέρων τὸν ἀριθμήσαντα σημαίνων καὶ τὸν ὀνομάσαντα δεικνύων, ζῶα τὸν ψυχώσαντα, δένδρα τὸν ἐκφύσαντα· ἅπερ ἅπαντα τῷ σῷ λόγῳ γενόμενα παριστᾷ τῆς σῆς δυνάμεως τὸ κράτος. 6. διὸ καὶ ὀφείλει πᾶς ἄνθρωπος ἐξ αὐτῶν τῶν στέρνων σοὶ διὰ Χριστοῦ τὸν ὑπὲρ πάντων ὕμνον ἀναπέμπειν, διὰ σὲ

"There is one holy one." And the holy Seraphim together with the six-winged Cherubim singing the victory ode to you cry out with never-ceasing voices, "Holy, holy, holy Lord Sabaoth, heaven and earth are full of your glory."[7] And the other multitudes of the orders: angels,[8] archangels, thrones, dominions, rulers, authorities, powers,[9] cry out and say, "Blessed is the glory of the Lord from his place."[10]

4. But Israel, your earthly assembly from the nations, competing night and day with the powers in heaven sings with full heart and willing soul,[11] "The chariot of God is ten thousand-fold thousands of flourishing ones. The Lord is among them on Sinai, in his holy place."[12]

5. Heaven knows the one who vaulted it upon nothing as a stony cube and who united earth and water with themselves and scattered air which nourishes animals and combined fire with it[13] for heat and for consolation in darkness. The chorus of stars amaze (us), pointing to the one who counted (them), declaring the one who named (them). The living creatures (declare) the one who animated them, and the trees, the one who germinated them, as everything which has been created by your word presents the might of your power.

6. Wherefore also every man ought to send up through Christ the hymn to you from their breasts for all things, since on account

---

[7] Isa 6:3.

[8] The word "angels" is in d, e and the corrector of a. Funk left it out. It is in Migne and Bunsen.

[9] Col 1:16. Similar lists of heavenly beings are found in 1 En 61:10, 71:7, 2 En 20 and T Adam 4, among Jewish sources and in Eph 3:10, 1:21, 1 Pet 3:22, Rom 8:28, and Ps-Dionysius *De Cael. hierarch.* 6.2 in Christian sources.

[10] Ezek 3:12. This scripture plus the one just quoted (Isa 6:3) comprise the Kedusha or sanctification hymn which is found in the modern Jewish prayer book in three places: the Amida, the Yotzer, the Kedusha de Sidra (Birnbaum, *Daily Prayer Book*, 74, 84, 131). The earliest reference to the Kedushah is T. Ber 1:9. The *tersanctus* however is fairly common in both Christian and Jewish literature dating before the Tosephta: 1 En 39:12, 2 En 21:1, Rev 4:8, 1 Clem 34. The idea that heavenly beings of various types sing praises to God is even more common: 1 En 40:7, 71:7, 2 Bar 51:11, 2 En 8:8, 17:1, 19:6, 20:3, 21:1, 22:3, 31:1f, 42:4, Ap Mos 17, Ap Abe 17, T Abe (B) 4, 4Q Šir Šabb (Angelic Liturgy), Ascen Isa 7.

[11] 2 Macc 1:3.

[12] Ps 68:18.

[13] I.e. air?

τῶν ἀπάντων κρατῶν. 7. σὺ γὰρ εἶ ὁ χρηστὸς ἐν εὐεργεσίαις καὶ φιλόδωρος ἐν οἰκτιρμοῖς, ὁ μόνος παντοκράτωρ· ὅτε γὰρ θέλεις, πάρεστί σοι τὸ δύνασθαι· τὸ γὰρ σὸν αἰώνιον κράτος καὶ φλόγα καταψύχει καὶ λέοντας φιμοῖ καὶ κήτη καταπραΰνει καὶ νοσοῦντας ἐγείρει καὶ δυνάμεις μετατρέπει καὶ στρατὸν ἐχθρῶν καὶ λαὸν ἀριθμούμενον ἐν τῷ ὑπερηφανεύεσθαι καταστρώννυσιν. 8. σὺ εἶ ὁ ἐν οὐρανῷ, ὁ ἐπὶ γῆς, ὁ ἐν θαλάσσῃ, ὁ ἐν περατουμένοις ὑπὸ μηδενὸς περατούμενος, τῆς γὰρ μεγαλοσύνης σου οὐκ ἔστιν πέρας. μὴ γὰρ ἡμέτερόν ἐστιν τοῦτο, δέσποτα, τοῦ θεράποντός σου λόγιόν ἐστιν φάσκοντος· "Καὶ γνώσῃ τῇ καρδίᾳ σου, ὅτι κύριος ὁ θεός σου, θεὸς ἐν οὐρανῷ ἄνω καὶ ἐπὶ γῆς κάτω, καὶ οὐκ ἔστιν ἔτι πλὴν αὐτοῦ". 9. οὐδὲ γὰρ ἔστι θεὸς πλὴν σοῦ μόνου, ἅγιος οὐκ ἔστι πλὴν σοῦ, κύριος θεὸς γνώσεων, θεὸς ἁγίων, ἅγιος ὑπὲρ πάντας ἁγίους, οἱ γὰρ ἡγιασμένοι ὑπὸ τὰς χεῖράς σού εἰσιν· ἔνδοξος καὶ ὑπερυψούμενος, ἀόρατος τῇ φύσει, ἀνεξιχνίαστος κρίμασιν· οὗ ἀνενδεὴς ἡ ζωή, ἄτρεπτος καὶ ἀνελλιπὴς ἡ διαμονή, ἀκάματος ἡ ἐνέργεια, ἀπερίγραφος ἡ μεγαλειότης, ἀέναος ἡ εὐπρέπεια, ἀπρόσιτος ἡ κατοικία, ἀμετανάστευτος ἡ κατασκήνωσις, ἄναρχος ἡ γνῶσις, ἀναλλοίωτος ἡ ἀλήθεια, ἀμεσίτευτον τὸ ἔργον, ἀνεπιβούλευτον τὸ κράτος, ἀδιάδοχος ἡ μοναρχία, ἀτελεύτητος ἡ βασιλεία, ἀνανταγώνιστος ἡ ἰσχύς, πολυάριθμος ἡ στρατιά. 10. σὺ γὰρ εἶ ὁ σοφίας πατήρ, ὁ δημιουργίας τῆς διὰ μεσίτου κτίστης ὡς αἴτιος, ὁ προνοίας χορηγός, ὁ νόμων δοτήρ, ὁ ἐνδείας πληρωτής, ὁ τῶν ἀσεβῶν τιμωρὸς καὶ τῶν δικαίων μισθαποδότης, ὁ τοῦ Χριστοῦ θεὸς

of you he has power over all things. 7. For you are beneficial in kindness and bountiful in mercies, the only almighty; for when you wish, ability is yours (to ccomplish); for your eternal power cools the flame, muzzles the lions, pacifies sea monsters, raises up those who are sick, turns back powers and lays low the army of enemies and the people numbered with those who behave arrogantly.

8. You are the one in heaven, on the earth, in the sea, the one among those delimited who is delimited by nothing;[14] for of your magnitude there is no limit; for this is not our (oracle) Master, it is your servant's oracle who says, "And know in your heart that the Lord your God is God in heaven above, earth below and there is none except him."[15]

9. For there is no God except you alone, no holy one but you, Lord God of knowledge,[16] God of holy ones, holy above all holy ones; for they are sanctified by your hands. Glorious and exceedingly exalted,[17] invisible by nature, inscrutable in judgments. Whose life is in want of nothing, whose continuity is unchangeable and unceasing, whose activity is untiring, whose majesty is not circumscribed, whose beauty is everflowing, whose habitation is inaccessible, whose encamping is unmoving, whose knowledge is without beginning, whose truth is unchangeable, whose work is without meditation, whose might is not liable to attack,[18] whose monarchy is without successor, whose kingdom is without end, whose strength is irresistable, whose army is numerous.

10. You are the Father of Wisdom[19] the Craftsman of the creation as cause, through a mediator, the supplier[20] of providence, the Giver of the Law, the Provider in want,[21] the avenger of the impious ones, and rewarder of the righteous ones, the God of Christ

---

[14] I.e. nothing which is defined can define him.

[15] Deut 4:39, Isa 45:5.

[16] γνῶσις is plural here as in 1 Sam 2:3; cf. 1QS 3:15.

[17] Deut 33:3, Dan 3:28, 30.

[18] Or "can not be plotted against" (LSJM).

[19] "Wisdom" may be personified here. In AC 7.36.1 God is called the creator of Wisdom. This phrase may only mean, however, that God is the source of all wisdom.

[20] The χορηγός in classical Greece was the one who paid for the expenses of the chorus (LSJM).

[21] Literally the "treasurer for want."

καὶ πατὴρ καὶ τῶν εἰς αὐτὸν εὐσεβούντων κύριος, οὗ ἀδιάψευστος ἡ ἐπαγγελία, ἀδωροδόκητος ἡ κρίσις, ἀμετάπιστος ἡ γνώμη, ἄπαυστος ἡ εὐσέβεια, ἀΐδιος ἡ εὐχαριστία, δι' οὗ σοι καὶ ἡ ἐπάξιος προσκύνησις ὀφείλεται παρὰ πάσης λογικῆς καὶ ἁγίας φύσεως.

and Father and Lord of those who act reverently toward him. Whose promise is not deceitful, whose judgment is not corruptible, whose decision[22] is not moved by persuasion, whose piety is unceasing, whose thankfulness is everlasting, through whom rightful worship is owed to you from every rational and holy nature.

---

[22]So translates ANF. "Judgment" would be better here but we have just translated κρίσις as "judgment." γνώμη can also mean "opinion."

7.36.1-7

Κύριε παντοκράτορ, κόσμον ἔκτισας διὰ Χριστοῦ καὶ σάββατον ὥρισας εἰς μνήμην τούτου, ὅτι ἐν αὐτῷ κατέπαυσας ἀπὸ τῶν ἔργων εἰς μελέτην τῶν σῶν νόμων, καὶ ἑορτὰς διετάξω εἰς εὐφροσύνην τῶν ἡμετέρων ψυχῶν, ὅπως εἰς μνήμην ἐρχώμεθα τῆς ὑπὸ σοῦ κτισθείσης σοφίας· 2. ὡς δι᾽ ἡμᾶς γένεσιν ὑπέστη τὴν διὰ γυναικός, ἐπεφάνη τῷ βίῳ ἀναδεικνὺς ἑαυτὸν ἐν τῷ βαπτίσματι, ὡς θεός ἐστι καὶ ἄνθρωπος ὁ φανείς, ἔπαθεν δι᾽ ἡμᾶς σῇ συγχωρήσει καὶ ἀπέθανεν καὶ ἀνέστη σῷ κράτει· διὸ καὶ τὴν ἀναστάσιμον ἑορτὴν πανηγυρίζοντες τῇ κυριακῇ χαίρομεν ἐπὶ τῷ νικήσαντι μὲν τὸν θάνατον, φωτίσαντι δὲ ζωὴν καὶ ἀφθαρσίαν· δι᾽ αὐτοῦ γὰρ

7.36.1-7

1. Lord, almighty, you created the world through Christ and set apart the Sabbath to remember this[1]--because on it you rested[2] from (your) works--for meditation on your laws, and you ordained feasts for the gladdening of our souls, so that we may be reminded[3] of the Wisdom[4] created[5] by you: 2. How he[6] submitted to birth by a woman on account of us, he appeared in life manifesting himself in (his) baptism, how[7] the one who appeared is God and man, by your consent he suffered on our behalf and died and arose by your power. Wherefore also we celebrate the resurrection festival on the Lord's Day and rejoice because of the one who not only conquered death but brought to light life and incorruption.[8] For through him you

---

[1]Lit. "for the remembrance of this."

[2]καταπαύω may be transitive (i.e. causal) or intransitive. Thus we might translate with ANF (and Bouyer, *Eucharistie*, 131): "on that day Thou hast made us rest from our works." However, it seems more reasonable to say that God appointed the Sabbath as a memorial because *he* rested on the sixth day not because he caused us to rest. Further the phrase needs to be set off by dashes since it would also seem obvious that "for meditation on your laws" continues the thought "set apart the Sabbath to remember this..." which has been interrupted by the parenthetical phrase (i.e. "because on it you rest" etc.). Otherwise we must assume that the author is claiming God set apart the Sabbath so that God himself could meditate on his laws (as Darnell has rendered it). This appears unlikely. For the Sabbath as the day for meditating on the Law see Philo, *Spec. Leg.* 2.59-62.

[3]Lit. "so that we may come into remembrance...."

[4]Here "Wisdom" seems to be personified and is therefore capitalized.

[5]To say Wisdom was created would appear to be heresy since Wisdom is next identified with Christ (as Bousett, *Nachrichten*, 443, pointed out). For Wisdom as a creation of God see Sir 1:4, 1:15, 24:8. MS d sought to correct this theological aberration by reading ὑπὸ θεοῦ γενηθείσης σοφίας, "the Wisdom begotten by God."

[6]Although "Wisdom" is feminine the pronouns and participles which follow referring to Wisdom are masculine.

[7]Bouyer (*Eucharistie*, 132) combines the previous clause with this one: "se montrant dans le baptême comme Dieu et homme."

[8]2 Tim 1:10.

προσηγάγου τὰ ἔθνη ἑαυτῷ εἰς λαὸν περιούσιον, τὸν ἀληθινὸν Ἰσραήλ, τὸν θεοφιλῆ, τὸν ὁρῶντα θεόν. 3. σὺ γάρ, κύριε, καὶ τοὺς πατέρας ἡμῶν ἐξήγαγες ἐκ γῆς Αἰγύπτου καὶ ἐρρύσω ἐκ καμίνου σιδηρᾶς καὶ ἐκ πηλοῦ καὶ πλινθουργίας, ἐλυτρώσω ἐκ χειρὸς Φαραῶ καὶ τῶν ὑπ᾽ αὐτὸν καὶ διὰ θαλάσσης ὡς διὰ ξηρᾶς αὐτοὺς παρήγαγες καὶ ἐτροποφόρησας αὐτοὺς ἐν τῇ ἐρήμῳ παντοίοις ἀγαθοῖς. 4. νόμον αὐτοῖς ἐδωρήσω δέκα λογίων σῇ φωνῇ φθεγχθέντα καὶ χειρὶ σῇ καταγραφέντα· σαββατίζειν ἐνετείλω, οὐ πρόφασιν ἀργίας διδούς, ἀλλ᾽ ἀφορμὴν εὐσεβείας, εἰς γνῶσιν τῆς σῆς δυνάμεως, εἰς κώλυσιν κακῶν ὡς ἐν ἱερῷ καθείρξας περιβόλῳ διδασκαλίας χάριν εἰς ἀγαλλίαμα ἑβδομάδος· διὰ τοῦτο ἑβδομὰς μία καὶ ἑβδομάδες ἑπτὰ καὶ μὴν ἕβδομος καὶ ἐνιαυτὸς ἕβδομος καὶ τούτου κατὰ

brought the gentiles to yourself for a special[9] people, the true Israel, the beloved of God, the one who sees God.[10]

3. For you, Lord, led our fathers out of Egypt and saved (them) from the iron furnace and from the clay and the making of bricks. You redeemed them from the hands of Pharoah and those under him, and you brought them through the sea as through dry land, and you endured their character in the wilderness[11] with all sorts of good things.[12] 4. You gave them the Law of ten oracles clearly expressed by your voice and written by your hand. You commanded (them) to keep the Sabbath, not giving a pretext for idleness but an opportunity for piety, for the knowledge of your power, for prevention of evil. Therefore[13] you confined (them) in the sacred precinct[14] for the sake of teaching, for exultation in the number seven.[15] On account of this (there are) one seven and seven sevens[16] and a seventh month and a seventh year and according

---

[9]Deut 7:6.

[10]The notion of Israel as the one who sees God is common in Philo: *Leg. All.* 2.34, 3.186, 212, *Sacr.* 134, *Post.* 62, 92, *Conf.* 56, 72, 146, 148, *Migr.* 113, 125, 201, *Heres.* 78, *Congr.* 51, *Fuga.* 208, *Somm.* 1.173, 2:44, 173, *Abr.* 57, *Quaes. Gen.* 3.49, 4.233. See also Christian sources: Clement *Paid.* 1.9, Origen, *Princ.* 4.3, Eusebius *Pr. Ev.* 11.6.519b, and elsewhere in AC 8.15.7.

[11]Acts 13:8.

[12]I.e. probably as ANF has rendered it "(Thou) didst bear their manners in the wilderness, and bestow on them all sorts of good things."

[13]ὡς here must be translated as a consecutive. See LSJM.

[14]The phrase ἱερος περίβολος ordinarily meant the "temple precinct." See Sir 50:2, 2 Macc 6:4, 4 Macc 4:11, Josephus, *Ant.* 15.11.5 (LSJM). This meaning would seem to make no sense, since one was not confined to the temple on the Sabbath, but to the Sabbath "limit" around each town. The phrase, then, as Kohler maintained ("The Essene Version," 419), probably refers to the Sabbath limit (תחום) which one could travel (2000 cubits, Erubim 4:3). περίβολος would seem to be the logical translation of תחום, since both meant basically a "district" or "precinct" (LSJM; M. Jastrow, *A Dictionary of the Targumim, the Talmud Babli and Yerushalmi, and the Midrashic Literature* [New York: Judaica Press, 1975] 1660).

[15]Bouyer (*Eucharistie*, 132) translates: "les réjouir de la semaine." The Greek ἕβδομας can mean the number seven, a week or a seven-year period (LSJM). It rather seems that the number seven is meant here since the author continues by listing several notable sevens. The emphasis on the number seven is found in the Alexandrian Aristobulus (in Eusebius *Pr. Ev.* 13.12.9-16) and Philo (*Leg. All.* 1.8-16).

[16]Or "one week and seven weeks."

ἀνακύκλησιν ἔτος πεντηκοστὸν εἰς ἄφεσιν. 5. ὅπως μηδεμίαν ἔχωσιν πρόφασιν ἄνθρωποι ἄγνοιαν σκήψασθαι, τούτου χάριν πᾶν σάββατον ἐπέτρεψας ἀργεῖν, ὅπως μηδὲ λόγον τις ἐν ὀργῇ ἐκ τοῦ στόματος αὐτοῦ προέσθαι θελήσῃ ἐν τῇ ἡμέρᾳ τῶν σαββάτων· σάββατον γάρ ἐστιν κατάπαυσις δημιουργίας, τελείωσις κόσμου, νόμων ζήτησις, αἶνος εἰς θεὸν εὐχάριστος ὑπὲρ ὧν ἀνθρώποις ἐδωρήσατο. 6. ὧν ἁπάντων ἡ κυριακὴ προὔχουσα, αὐτὸν τὸν μεσίτην, τὸν προνοητήν, τὸν νομοθέτην, τὸν ἀναστάσεως αἴτιον, τὸν πρωτότοκον πάσης κτίσεως, τὸν θεὸν λόγον καὶ ἄνθρωπον τὸν ἐκ Μαρίας γεννηθέντα μόνον δίχα ἀνδρός, τὸν πολιτευσάμενον ὁσίως, τὸν σταυρωθέντα ἐπὶ Ποντίου Πιλάτου καὶ ἀποθανόντα καὶ ἀναστάντα ἐκ νεκρῶν ὑποδεικνύουσα, ὡς κυριακὴ παρακελεύεταί σοι, δέσποτα, τὴν ὑπὲρ πάντων εὐχαριστίαν προσφέρειν. 7. αὕτη γὰρ ἡ ὑπὸ σοῦ παρασχεθεῖσα χάρις, ἥτις διὰ μέγεθος πᾶσαν εὐεργεσίαν ἐκάλυψεν.

to this cycle the fiftieth year[17] is for remission. 5. (This is) so that men may have no excuse to plead ignorance. On account of this you entrusted (them) to keep[18] every Sabbath that no one may desire to send forth a word from his mouth in anger on the day of the Sabbath.[19] For the Sabbath is rest from creation, the completion of the world, the seeking of laws, thankful praise to God for (those things) which were given to men. 6. All of which the Lord's day surpasses, pointing to the Mediator himself, the Administrator, the Lawgiver, the Cause of resurrection, the Firstborn of all creation,[20] God the Word and a man born of Mary, the only one begotten without a man, the one who lived a holy life;[21] who was crucified under Pontius Pilate and died and rose from the dead. The Lord's day was commanded by you, Master, to offer thanks for all (these) things.

7. For your grace alone[22] by its magnitude has obscured every (other) benefit.[23]

---

[17]MS a, Migne and Bunsen((but he reads κατακύκλησις) read ἀντανακύκλησις ἰοβηλαῖος ὅ ἐστιν. ANF translates "and the revolution of these, the jubilee, which is the fiftieth year...."

[18]ἀργέω "to do nothing" also has the special meaning "to keep the Sabbath." See 2 Macc 6:25, Josephus, *War* 7.3.3. (LSJM).

[19]Here as often in the NT, Sabbath is plural. Cf. Matt 28:1, Mark 16:2, Luke 24:1, John 20:1, Acts 20:7, 1 Cor 16:2.

[20]Col 1:15.

[21]Lit. "practised a holy citizenship."

[22]See Smyth, *Greek Grammar*, §1209a.

[23]A difficult sentence. Lit. "for it is the grace alone which is furnished by you which by magnitude covers every benefit."

7.37.1-5

Ὁ τὰς ἐπαγγελίας τὰς διὰ τῶν προφητῶν πληρώσας καὶ ἐλεήσας τὴν Σιὼν καὶ οἰκτειρήσας τὴν Ἱερουσαλὴμ τῷ τὸν θρόνον Δαυὶδ τοῦ παιδός σου ἀνυψῶσαι ἐν μέσῳ αὐτῆς τῇ γενέσει τοῦ Χριστοῦ τοῦ ἐκ σπέρματος αὐτοῦ τὸ κατὰ σάρκα γεννηθέντος ἐκ μόνης παρθένου· αὐτὸς καὶ νῦν, δέσποτα ὁ θεός, πρόσδεξαι τὰς διὰ χειλέων δεήσεις τοῦ λαοῦ σου τοῦ ἐξ ἐθνῶν, τῶν ἐπικαλουμένων σε ἐν ἀληθείᾳ, καθὼς προσεδέξω τὰ δῶρα τῶν δικαίων ἐν ταῖς γενεαῖς αὐτῶν.
2. Ἄβελ ἐν πρώτοις τὴν θυσίαν ἐπεῖδες καὶ προσεδέξω, Νῶε ἐξελθόντος τῆς κιβωτοῦ, Ἀβραὰμ μετὰ τὸ ἐξελθεῖν ἐκ γῆς Χαλδαίων, Ἰσαὰκ ἐν τῷ φρέατι τοῦ ὅρκου, Ἰακὼβ ἐν Βηθλεέμ, Μωσέως ἐκ τῇ ἐρήμῳ, Ἀαρὼν ἀνὰ μέσον τῶν ζώντων καὶ τῶν τεθνεώτων, Ἰησοῦ τοῦ Ναυῆ ἐν Γαλγάλοις, Γεδεὼν ἐπὶ τῆς πέτρας καὶ τῶν πόκων πρὸ τῆς ἁμαρτίας, Μανωὲ καὶ τῆς αὐτοῦ γυναικὸς ἐν τῷ πεδίῳ, Σαμψὼν ἐν τῷ δίψει πρὸ τῆς πλημμελείας, Ἰεφθάε ἐν

7.37.1-5

1. You who have fulfilled the promises of the prophets and had mercy on Zion and compassion on Jerusalem by exalting the throne of David your servant in its midst, by the birth of Christ who was born of his seed according to the flesh[1] from a virgin only, you yourself also now,[2] O Master, God, accept the entreaties from the lips of your people which are out of the gentiles, which call[3] upon you in truth,[4] as you accepted the gifts of the righteous in their generations: 2. In the first place you beheld the sacrifice of Abel[5] and accepted (it). (You also accepted the sacrifice of) Noah[6] when he had departed from the ark, of Abraham[7] after he left the land of the Chaldees, of Isaac[8] at the well of the oath, of Jacob[9] at Bethlehem,[10] of Moses in the wilderness,[11] of Aaron (when he was) between the living and the dead,[12] of Joshua the Son of Nun at Gilgal,[13] of Gideon at the rock and of the fleeces before his sin,[14] of Manoa and his wife on the plain,[15] of Sampson (when he was) thirsty before his error,[16] of Jephthah in

---

[1]Rom 1:3.

[2]See the note on 8.37.2.

[3]I.e. the lips "call upon you in truth."

[4]Ps 144:18 LXX.

[5]Genesis 4.

[6]Gen 8:20-22.

[7]Gen 12:7.

[8]Gen 26:23-25.

[9]Genesis 35.

[10]Obviously an error, which seems to have endured in all MSS, for Bethel. Bunsen reads βηθέλ.

[11]The wilderness story is narrated from Exodus through Deuteronomy.

[12]Num 16:48.

[13]Joshua 5.

[14]Judges 6, 8.

[15]Judges 13.

[16]Judg 15:18f.

τῷ πολέμῳ πρὸ τῆς ἀκρίτου ἐπαγγελίας, Βαρὰκ καὶ Δεββώρας ἐπὶ τοῦ Σισάρα. Σαμουὴλ ἐν Μασσηφά· 3. Δαυὶδ ἐν ἅλῳ Ὀρνὰ τοῦ Ἰεβουσαίου, Σολομῶνος ἐν Γαβαὼν καὶ ἐν Ἱερουσαλήμ, Ἠλία ἐν τῷ ὄρει τῷ Καρμηλίῳ, Ἐλισσαίου ἐπὶ τῆς ἀτεκνούσης πηγής, Ἰωσαφὰτ ἐν τῷ πολέμῳ, Ἐζεκία ἐν ἀρρωστίᾳ καὶ ἐπὶ τοῦ Σενναχηρείμ, Μανασσῆ ἐν γῇ Χαλδαίων μετὰ τὴν πλημμέλειαν, Ἰωσία ἐν τῷ Φασσᾶ, Ἔσδρα ἐν τῇ ἐπανόδῳ· 4. Δανιὴλ ἐν τῷ λάκκῳ τῶν λεόντων, Ἰωνᾶ ἐν τῇ κοιλίᾳ τοῦ κήτους, τῶν τριῶν παίδων ἐν καμίνῳ πυρός, Ἄννας ἐν τῇ σκηνῇ ἐνώπιον τῆς κιβωτοῦ, Νεεμία ἐπὶ τῇ ἀνεγέρσει τῶν τειχῶν καὶ τοῦ Ζοροβάβελ, Ματταθία καὶ τῶν υἱῶν αὐτοῦ ἐν τῷ ζήλῳ σου, Ἰαὴλ ἐν εὐλογίαις. 5. καὶ νῦν οὖν πρόσδεξαι τὰς τοῦ λαοῦ σου προσευχὰς μετ' ἐπιγνώσεώς σοι διὰ Χριστοῦ προσφερομένας ἐν τῷ πνεύματι.

war before his foolish[17] promise,[18] of Barak and Deborah in the time of Sisera,[19] of Samuel[20] at Mizpah, 3. of David on the threshing floor, of Ornan the Jebusite,[21] of Solomon at Gibeon and at Jerusalem,[22] of Elijah at Mount Carmel,[23] of Elisha at the barren fountain,[24] of Jehoshaphat in war,[25] of Hezekiah in sickness and at the time of Sennacherib,[26] of Manasseh in the land of the Chaldeans after his error,[27] of Josiah at Phassa,[28] of Ezra[29] in the return, 4. of Daniel in the den of lions,[30] of Jonah in the whale's belly,[31] of the three youths in the furnace of fire,[32] of Hannah in the tent before the ark,[33] of Nehemiah at the raising of the walls and of Zerubabel,[34] of Mattathias and of his sons in (their) zeal,[35] of Jael in blessings.[36]

5. And now, therefore, accept the prayers of your people which are offered in the spirit (and) with knowledge to you through Christ.

---

[17]Lit. "undiscriminating" (LSJM).

[18]Judges 11.

[19]Judges 4, 5.

[20]1 Samuel 7.

[21]1 Chronicles 21.

[22]1 Kings 3, 8.

[23]1 Kings 18.

[24]2 Kings 2:19-22.

[25]2 Chronicles 18.

[26]2 Kings 20, 19.

[27]2 Chr 33:10-13.

[28]This appears to be a mistake for πάσχα (see 2 Chronicles 35) as Cotelerius suggested (ANF, 475). Bunsen reads πάσχα and notes that his MSS (he used 4 MSS: Vindovonensis Gk. 64, Petropolitano Gk. xv, Parisino 931, and Montefalconio, see *Analecta*, 35) all have φάσκᾳ ("*vulgo* φάσκᾳ"). Funk only notes that MSS d and e read σάφφα but d has been corrected in the margin to φάσσα. Evidently most of Funk's MSS read φασσᾶ (Bunsen's MSS are all sixteenth and seventeenth century. See Funk, *Constitutiones*, xxixf). σάφφα could refer to Shaphan the scribe of Josiah (2 Kgs 22:3-20=2 Chr 34:8-28) who played a prominent role at the time the book of the law was found. Either suggestion is possible since both Shaphan and a notable passover were contemporaneous with Josiah. The passover, however, would seem to fit this context better, i.e. God accepts the gift of Josiah (2 Chr 35:1). The spelling for passover is a problem. The LXX uses πάσχα (e.g. Exod 12:11, 34:25, Lev 23:5) and φασέκ (e.g. 2 Chr 30:1, 35:1, 6, 7, Jer 38:8) which we would expect to find used here if the author referred to 2 Chronicles 35. The reading of Bunsen's MSS must be viewed as copyist corrections. It is interesting that Aquila customarily rendered פסח as φασέ or φεσά. See Reider and Turner, *Index*, 249, 322.

[29]Ezra 8.

[30]Dan 6:14.

[31]Jonah 2.

[32]Daniel 3.

[33]1 Samuel 1.

[34]Nehemiah 3.

[35]1 Macc 2-16.

[36]Judges 4, 5.

7.38.1-8

Εὐχαριστοῦμέν σοι περὶ πάντων, δέσποτα παντοκράτορ, ὅτι οὐκ ἐγκατέλιπες τὰ ἐλέη σου καὶ τοὺς οἰκτιρμούς σου ἀφ' ἡμῶν, ἀλλὰ καθ' εκάστην γενεὰν καὶ γενεὰν σώζεις, ῥύῃ, ἀντιλαμβάνῃ, σκεπάζεις. 2. ἀντελάβου γὰρ ἐν ἡμέραις Ἐνὼς καὶ Ἐνώχ, ἐν ἡμέραις Μωσῆ καὶ Ἰησοῦ, ἐν ἡμέραις τῶν κριτῶν, ἐν ἡμέραις Σαμουὴλ καὶ Ἠλία καὶ τῶν προφητῶν, ἐν ἡμέραις Δαυὶδ καὶ τῶν βασιλέων, ἐν ἡμέραις Ἐσθὴρ καὶ Μαρδοχαίου, ἐν ἡμέραις Ἰουδίθ, ἐν ἡμέραις Ἰούδα Μακκαβαίου καὶ τῶν ἀδελφῶν αὐτοῦ. 3. καὶ ἐν ταῖς ἡμέραις ἡμῶν ἀντελάβου ἡμῶν διὰ τοῦ μεγάλου σου ἀρχιερέως Ἰησοῦ Χριστοῦ τοῦ παιδός σου· καὶ ἀπὸ μαχαίρας γὰρ ἐρρύσατο καὶ ἐκ λιμοῦ ἐξείλατο διαθρέψας, ἐκ νόσου ἰάσατο, ἐκ γλώσσης πονηρᾶς ἐσκέπασεν. 4. περὶ πάντων σοι διὰ Χριστοῦ εὐχαριστοῦμεν, ὁ καὶ φωνὴν ἔναρθρον εἰς ἐξομολόγησιν δωρησάμενος καὶ γλῶσσαν εὐάρμοστον δίκην πλήκτρου ὡς ὄργανον ὑποθείς, καὶ γεῦσιν πρόσφορον καὶ ἀφὴν κατάλληλον καὶ ὅρασιν θέας καὶ ἀκοὴν φωνῆς καὶ ὄσφρησιν ἀτμῶν καὶ χεῖρας εἰς ἔργον καὶ πόδας πρὸς ὁδοιπορίαν. 5. καὶ ταῦτα πάντα ἐκ μικρᾶς σταγόνος διαπλάσας ἐν μήτρᾳ καὶ ψυχὴν ἀθάνατον μετὰ τὴν μόρφωσιν χαρίζῃ καὶ προάγεις εἰς φῶς τὸ λογικὸν ζῶον, τὸν ἄνθρωπον· νόμοις ἐπαίδευσας, δικαιώμασιν εφαίδρυνας· πρὸς ὀλίγον ἐπάγων διάλυσιν, τὴν ἀνάστασιν ἐπηγγείλω. 6. ποῖος τοιγαροῦν αὐτάρκης βίος, αἰώνων δὲ μῆκος πόσον διαρκέσει ἀνθρώποις πρὸς εὐχαριστίαν; ἢ τὸ μὲν πρὸς ἀξίαν ἀδύνατον, τὸ δὲ κατὰ δύναμιν ευαγές. 7. ἐρρύσω γὰρ ἀσεβείας πολυθέων, καὶ χριστοκτόνων αἱρέσεως ἐξείλω, πεπλανημένης ἀγνοίας ἠλευθέρωσας· τὸν Χριστὸν ἀπέστειλας εἰς ἀνθρώπους ὡς ἄνθρωπον, θεὸν ὄντα μονογενῆ, τὸν παράκλητον ἐνῴκισας ἡμῖν, ἀγγέλους ἐπέστησας, τὸν διάβολον

7.38.1-8

1. We give thanks to you for all things, Master, almighty, because you have not taken your mercies and compassions from us, but in each and every generation you save, rescue, help (and) protect. 2. For you helped in the days of Enos, in the days of Enoch, in the days of Moses and Joshua, in the days of the judges, in the days of Samuel and Elijah and the prophets, in the days of David and of the kings, in the days of Esther and Mordecai, in the days of Judith, in the days of Judas Maccabeus and his brothers; 3. and in our days you helped us through your great High Priest, Jesus Christ your child. For he rescued (us) even from the sword and he removed (us) from hunger and nourished (us), he healed (us) from disease, he protected (us) from an evil tongue. 4. For all things we give thanks to you through Christ, who also has given (us) an articulate voice for confessing (you) and who has also added a harmonious tongue in the manner of a plectrum as an instrument; and useful taste, appropriate touch, sight for seeing, the hearing of a sound, the ability to smell vapors, hands for works and feet for walking.

5. And you formed all these things from a small drop in the womb and endowed it after the formation with an immortal soul and led forth into light the rational creature, man. You have educated (him) with laws, cleansed (him)[1] with statues. You bring on dissolution for a short while, but you promised the resurrection.[2]

6. Therefore what life is sufficient and what length of the ages adequate to men to give thanks? Although it is impossible to give thanks as one ought, it is right to give thanks as one can.[3]

7. For you rescued (us) from the impiety of polytheism and you removed (us) from the heresy of the Christ murderers. You freed (us) from ignorance which went astray. You sent Christ among men as a man, being only begotten God. You caused the paraclete to dwell among us, you set angels over us, you put the devil

---

[1]φαιδρύνω to "make bright or cleanse" (LSJM). Bouyer (*Eucharistie*, 136) "tu l'as éclairé." ANF, "(thou hast) improved." Warren (*Liturgy*, 251) "brighten." Darnell, "cleanse."

[2]Cf. AC 7.34.8 in a very similar passage where παλιγγενεσία is used, while here ἀνάστασις is used.

[3]Lit. "on the one hand it is impossible for worthiness, but on the other hand it is lawful according to power." MS d reads instead of εὐαγές ("lawful"): ἁγνόν· εὐσεβές· ὅσιον· θειότατον, "pure, pious, holy (and) godly," an obvious pietistic gloss.

ᾔσχυνας· οὐκ ὄντας ἐποίησας, γενομένους φυλάσσεις, ζωὴν ἐπιμετρεῖς, χορηγεῖς τροφήν, μετάνοιαν ἐπηγγείλω. 8. ὑπὲρ ἁπάντων σοι ἡ δόξα καὶ τὸ σέβας διὰ Ἰησοῦ Χριστοῦ νῦν καὶ ἀεὶ καὶ εἰς τοὺς αἰῶνας· ἀμήν.

to shame. You made what did not exist, you guard what has come into being, you measure out life, you supply abundant nourishment, you promised repentance.

8. For all things may glory and reverence be to you through Jesus[4] Christ now and forever and ever. Amen.

---

[4]MS d reads μετὰ χριστοῦ καὶ πνεύματος ἁγίου "may glory and reverence be to you *with Christ and the Holy Spirit*."

7.39.2-4

2. Ὁ μέλλων τοίνυν κατηχεῖσθαι τὸν λόγον τῆς εὐσεβείας παιδευέσθω πρὸ τοῦ βαπτίσματος τὴν περὶ θεοῦ τοῦ ἀγεννήτου γνῶσιν, τὴν περὶ υἱοῦ μονογενοῦς ἐπίγνωσιν, τὴν περὶ τοῦ ἁγίου πνεύματος πληροφορίαν· μανθανέτω δημιουργίας διαφόρου τάξιν, προνοίας εἱρμόν, νομοθεσίας διαφόρου δικαιωτήρια· παιδευέσθω, διὰ τί κόσμος γέγονεν καὶ δι' ὃ κοσμοπολίτης ὁ ἄνθρωπος κατέστη· ἐπιγινωσκέτω τὴν ἑαυτοῦ φύσιν, οἵα τις ὑπάρχει· 3. παιδευέσθω, ὅπως ὁ θεὸς τοὺς πονηροὺς ἐκόλασεν ὕδατι καὶ πυρί, τοὺς δὲ ἁγίους ἐδόξασεν καθ' ἑκάστην γενεάν, λέγω δὴ τὸν Σήθ, τὸν Ἐνώς, τὸν Ἐνώχ, τὸν Νῶε, τὸν Ἀβραὰμ καὶ τοὺς ἐκγόνους αὐτοῦ, τὸν Μελχισεδὲκ καὶ τὸν Ἰὼβ καὶ τὸν Μωσέα, Ἰησοῦν τε καὶ Χαλὲβ καὶ Φινεὲς τὸν ἱερέα καὶ τοὺς καθ' ἑκάστην γενεὰν ὁσίους, ὅπως τε προνοούμενος οὐκ ἀπεστράφη ὁ θεὸς τὸ τῶν ἀνθρώπων γένος, ἀλλ' ἀπὸ πλάνης καὶ ματαιότητος εἰς ἐπίγνωσιν ἀληθείας ἐκάλει κατὰ διαφόρους καιρούς, ἀπὸ τῆς δουλείας καὶ ἀσεβείας εἰς ἐλευθερίαν καὶ εὐσέβειαν ἐπανάγων, ἀπὸ ἀδικίας εἰς δικαιοσύνην, ἀπὸ θανάτου αἰωνίου εἰς ζωὴν ἀΐδιον. 4. ταῦτα καὶ τὰ τούτοις ἀκόλουθα μανθανέτω ἐν τῇ κατηχήσει ὁ προσιών.

7.39.2-4

2. Let the one who is to be instructed in piety[1] be taught before baptism knowledge concerning the unbegotten God, knowledge[2] concerning the only begotten son, full assurance concerning the Holy Spirit. Let him learn the order of a diverse creation,[3] the sequence of providence,[4] the judgment seats of different legislation,[5] why the world came to be and why man was appointed a cosmopolitan.[6] Let him understand his own nature, of what sort it is. 3. Let him be educated in how God punished the wicked by water and fire, and glorified the saints in each generation: I mean Seth, Enos, Enoch, Noah, Abraham and his descendants, Melchizedek, Job, Moses, both Joshua and Chaleb, Phineas the priest, and the holy ones in each generation, and how God, provided for and[7] did not abandon the race of men, but summoned them at various times from error and folly into the understanding of truth,[8] leading them from servitude and impiety into freedom and piety, from iniquity into righteousness, from eternal death into everlasting life. 4. Let the one who offers himself learn during his instruction these things and those that are related to them.

---

[1]Lit. "be instructed regarding the teaching of piety." For this use of λόγος see Lampe.

[2]The Greek word here is ἐπιγνῶσις. Cf. this with γνῶσις used above. ἐπιγνῶσις can also mean "recognition" (LSJM), but such a meaning does not seem appropriate here.

[3]ANF translates, "the order of the several parts of the creation." But it is doubtful if διάφορος in the singular can mean "several." See LSJM. For the emphasis on the order of creation in Philo, see *Opf*. 13-83.

[4]This phrase may be equal to the Stoic belief in the chain of destiny which continuously connects the causes of each event. See Arnim 2.918 (εἱμαρμένη εἱρμός τις οὖσα αἰτιῶν). See F. H. Colson's notes in *Philo* (LCL; Cambridge: Harvard, 1965-68) vols. 5, 210f and 9, 236f. See also *Mut*. 135, *De Aet*. 75.

[5]The different legislation is, according to Goodenough (*By Light, Light*, 327) the law as implanted and as written.

[6]Cf. note on 7.34.6.

[7]προνοέω can also mean "to foresee." We might then translate the participle as concessive, "And how God, though he foresaw that man would sin, he did not abandon him." Nevertheless, the repeated emphasis on God's providential care in the AC makes it likely that the former translation is correct.

[8]1 Tim 2:4.

8.5.1-4

1. Ὁ ὤν, δέσποτα κύριε ὁ θεὸς ὁ παντοκράτωρ, ὁ μόνος ἀγέννητος καὶ ἀβασίλευτος, ὁ ἀεὶ ὢν καὶ πρὸ τῶν αἰώνων ὑπάρχων, ὁ πάντη ἀνενδεὴς καὶ πάσης αἰτίας καὶ γενέσεως κρείττων, ὁ μόνος ἀληθινός, ὁ μόνος σοφός, ὁ ὢν μόνος ὕψιστος, ὁ τῇ φύσει ἀόρατος, οὗ ἡ γνῶσις ἄναρχος, ὁ μόνος ἀγαθὸς καὶ ἀσύγκριτος, ὁ τὰ πάντα εἰδὼς πρὶν γενέσεως αὐτῶν, ὁ τῶν κρυπτῶν γνώστης, ὁ ἀπρόσιτος, ὁ ἀδέσποτος· 2. ὁ θεὸς καὶ πατὴρ τοῦ μονογενοῦς υἱοῦ σου τοῦ θεοῦ καὶ σωτῆρος ἡμῶν, ὁ δημιουργὸς τῶν ὅλων δι' αὐτοῦ, ὁ προνοητής, ὁ κηδεμών, ὁ πατὴρ τῶν οἰκτιρμῶν καὶ θεὸς πάσης παρακλήσεως, ὁ ἐν ὑψηλοῖς κατοικῶν καὶ τὰ ταπεινὰ ἐφορῶν· 3. σὺ ὁ δοὺς ὅρους ἐκκλησίας διὰ τῆς ἐνσάρκου παρουσίας τοῦ Χριστοῦ σου ὑπὸ μάρτυρι τῷ παρακλήτῳ διὰ τῶν σῶν ἀποστόλων καὶ ἡμῶν τῶν χάριτι σῇ παρεστώτων ἐπισκόπων, ὁ προορίσας ἐξ ἀρχῆς ἱερεῖς εἰς ἐπιστασίαν λαοῦ σου, Ἄβελ ἐν πρώτοις, Σὴθ καὶ Ἐνὼς καὶ Ἐνὼχ καὶ Νῶε καὶ Μελχισεδὲκ καὶ Ἰώβ· 4. ὁ ἀναδείξας Ἀβραὰμ καὶ τοὺς λοιποὺς πατριάρχας σὺν τοῖς πιστοῖς σου θεράπουσιν Μωϋσεῖ καὶ Ἀαρὼν καὶ Ἐλεαζάρῳ καὶ Φινεές, ὁ ἐξ αὐτῶν προχειρισάμενος ἄρχοντας καὶ ἱερεῖς ἐν τῇ σκηνῇ τοῦ μαρτυρίου, ὁ τὸν Σαμουὴλ ἐκλεξάμενος εἰς ἱερέα καὶ προφήτην, ὁ τὸ ἁγίασμά σου ἀλειτούργητον μὴ ἐγκαταλιπών, ὁ εὐδοκήσας ἐν οἷς ἠρετίσω δοξασθῆναι·

8.5.1-4

1. The one who is Master, Lord, God the Almighty, the only begotten and unruled, who always is, and existed before the ages, who is in need of nothing in any way, before[1] every cause and beginning, the only true, the only wise, the one who alone is most high, who is invisible by nature, whose knowledge is without beginning, the only good and incomparable, who knows all things before their beginning, the knower of secret things, unapproachable, without master. 2. The God and Father of your only begotten son, our God and Savior, the creator of the universe through him, the Supervisor, the Preserver, the Father of compassions and God of all consolation, who dwells on high and looks down upon the lowly. 3. You are the one who gave decrees[2] to the church through the coming of your Christ in the flesh by the witness[3] of the Paraclete through your apostles and our[4] bishops who are present by your grace; you are the one who foreordained from the beginning priests for the oversight[5] of your people: Abel first, Seth and Enos and Enoch and Noah and Melchizedek and Job. 4. You are the one who appointed[6] Abraham and the rest of the patriarchs with your faithful servants Moses and Aaron and Eleazar and Phinehas, who chose from them rulers and priests in the tent of witness, who elected Samuel as a priest and prophet, who did not leave your holy place without a minister, who was well pleased with those by whom[7] you selected to be glorified.

---

[1]Lit. "superior to." Cf. Darnell, "greater than."

[2]See Lampe. ANF renders it "rules."

[3]Lit. "by the power of the witness...." For this use of the dative with ὑπό see LSJM.

[4]Darnell's "us bishops" is not a good rendering.

[5]Lampe defines ἐπιστασία as "control" or "authority."

[6]Lampe gives the definition "announce as appointed" for ἀναδείκνυμι.

[7]Lit. "well pleased in whom you selected...." The idea is that God is well pleased with those whom he selected to bring him glory.

8.6.5-8

5. Ὑπὲρ τῶν κατηχουμένων πάντες ἐκτενῶς τὸν θεὸν παρακαλέσωμεν, ἵνα ὁ ἀγαθὸς καὶ φιλάνθρωπος εὐμενῶς εἰσακούσῃ τῶν δεήσεων αὐτῶν καὶ τῶν παρακλήσεων, καὶ προσδεξάμενος αὐτῶν τὴν ἱκεσίαν ἀντιλάβηται αὐτῶν καὶ δῷ αὐτοῖς τὰ αἰτήματα τῶν καρδιῶν αὐτῶν πρὸς τὸ συμφέρον, ἀποκαλύψῃ αὐτοῖς τὸ εὐαγγέλιον τοῦ Χριστοῦ αὐτοῦ, φωτίσῃ αὐτοὺς καὶ συνετίσῃ, παιδεύσῃ αὐτοὺς τὴν θεογνωσίαν, διδάξῃ αὐτοὺς τὰ προστάγματα αὐτοῦ καὶ τὰ δικαιώματα, ἐγκαταφυτεύσῃ ἐν αὐτοῖς τὸν ἁγνὸν αὐτοῦ καὶ σωτήριον φόβον, διανοίξῃ τὰ ὦτα τῶν καρδιῶν αὐτῶν πρὸς τὸ ἐν τῷ νόμῳ αὐτοῦ καταγίνεσθαι ἡμέρας καὶ νυκτός· 6. βεβαιώσῃ δὲ αὐτοὺς ἐν τῇ εὐσεβείᾳ, ἑνώσῃ καὶ ἐγκαταριθμήσῃ αὐτοὺς τῷ ἁγίῳ αὐτοῦ ποιμνίῳ, καταξιώσας αὐτοὺς τοῦ λουτροῦ τῆς παλιγγενεσίας, τοῦ ἐνδύματος τῆς ἀφθαρσίας, τῆς ὄντως ζωῆς· ῥύσηται δὲ αὐτοὺς ἀπὸ πάσης ἀσεβείας καὶ μὴ δῷ τόπον τῷ ἀλλοτρίῳ κατ᾽ αὐτῶν, καθαρίσῃ δὲ αὐτοὺς ἀπὸ παντὸς μολυσμοῦ σαρκὸς καὶ πνεύματος, ἐνοικήσῃ τε ἐν αὐτοῖς καὶ ἐμπεριπατήσῃ διὰ τοῦ Χριστοῦ αὐτοῦ, εὐλογήσῃ τὰς εἰσόδους αὐτῶν καὶ τὰς ἐξόδους καὶ κατευθύνῃ αὐτοῖς τὰ προκείμενα εἰς τὸ συμφέρον. 7. ἔτι ἐκτενῶς ὑπὲρ αὐτῶν ἱκετεύσωμεν, ἵνα ἀφέσεως τυχόντες τῶν πλημμελημάτων διὰ τῆς μυήσεως

8.6.5-8

5. Let us all earnestly entreat God on behalf of the catechumens: That the one who is good and loves mankind will kindly hear their prayers; and having received their supplication, may assist them and grant them for their good the requests of their hearts;[1] that he may reveal to them the Gospel of his Christ, illumine them, and give them understanding, educate them in the knowledge of God, teach them his ordinances and judgments,[2] implant in them his pure and saving fear, open the ears of their hearts to engage in his Law day and night;[3] 6. and that he may establish them in piety, unify and number them among his holy flock, grant them the washing of regeneration,[4] of the garment of incorruption,[5] of real life; and that he may save them from all impiety, and give place to no adversary against them; and that he may cleanse them from all pollution of flesh and spirit,[6] and dwell in them, and walk (among them) through his Christ; and bless their comings in and their goings out,[7] and guide their affairs for their good.

7. Let us still earnestly supplicate for them that, obtaining remission of their trespasses through initiation,[8] they may be

---

[1]Ps 37:4.

[2]Ps 119:12.

[3]Ps 1:2.

[4]Tit 3:5. See the note on 7.33.3. παλιγγενεσία is translated "regeneration" here instead of "rebirth" out of conformity to the RSV.

[5]The notion that initiates wear a garment of incorruption is also found in Chrysostom's liturgy (Brightman, *Liturgies*, 374). The idea is found in Jewish and Christian apocalyptic literature where God grants a new garment in paradise or heaven (e.g. 1 En 62: 15f, 2 En 22:8, Rev 3:5, Ascen Isa 8:14, Apoc Thomas in E. Hennecke, W. Schneemelcher, and R. McL. Wilson, *New Testament Apocrypha* [Philadelphia: Westminster, 1976] vol. 2, 802), as well as in the pagan mysteries where the initiate supposedly wore celestial garments (e.g. Plutarch, *De Is. et Os.* 77; see Reitzenstein, *Hellenistic Mystery Religions*, 43, 98). See also Acts of Thomas 6, 7, and Odes of Solomon 8:9, 11:11.

[6]2 Cor 7:1.

[7]Ps 121:8; cf. AC 8.15.8.

[8]This word and the related word in the same verse, μυστήριον, are terms from the pagan mystery religions (Reitzenstein, *Hellenistic Mystery Religions*, 241; also see LSJM) but are also found in Philo (e.g. *Leg. All.* 3.100, *Quaes. Gen.* 4.8, *Sac* 60). But the terms were appropriated by Christians also, and μυστήριον is the ordinary term for "sacrament" which is the meaning here. See Lampe.

ἀξιωθῶσιν τῶν ἁγίων μυστηρίων καὶ τῆς μετὰ τῶν ἁγίων διαμονῆς.
8. ἐγείρεσθε, οἱ κατηχούμενοι· τὴν εἰρήνην τοῦ θεοῦ διὰ τοῦ Χριστοῦ αὐτοῦ αἰτήσασθε, εἰρηνικὴν τὴν ἡμέραν καὶ ἀναμάρτητον καὶ πάντα τὸν χρόνον τῆς ζωῆς ὑμῶν, χριστιανὰ ὑμῶν τὰ τέλη, ἵλεω καὶ εὐμενῆ τὸν θεόν, ἄφεσιν πλημμελημάτων· ἑαυτοὺς τῷ μόνῳ ἀγεννήτῳ θεῷ διὰ τοῦ Χριστοῦ αὐτοῦ παράθεσθε. κλίνατε καὶ εὐλογεῖσθε.

deemed worthy of the holy mysteries and remaining constantly with the saints.

8. Arise, catechumens, request the peace of God through his Christ, that the day be peaceable and free from sin, even the entire time of your life, that your end[9] be Christian, that God be gracious and kind, the forgiveness of trespasses. Dedicate yourselves to the only unbegotten God through his Christ. Bow down and receive a blessing.

---

[9]Or "your death be Christian."

8.9.8-9

8. Παντοκράτορ θεὲ αἰώνιε, δέσποτα τῶν ὅλων, κτίστα καὶ πρύτανι τῶν πάντων, ὁ τὸν ἄνθρωπον κόσμου κόσμον ἀναδείξας διὰ Χριστοῦ καὶ νόμον δοὺς αὐτῷ ἔμφυτον καὶ γραπτὸν πρὸς τὸ ζῆν αὐτὸν ἐνθέσμως ὡς λογικόν, καὶ ἁμαρτόντι ὑποθήκην δοὺς πρὸς μετάνοιαν τὴν σαυτοῦ ἀγαθότητα· ἔπιδε ἐπὶ τοὺς κεκλικότας σοι αὐχένα ψυχῆς καὶ σώματος, ὅτι οὐ βούλει τὸν θάνατον τοῦ ἁμαρτωλοῦ, ἀλλὰ τὴν μετάνοιαν, ὥστε ἀποστρέψαι αὐτὸν ἀπὸ τῆς ὁδοῦ αὐτοῦ τῆς πονηρᾶς καὶ ζῆν. 9. ὁ Νινευιτῶν προσδεξάμενος τὴν μετάνοιαν, ὁ θέλων πάντας ἀνθρώπους σωθῆναι καὶ εἰς ἐπίγνωσιν ἀληθείας ἐλθεῖν, ὁ τὸν υἱὸν προσδεξάμενος τὸν καταφαγόντα τὸν βίον αὐτοῦ ασώτως κατρικοῖς σπλάγχνοις διὰ τὴν μετάνοιαν, αὐτὸς καὶ νῦν πρόσδεξαι τῶν ἱκετῶν σου τὴν μετάγνωσιν, ὅτι οὐκ ἔστιν, ὃς οὐχ ἁμαρτήσεταί σοι· ἐὰν γὰρ ἀνομίας παρατηρήσῃ, κύριε, κύριε, τίς ὑποστήσεται; ὅτι παρὰ σοὶ ὁ ἱλασμός ἐστιν·

8.9.8-9

8. Almighty God, Eternal, Master of the universe, Creator and Principal of beings,[1] who exhibited man as an ornament of the world through Christ and gave to him a law implanted and written[2] that he might live lawfully as a rational being and to the sinner gave your own goodness (as) a pledge of repentance;[3] look down upon those who have bowed the neck of soul and body to you, because you do not desire the death of the sinner, but the repentance, to turn him from his way of evil and that he might live.

9. (You are the one) who accepted the repentance of the Ninevites, who desires that all men be saved and that (all) come into knowledge of the truth, who accepted the son with paternal affections who dissolutely consumed his livelihood, because of (his) repentance. You yourself also now accept the change of mind of your supplicants[4] because there is no one who will not sin against you. For if you should watch iniquities closely, O Lord; O Lord[5] who would stand? For with you is expiation.

---

[1]Reading with MS d ὄντων. Funk has πάντων "of all."

[2]The idea of law as implanted and written is also found in 8.12.25. See also the note on 7.33.3.

[3]A difficult phrase. Darnell understands it to mean that God's goodness leads man to repent. It seems more likely that God's goodness is a pledge that he will accept man's repentance.

[4]MS d reads οἰκετῶν, "household," probably a hearing error on the part of the copyist, since the diphthong omicron-iota sounded like iota. See B. M. Metzger, *The Text of the New Testament* (Oxford: University, 1968) 193.

[5]"Lord" is repeated, evidently, for emphasis.

8.12.6-27

6. Ἄξιον ὡς ἀληθῶς καὶ δίκαιον πρὸ πάντων ἀνυμνεῖν σε τὸν ὄντως ὄντα θεὸν τὸν πρὸ τῶν γενητῶν ὄντα, ἐξ οὗ πᾶσα πατριὰ ἐν οὐρανῷ καὶ ἐπὶ γῆς ὀνομάζεται, τὸν μόνον ἀγέννητον καὶ ἄναρχον καὶ ἀβασίλευτον καὶ ἀδέσποτον, τὸν ἀνενδεῆ, τὸν παντὸς ἀγαθοῦ χορηγόν, τὸν πάσης αἰτίας καὶ γενέσεως κρείττονα, τὸν πάντοτε κατὰ τὰ αὐτὰ καὶ ὡσαύτως ἔχοντα· ἐξ οὗ τὰ πάντα, καθάπερ ἔκ τινος ἀφετηρίας, είς τὸ εἶναι παρῆλθεν. 7. σὺ γὰρ εἶ ἡ ἄναρχος γνῶσις, ἡ ἀΐδιος ὅρασις, ἡ ἀγέννητος ἀκοή, ἡ ἀδίδακτος σοφία, ὁ πρῶτος τῇ φύσει καὶ μόνος τῷ εἶναι καὶ κρείττων παντὸς ἀριθμοῦ· ὁ τὰ πάντα ἐκ τοῦ μὴ ὄντος είς τὸ εἶναι παραγαγὼν διὰ τοῦ μονογενοῦς σου υἱοῦ, αὐτὸν δὲ πρὸ πάντων αἰώνων γεννήσας βουλήσει καὶ δυνάμει καὶ ἀγαθότητι ἀμεσιτεύτως, υἱὸν μονογενῆ, λόγον θεόν, σοφίαν ζῶσαν, πρωτότοκον πάσης κτίσεως, ἄγγελον τῆς μεγάλης βουλῆς σου, ἀρχιερέα σόν, βασιλέα δὲ καὶ κύριον πάσης νοητῆς καὶ αἰσθητῆς φύσεως, τὸν πρὸ πάντων, δι᾽ οὗ τὰ πάντα. 8. σὺ γάρ, θεὲ αἰώνιε, δι᾽ αὐτοῦ τὰ πάντα πεποίηκας καὶ δι᾽ αὐτοῦ τῆς προσηκούσης προνοίας τὰ ὅλα ἀξιοῖς· δι᾽ οὗ γὰρ τὸ εἶναι ἐχαρίσω,

8.12.6-27

6. It is truly meet and right above all[1] things to sing a hymn to you who are truly God (and) before all (created) beings, from whom every family[2] in heaven or on earth is named, the only unbegotten, without beginning, not ruled and without a master, in want of nothing, the supplier of every good (thing), the one greater than any cause or beginning, the one who is always the same and unchangeable,[3] (and the one) from whom all things[4] as from a certain starting point[5] pass into being. 7. For you are knowledge without beginning, everlasting sight, unbegotten hearing, untaught wisdom, the first by nature and alone[6] in being and greater than any number: who brings all things into being from nothing through your only begotten son, and who has begotten him before all ages by (your) will and power and goodness, the only begotten son, divine Word,[7] living Wisdom, the first born of all creation,[8] the angel of your great counsel,[9] your High Priest,[10] and King and Lord of every intelligible and sensible nature,[11] the one before all things, through whom are all things.[12]

8. For you, eternal God, have made all things through him and you have deemed the whole (world) worthy of your suitable providence.[13] For through (that one by) which you bestowed being,

---

[1]Lit. "before all things."

[2]Eph 3:15.

[3]Lit. "always the same, even thus."

[4]1 Cor 8:6.

[5]ἀφετηρία, "the starting point of a race" (LSJM).

[6]Migne reads νόμος here for μόνος (thus "the Law of being"). Bunsen and Brightman agree with Funk.

[7]Migne reads λόγον θεοῦ "word of God." Bunsen and Brightman agree with Funk.

[8]Col 1:15.

[9]Isa 9:6.

[10]MS d adds after ἀρχιερέα σόν: καὶ προσκυνήτην ἀξιόχρεων, "and a sufficient worshipper." This appears to be a gloss.

[11]See Philo's conception of the sensible and intelligible worlds, *Conf.* 34, 172. The notion is derived from Plato (e.g. *Timaeus* 39E).

[12]Col 1:17, 1 Cor 8:6.

[13]See above on 7.33.2 for "providence."

δι᾽ αὐτοῦ καὶ τὸ εὖ εἶναι ἐδωρήσω· ὁ θεὸς καὶ πατὴρ τοῦ μονογενοῦς υἱοῦ σου, ὁ δι᾽ αὐτοῦ πρὸ πάντων ποιήσας τὰ Χερουβὶμ καὶ
τὰ Σεραφίμ, αἰῶνάς τε καὶ στρατιάς, δυνάμεις τε καὶ ἐξουσίας,
ἀρχάς τε καὶ θρόνους, ἀρχαγγέλους τε καὶ ἀγγέλους, καὶ μετὰ ταῦτα
πάντα ποιήσας δι᾽ αὐτοῦ τὸν φαινόμενον τοῦτον κόσμον καὶ πάντα
τὰ ἐν αὐτῷ. 9. σὺ γὰρ εἶ ὁ τὸν οὐρανὸν ὡς καμάραν στήσας καὶ
ὡς δέρριν ἐκτείνας καὶ τὴν γῆν ἐπ᾽ οὐδενὸς ἱδρύσας γνώμῃ μόνῃ,
ὁ πήξας στερέωμα καὶ νύκτα καὶ ἡμέραν κατασκευάσας, ὁ ἐξαγαγὼν
φῶς ἐκ θησαυρῶν καὶ τῇ τούτου συστολῇ ἐπαγαγὼν τὸ σκότος εἰς
ἀνάπαυλαν τῶν ἐν τῷ κόσμῳ κινουμένων ζώων, ὁ τὸν ἥλιον τάξας
εἰς ἀρχὰς τῆς ἡμέρας ἐν οὐρανῷ καὶ τὴν σελήνην εἰς ἀρχὰς τῆς
νυκτὸς καὶ τὸν χορὸν τῶν ἀστέρων ἐν οὐρανῷ καταγράψας εἰς αἶνον
τῆς σῆς μεγαλοπρεπείας· 10. ὁ ποιήσας ὕδωρ πρὸς πόσιν καὶ
κάθαρσιν, ἀέρα ζωτικὸν πρὸς εἰσπνοὴν καὶ ἀναπνοὴν καὶ φωνῆς
ἀπόδοσιν διὰ γλώττης πληττούσης τὸν ἀέρα καὶ ἀκοὴν συνεργουμένην
ὑπ᾽ αὐτοῦ ὡς ἐπαΐειν εἰσδεχομένην τὴν προσπίπτουσαν αὐτῇ λαλιάν·
11. ὁ ποιήσας πῦρ πρὸς σκότους παραμυθίαν, πρὸς ἐνδείας
ἀναπλήρωσιν καὶ τὸ θερμαίνεσθαι ἡμᾶς καὶ φωτίζεσθαι ὑπ᾽ αὐτοῦ·
12. ὁ τὴν μεγάλην θάλασσαν χωρίσας τῆς γῆς καὶ τὴν μὲν
ἀναδείξας πλωτήν,

through him also you granted well-being. God and Father of your only begotten son, who made through him before all things the Cherubim and Seraphim, aeons and hosts, powers and authorities, rulers and thrones,[14] archangels and angels,[15] and after all these things you made through him this visible world and all in it.

9. For you are the one who set up heaven like an arch,[16] stretched it out like a curtain[17] and established the earth upon nothing[18] by (your) will alone, who fixed the firmament and prepared night and day, who brought out light from the treasuries[19] and brought forth darkness by its dimming[20] for rest for living creatures that move on the earth, who arranged in heaven the sun for ruling of the day and the moon for ruling of the night[21] and who inscribed the chorus of stars in heaven to praise your magnificence. 10. (You are the one) who made water for drinking and cleansing, living air[22] for breathing in and out[23] and rendering sound by the tongue striking[24] the air and the sense of hearing which is helped by it so as to have perception when it receives the voice which falls upon it. 11. (You are the one) who made fire for consolation in darkness, for satisfying of want and to warm us and for us to be illuminated by it. 12. (You are the one) who separated the great sea from the land and showed one navigable and

---

[14]Col 1:16.

[15]The pairing of the heavenly beings with τὲ...καί (Smyth, *Greek Grammar*, §2974) may suggest the Gnostic notion of pairs at each level of the universe.

[16]Isa 40:22. The parallels between 7.34 and 8.12.9-20 are striking.

[17]Ps 103:2.

[18]Job 16:7.

[19]For a similar idea of the heavenly treasuries see: 1 En 17:1, 18:1, 41:4f, 60:12, 60:14, 4 Ezra 4:5, 5:37 and R. H. Charles, *Apocrypha and Pseudepigraph of the Old Testament* (Oxford: Clarendon, 1976) vol. 2, 564, 572.

[20]συστολή, "contraction, abasing" (LSJM).

[21]Gen 1:16.

[22]"Living air" may derive from the stoic idea of air as an active element. See e.g. Cicero, *De Nat. De.* 2.27.

[23]MS a and Migne omit ἀναπνοή.

[24]Notice the atticisms here: γλώττα and πλήττω, double tau for double sigma (LSJM).

τὴν δὲ ποσὶ βάσιμον ποιήσας, καὶ τὴν μὲν ζώοις μικροῖς καὶ μεγάλοις πληθύνας, τὴν δὲ ἡμέροις καὶ ἀτιθάσσοις πληρώσας, φυτοῖς τε διαφόροις στέψας καὶ βοτάναις στεφανώσας καὶ ἄνθεσι καλλύνας καὶ σπέρμασι πλουτίσας· 13. ὁ συστησάμενος ἄβυσσον καὶ μέγα κύτος αὐτῇ περιθείς, ἁλμυρῶν ὑδάτων σεσωρευμένα πελάγη, περιφράξας δὲ αὐτὴν πύλαις ἄμμου λεπτοτάτης· ὁ πνεύμασί ποτε μὲν αὐτὴν κορυφῶν εἰς ὀρέων μέγεθος, ποτὲ δὲ στρωννύων αὐτὴν εἰς πεδίον, καί ποτε μὲν ἐκμαίνων χειμῶνι, ποτὲ δὲ πραΰνων γαλήνῃ ὡς ναυσιπόροις πλωτῆρσιν εὔκολον εἶναι πρὸς πορείαν· 14. ὁ ποταμοῖς διαζώσας τὸν ὑπὸ σοῦ διὰ Χριστοῦ γενόμενον κόσμον καὶ χειμάρροις ἐπικλύσας καὶ πηγαῖς ἀενάοις μεθύσας, ὄρεσιν δὲ περισφίγξας εἰς ἕδραν ἀτρεμῆ γῆς ἀσφαλεστάτην. 15. ἐπλήρωσας γάρ σου τὸν κόσμον καὶ διεκόσμησας αὐτὸν βοτάναις εὐόσμοις καὶ ἰασίμοις, ζώοις πολλοῖς καὶ διαφόροις, ἀλκίμοις καὶ ἀσθενεστέροις, ἐδωδίμοις καὶ ἐνεργοῖς, ἡμέροις καὶ ἀτιθάσσοις, ἑρπετῶν συριγμοῖς, πτηνῶν ποικίλων κλαγγαῖς, ἐνιαυτῶν κύκλοις, μηνῶν καὶ ἡμερῶν ἀριθμοῖς, τροπῶν τάξεσιν, νεφῶν ὀμβροτόκων διαδρομαῖς εἰς καρπῶν γονὰς καὶ ζώων σύστασιν, σταθμὸν ἀνέμων διαπνεόντων ὅτε προσταχθῶσιν παρὰ σοῦ, τῶν φυτῶν καὶ τῶν βοτανῶν τὸ πλῆθος. 16. καὶ οὐ μόνον τὸν κόσμον ἐδημιούργησας, ἀλλὰ καὶ τὸν κοσμοπολίτην ἄνθρωπον ἐν αὐτῷ ἐποίησας, κόσμου κόσμον αὐτὸν ἀναδείξας εἶπας γὰρ τῇ σῇ σοφίᾳ "Ποιήσωμεν ἄνθρωπον

and made the other passable on foot; and the one you made numerous with animals small and large[25] and the other you filled with animals tame and wild, crowning it with various plants, wreathing it with herbs, beautifying it with flowers and enriching it with seeds.

13. (You are the one) who set up the abyss and surrounded it with a great cavity[26] when the sea was heaped up with salty water. But you circumscribed it[27] with the gates[28] of the lightest sand. (You are the one) who by the winds sometimes arches it[29] as high as mountains, while at other times you spread it out like a plain. Also sometimes it[30] rages in a storm, while at other times it[31] is meek and calm so as to be gentle for traveling for seafaring sailors. 14. (You are the one) who girds the world which was created by you through Christ with rivers and flooded (it) with torrents and drenched (it) with everlasting springs, and bound (it) round with mountains for a firm (and) very sure foundation. 15. For you filled your world and adorned it with herbs, fragrant and healing, with many and varied animals, both strong and weak, for food and for working, tame and wild, with hissing of serpents, with flapping of various flying creatures, with cycles of years, with enumeration of months and days, with the order of seasons, with the procession[32] of rain clouds for generating fruits and sustaining animals, for the station of winds which blow when commanded by you (and) for the multitude of plants and herbs.

16. And not only did you create the world but you also made man in it the cosmopolitan, exhibiting him an ornament of the world.[33] For you said to your Wisdom,[34] "Let us make man in our

---

[25]Ps 103:25.

[26]MS a and Migne read κῆτος ("sea monster") for κύτος ("cavity").

[27]I.e. the sea. [28]Ps 64:8. [29]I.e. the sea.

[30]Probably the person shifts to third here and refers to the sea, but one could read it "you rage...." But see the following note.

[31]Or we could translate "you are meek...." But this is unlikely. The person probably shifts and refers to the sea and not to God.

[32]διαδρομή "running to and fro" or "a parade" (LSJM).

[33]See the notes on 7.34.6.

[34]For Wisdom as creator see Wisdom of Solomon 9:1f, 9:9. Cf. the similar passage in 7.34.6 where it is not clear that "wisdom" is personified.

κατ' εἰκόνα ἡμετέραν καὶ καθ' ὁμοίωσιν καὶ ἀρχέτωσαν τῶν ἰχθύων τῆς θαλάσσης καὶ τῶν πετεινῶν τοῦ οὐρανοῦ". 17. διὸ καὶ πεποίηκας αὐτὸν ἐκ ψυχῆς ἀθανάτου καὶ σώματος σκεδαστοῦ, τῆς μὲν ἐκ τοῦ μὴ ὄντος, τοῦ δὲ ἐκ τῶν τεσσάρων στοιχείων· καὶ δέδωκας αὐτῷ κατὰ μὲν τὴν ψυχὴν τὴν λογικὴν διάγνωσιν, εὐσεβείας καὶ ἀσεβείας διάκρισιν, δικαίου καὶ ἀδίκου παρατήρησιν, κατὰ δὲ τὸ σῶμα τὴν πένταθλον ἐχαρίσω αἴσθησιν καὶ τὴν μεταβατικὴν κίνησιν. 18. σὺ γάρ, θεὲ παντοκράτορ, διὰ Χριστοῦ παράδεισον ἐν 'Εδὲμ κατὰ ἀνατολὰς ἐφύτευσας παντοίων φυτῶν ἐδωδίμων κόσμῳ, καὶ ἐν αὐτῷ, ὡς ἂν ἐν ἑστίᾳ πολυτελεῖ, εἰσήγαγες αὐτόν, κἂν τῷ ποιεῖν νόμον δέδωκας αὐτῷ ἔμφυτον, ὅπως οἴκοθεν καὶ παρ' ἑαυτοῦ ἔχοι τὰ σπέρματα τῆς θεογνωσίας. 19. εἰσαγαγὼν δὲ εἰς τὸν τῆς τρυφῆς παράδεισον, πάντων μὲν ἀνῆκας αὐτῷ τὴν ἐξουσίαν πρὸς μετάληψιν, ἑνὸς δὲ μόνου τὴν γεῦσιν ἀπεῖπας ἐπ' ἐλπίδι κρειττόνων, ἵνα, ἐὰν φυλάξῃ τὴν ἐντολήν, μισθὸν ταύτης τὴν ἀθανασίαν κομίσηται. 20. ἀμελήσαντα δὲ τῆς ἐντολῆς καὶ γευσάμενον ἀπηγορευμένου καρποῦ ἀπάτῃ ὄφεως καὶ συμβουλίᾳ γυναικὸς τοῦ μὲν παραδείσου δικαίως ἐξῶσας αὐτόν, ἀγαθότητι δὲ εἰς τὸ παντελὲς ἀπολλύμενον οὐχ ὑπερεῖδες, σὸν γὰρ ἦν δημιούργημα, ἀλλὰ καθυποτάξας αὐτῷ τὴν κτίσιν δέδωκας αὐτῷ οἰκείοις ἱδρῶσιν καὶ πόνοις πορίζειν ἑαυτῷ τὴν τροφήν, σοῦ πάντα φύοντος καὶ αὔξοντος καὶ πεπαίνοντος· χρόνῳ δὲ πρὸς ὀλίγον αὐτὸν κοιμίσας ὅρκῳ εἰς παλιγγενεσίαν εκάλεσας, ὅρον θανάτου λύσας ζωὴν ἐξ ἀναστάσεως ἐπηγγείλω.

image and likeness, and let them rule over the fish of the sea and the birds of the heaven."[35] 17. Wherefore also you have made him from an immortal soul and a dissoluble body, the one from nothing, the other from the four elements. You have given to him with respect to his soul rational discernment between piety and impiety, observation of justice and iniquity; but with respect to his body you have bestowed the five senses,[36] motion and mobility.[37] 18. For you, O God almighty, planted through Christ a paradise in Eden to the East[38] adorned with all sorts of edible plants and in it as if in a very costly home, you brought him. And when you made (him) you gave (him) a law implanted[39] in him that originally he might have in himself the seeds of divine knowledge. 19. And when you brought (him) into the paradise of pleasure you allowed him the power to participate in everything except you forbade him to taste of one (tree) only, in hope of greater things,[40] that if he keep the commandment he would receive[41] immortality as the reward.

20. But when he ignored the commandment and tasted the forbidden fruit by the deceit of a serpent and counsel of his wife, you justly drove him out of paradise. But in (your) goodness you did not completely overlook (him) when he was lost. For he was your creation. But subjecting creation to him, you have granted to him to provide food for his family by sweat and toil by himself, while you caused all things to grow and increase and become ripe. Although you caused him to sleep for a little while, by an oath, you called him into rebirth,[42] you loosed the bond of death and promised life by resurrection.

---

[35]Gen 1:26.

[36]The "pentathlon of sense perception." An unusual usage which we also saw in 7.34.6. See Darnell's translation: "the five-exercise senses." See also the note on 7.34.6.

[37]Lit. "motion which involves change of place."

[38]Gen 2:8.

[39]See the note on 7.33.3.

[40]We might paraphrase this: "holding out the hope of yet better things."

[41]κομίζω, "carry off as a prize" (LSJM).

[42]See note on 7.33.3.

21. καὶ οὐ τοῦτο μόνον, ἀλλὰ καὶ τοὺς ἐξ αὐτοῦ εἰς πλῆθος ἀνάριθμον χέας, τοὺς ἐμμείναντάς σοι ἐδόξασας, τοὺς δὲ ἀποστάντας σου ἐκόλασας, καὶ τοῦ μὲν Ἄβελ ὡς ὁσίου προσδεξάμενος τὴν θυσίαν, τοῦ δὲ ἀδελφοκτόνου Καΐν ἀποστραφεὶς τὸ δῶρον ὡς ἐναγοῦς· καὶ πρὸς τούτοις τὸν Σὴθ καὶ τὸν Ἐνὼς προσελάβου καὶ τὸν Ἐνὼχ μετατέθεικας. 22. σὺ γὰρ εἶ ὁ δημιουργὸς τῶν ἀνθρώπων καὶ τῆς ζωῆς χορηγὸς καὶ τῆς ἐνδείας πληρωτὴς καὶ τῶν νόμων δοτὴρ καὶ τῶν φυλαττόντων αὐτοὺς μισθαποδότης καὶ τῶν παραβαινόντων αὐτοὺς ἔκδικος, ὁ τὸν μέγαν κατακλυσμὸν ἐπαγαγὼν τῷ κόσμῳ διὰ τὸ πλῆθος τῶν ἀσεβησάντων, καὶ τὸν δίκαιον Νῶε ῥυσάμενος ἐκ τοῦ κατακλυσμοῦ ἐν λάρνακι σὺν ὀκτὼ ψυχαῖς, τέλος μὲν τῶν παρῳχηκότων, ἀρχὴν δὲ τῶν μελλόντων ἐπιγίνεσθαι· ὁ τὸ φοβερὸν πῦρ κατὰ τῆς σοδομηνῆς πενταπόλεως ἐξάψας καὶ γῆν καρποφόρον εἰς ἅλμην θέμενος ἀπὸ κακίας τῶν κατοικούντων ἐν αὐτῇ, καὶ τὸν ὅσιον Λὼτ ἐξαρπάσας τοῦ ἐμπρησμοῦ. 23. σὺ εἶ ὁ τὸν Ἀβραὰμ ῥυσάμενος προγονικῆς ἀσεβείας καὶ κληρονόμον τοῦ κόσμου καταστήσας καὶ ἐμφανίσας αὐτῷ τὸν Χριστόν σου, ὁ τὸν Μελχισεδὲκ ἀρχιερέα σῆς λατρείας προχειρισάμενος, τὸν πολύτλαν θεράποντά σου Ἰὼβ νικητὴν τοῦ ἀρχεκάκου ὄφεως ἀναδείξας, τὸν Ἰσαὰκ ἐπαγγελίας υἱὸν ποιησάμενος, τὸν Ἰακὼβ πατέρα δώδεκα παίδων καὶ τοὺς ἐξ αὐτοῦ εἰς πλῆθος χέας καὶ εἰσαγαγὼν εἰς Αἴγυπτον ἐν ἑβδομήκοντα πέντε ψυχαῖς. 24. σύ, κύριε, τὸν Ἰωσὴφ οὐχ ὑπερεῖδες, ἀλλὰ μισθὸν τῆς διὰ σὲ σωφροσύνης ἔδωκας αὐτῷ τὸ τῶν Αἰγυπτίων ἄρχειν· σύ, κύριε, Ἑβραίους ὑπὸ Αἰγυπτίων καταπονουμένους οὐ περιεῖδες διὰ τὰς πρὸς τοὺς πατέρας αὐτῶν ἐπαγγελίας, ἀλλ' ἐρρύσω, κολάσας Αἰγυπτίους.
25. παραφθειράντων δὲ τῶν ἀνθρώπων τὸν φυσικὸν νόμον καὶ τὴν κτίσιν ποτὲ μὲν αὐτόματον νομισάντων, ποτὲ δὲ πλεῖον ἢ δεῖ τιμησάντων

21. And not only this, but also you poured[43] them forth which came from him into an innumerable multitude. You glorified those which remained with you, and you punished those which apostatized from you, and you received the sacrifice of Abel as of a holy man, but you turned away from the gift of the fratricide Cain as from one cursed by bloodshed.[44] And in addition to these you received Seth and Enos and translated Enoch.

22. For you are the creator of men, the supplier of life, fulfiller of want, giver of laws, rewarder of those who keep them and avenger of those who transgress them, the one who brought the great flood upon the world because of the multitude of ungodly people and rescued the righteous Noah from the flood in an ark with eight souls. They were the end (of the generation) which had died, the beginning (of the generation) to be born.[45] You kindled a horrible fire upon the five cities of Sodom and made the fruitful earth into a sea because of the iniquity of those who were dwelling in it,[46] and you snatched the holy Lot from the conflagration. 23. You are the one who rescued Abraham from (his) ancestral impiety and appointed (him) heir of the world and manifested to him your Christ, the one who assigned Melchizedek to be the High Priest of your service, the one who showed your much enduring servant Job as a victor over the serpent, that prince of evil,[47] the one who made Isaac the son of promise, Jacob the father of twelve boys and poured them forth from him into a multitude and led (them) into Egypt with seventy-five people. 24. You, Lord, did not overlook Joseph but gave him, as reward of his chastity because of you, the rule of Egypt. You, Lord, because of the promise to their fathers did not overlook the Hebrews when they were oppressed by the Egyptians, but you rescued (them) and punished the Egyptians. 25. But when men corrupted the natural law and thought at sometime that creation was an accident, at another time honoring it more than was

---

[43]χέω is used in a colorful way for "increasing the offspring."

[44]ἐναγής, "under a curse due to bloodshed." Cf. Herodotus 1:61 (LSJM).

[45]Or it could be understood as: "(the flood) was the end for those which died, the beginning for those to be born." I.e. it marked a new age.

[46]Ps 106:34.

[47]ἀρχικακός is rendered by Darnell, "arch-evil."

καὶ σοί, τῷ θεῷ τῶν πάντων, συνταττόντων, οὐκ εἴασας πλανᾶσθαι, ἀλλὰ ἀναδείξας τὸν ἅγιόν σου θεράποντα Μωϋσῆν, δι' αὐτοῦ πρὸς βοήθειαν τοῦ φυσικοῦ τὸν γραπτὸν νόμον δέδωκας, καὶ τὴν κτίσιν ἔδειξας σὸν ἔργον εἶναι, τὴν δὲ πολύθεον πλάνην ἐξώρισας· τὸν Ἀαρὼν καὶ τοὺς ἐξ αὐτοῦ ἱερατικῇ τιμῇ ἐδόξασας, Ἑβραίους ἁμαρτόντας ἐκόλασας, ἐπιστρέφοντας ἐδέξω. 26. τοὺς Αἰγυπτίους δεκαπλήγῳ ἐτιμωρήσω, θάλασσαν διελὼν Ἰσραηλίτας διεβίβασας, Αἰγυπτίους ἐπιδιώξαντας ὑποβρυχίους ἀπώλεσας, ξύλῳ πικρὸν ὕδωρ ἐγλύκανας, ἐκ πέτρας ἀκροτόμου ὕδωρ ἀνέχεας, ἐξ οὐρανοῦ τὸ μάννα ὗσας, τροφὴν ἐξ ἀέρος ὀρτυγομήτραν, στῦλον πυρὸς τὴν νύκτα πρὸς φωτισμὸν καὶ στῦλον νεφέλης ἡμέρας πρὸς σκιασμὸν θάλπους· τὸν Ἰησοῦν στρατηγὸν ἀναδείξας, ἑπτὰ ἔθνη Χαναναίων δι' αὐτοῦ καθεῖλες, Ἰορδάνην διέρρηξας, τοὺς ποταμοὺς Ἠθὰμ ἐξήρανας, τείχη κατέρρηξας ἄνευ μηχανημάτων καὶ χειρὸς ἀνθρωπίνης.
27. ὑπὲρ ἁπάντων σοι ἡ δόξα, δέσποτα παντοκράτορ. σὲ προσκυνοῦσιν ἀνάριθμοι στρατιαὶ ἀγγέλων, ἀρχαγγέλων, θρόνων, κυριοτήτων, ἀρχῶν, ἐξουσιῶν, δυνάμεων, στρατιῶν αἰωνίων· τὰ Χερουβὶμ καὶ τὰ ἑξαπτέρυγα Σεραφὶμ ταῖς μὲν δυσὶν κατακαλύπτοντα τοὺς πόδας, ταῖς δὲ δυσὶ τὰς κεφαλάς, ταῖς δὲ δυσὶ πετόμενα, καὶ λέγοντα ἅμα χιλίαις χιλιάσιν ἀρχαγγέλων καὶ μυρίαις μυριάσιν ἀγγέλων ἀκαταπαύστως καὶ ἀσιγήτως βοώσαις, καὶ πᾶς ὁ λαὸς ἅμα εἰπάτω· "Ἅγιος, ἅγιος, ἅγιος κύριος Σαβαώθ, πλήρης ὁ οὐρανὸς καὶ ἡ γῆ τῆς δόξης αὐτοῦ· εὐλογητὸς εἰς τοὺς αἰῶνας· ἀμήν".

its due,[48] comparing[49] it to you, God of all things, you did not allow them to remain in error but you presented your holy servant Moses, through whom you gave the written law as an aid[50] to the natural, and you showed the creation to be your work, and you banished the error of polytheism. You glorified Aaron and his descendants with the honor of the priesthood, you punished the sinful Hebrews (and) received those who repented. 26. You chastised the Egyptians with ten plagues; you separated the sea and led the Israelites over; you destroyed the pursuing Egyptians underwater; you sweetened the bitter water with wood; you poured forth the water from the precipitous rock; you rained down the manna from heaven (and) the quails for food from the air, the pillar of fire for light at night and the pillar of clouds during the day[51] for a shelter[52] in the heat. You presented Joshua as a general and destroyed the seven nations of the Canaanites through him. You split the Jordan; you dried up the rivers of Etham;[53] you tore down walls without war engines and without human hand.

27. For all things may glory be to you, Master almighty. The innumerable hosts of angels, archangels, thrones, dominions, rulers, authorities,[54] powers (and) eternal armies worship you. Let the Cherubim and six-winged Seraphim--covering their feet with two, their heads with two and flying with two[55]--also speaking together with the thousand thousands of archangels and myriad myriads angels with cries unceasing and loud and all the people together say, "Holy, holy, holy, Lord Sabaoth. Heaven and earth are full of his glory.[56] Blessed (are you) forever. Amen."

---

[48]Lit. "more than necessary."

[49]Note the atticism, double tau.

[50]Isa 8:20 LXX. See the note on 7.33.3.

[51]Neh 9:19.

[52]σκιασμός, "shadow," can mean "shelter" in later Greek. See Lampe.

[53]See Ps 73:15 LXX which also transliterates the Hebrew word for "overflowing" as a place-name, ἠθάμ, as Darnell points out. MSS d, h, and v read ἰθάμ. The latter reading is probably due to a mistake by the copyist in hearing the reader since eta and iota sounded alike. See Metzger, *The Text of the New Testament*, 193.

[54]Col 1:16.

[55]Isa 6:2.

[56]Isa 6:3.

8.15.7-9

7. Ὁ θεὸς ὁ παντοκράτωρ, ὁ ἀληθινὸς καὶ ἀσύγκριτος, ὁ πανταχοῦ ὢν καὶ τοῖς πᾶσι παρὼν καὶ ἐν οὐδενὶ ὡς ἐνόν τι ὑπάρχων, ὁ τόποις μὴ περιγραφόμενος, ὁ χρόνοις μὴ παλαιούμενος, ὁ αἰῶσιν μὴ περατούμενος, ὁ λόγοις μὴ παραγόμενος, ὁ γενέσει μὴ ὑποκείμενος, ὁ φυλακῆς μὴ δεόμενος, ὁ φθορᾶς ἀνώτερος, ὁ τροπῆς ἀνεπίδεκτος, ὁ φύσει ἀναλλοίωτος, ὁ φῶς οἰκῶν ἀπρόσιτον, ὁ τῇ φύσει ἀόρατος, ὁ γνωστὸς πάσαις ταῖς μετ' εὐνοίας ἐκζητούσαις σε λογικαῖς φύσεσιν, ὁ καταλαμβανόμενος ὑπὸ τῶν ἐν εὐνοίᾳ ἐπιζητούντων σε, ὁ θεὸς Ἰσραὴλ τοῦ ἀληθινῶς ὁρῶντος, τοῦ εἰς Χριστὸν πιστεύσαντος λαοῦ σου· 8. εὐμενὴς γενόμενος ἐπάκουσόν μου διὰ τὸ ὄνομά σου καὶ εὐλόγησον τούς σοι κεκλικότας τοὺς ἑαυτῶν αὐχένας, καὶ δὸς αὐτοῖς τὰ αἰτήματα τῶν καρδιῶν αὐτῶν τὰ ἐπὶ συμφέροντι καὶ μηδένα αὐτῶν ἀπόβλητον ποιήσῃς ἐκ τῆς βασιλείας σου, ἀλλὰ ἁγίασον αὐτούς, φρούρησον, σκέπασον, ἀντιλαβοῦ, ῥῦσαι τοῦ ἀλλοτρίου, παντὸς ἐχθροῦ, τοὺς οἴκους αὐτῶν φύλαξον, τὰς εἰσόδους αὐτῶν καὶ τὰς ἐξόδους φρούρησον· 9. ὅτι σοὶ δόξα, αἶνος, μεγαλοπρέπεια, σέβας, προσκύνησις καὶ τῷ σῷ παιδὶ Ἰησοῦ τῷ Χριστῷ σου, τῷ κυρίῳ ἡμῶν καὶ θεῷ καὶ βασιλεῖ, καὶ τῷ ἁγίῳ πνεύματι νῦν καὶ ἀεὶ καὶ εἰς τοὺς αἰῶνας τῶν αἰώνων· ἀμήν.

8.15.7-9

7. O God almighty, the true and incomparable, who is everywhere and present in all things, and exists in nothing as something which is in it,[1] who is not circumscribed by places,[2] who does not age with times, who is not bounded[3] by ages, who is not averted[4] by words, who was not subject to a beginning, who has no need of a guardian, who is above corruption, who does not admit of change, who is immutable by nature, who dwells in unapproachable light,[5] who is invisible by nature, known to all reasonable natures with good will who seek you out, who is comprehended by those who seek after you in good will, the God of Israel which truly sees,[6] of your people who believe in Christ.

8. Be kindly and hearken to me because of your name, and bless those that have bowed their necks to you[7] and give them the petitions of their hearts which are for their benefit and do not make any of them castaways from your kingdom, but sanctify them, watch (them), protect (them), help (them), save (them) from the adversary, (from) every enemy, guard their houses, watch their comings in and goings out.[8]

9. For to you be glory, praise, magnificance, reverence, worship, and to your child Jesus, your Christ, our Lord and God and king, and to the Holy Spirit, now and always and forever and ever. Amen.

---

[1]Darnell translates: "Who is in nothing, as though being one certain thing." The point seems to be that God is not spatially (physically) in all things. This is contrary to Stoic doctrine which taught that God physically permeated the universe. As Darnell points out, Philo also denied that Stoic doctrine (*Leg. All.* 3.51).

[2]The plurals ("places," "times," "ages") are indefinite plurals (Smyth, *Greek Grammar*, §1000b). We might translate "not circumscribed by any place."

[3]Or we might translate "not brought to an end" (LSJM).

[4]Or "misled" (ANF, cf. Darnell, "deceived"). Probably, however, this means that God is not swayed or averted from justice.

[5]1 Tim 6:16.

[6]Cf. 7.36.2.

[7]See the note on 8.37.6.

[8]Ps 21:8.

8.16.3

Κύριε παντοκράτορ, ὁ θεὸς ἡμῶν ὁ διὰ Χριστοῦ τὰ πάντα δημιουργήσας καὶ δι' αὐτοῦ τῶν ὅλων προνοῶν καταλλήλως· ᾧ γὰρ δύναμις διάφορα ποιῆσαι, τούτῳ δύναμις καὶ διαφόρως προνοῆσαι· διὰ γὰρ αὐτοῦ, ὁ θεός, προνοεῖς τῶν μὲν ἀθανάτων φυλακῇ μόνῃ, τῶν δὲ θνητῶν διαδοχῇ, τῆς ψυχῆς φροντίδι νόμων, τοῦ σώματος ἀναπληρώσει τῆς ἐνδείας·

8.16.3

Lord almighty, our God who created all things through Christ and who through him appropriately provides for the universe; for he who has power to make different things also has power to provide for (them) differently;[1] for through him, O God, you provide for the immortal (beings) by merely guarding (them),[2] the mortal (beings) by succession,[3] the soul by the provision of laws, the body by supplying its needs.

---

[1]Cf. 7.34.5.

[2]Darnell renders "in a place of security, in a mansion," evidently reading μόνῃ not as an adjective describing φυλακῇ but a noun meaning "a station," or "apartment," (LSJM, see e.g. John 14:2). This is an interesting, but unlikely alternative, since φυλακῇ is juxtaposed beside μόνῃ. In such a case we would ordinarily suppose that μόνῃ is an adjective ("only," "alone," LSJM).

[3]Goodenough (*By Light, Light*, 335) understood διαδοχή as "a subordinate agency." I.e. God does not protect mortals directly, but through an intermediary. Darnell translates "in successive ways." The text seems to mean that God provides for immortals by preventing their death (guarding them), but God provides for mortals by giving them offspring to carry on the race (by succession).

8.37.1-4

1. Καὶ ὁ ἐπίσκοπος ἐπευχόμενος λεγέτω· 2. Ὁ ἄναρχος θεὸς καὶ ἀτελεύτητος, ὁ τῶν ὅλων ποιητὴς διὰ Χριστοῦ καὶ κηδεμών, πρὸ δὲ πάντων αὐτοῦ θεὸς καὶ πατήρ, ὁ τοῦ πνεύματος κύριος καὶ τῶν νοητῶν καὶ αἰσθητῶν βασιλεύς, ὁ ποιήσας ἡμέραν πρὸς ἔργα φωτὸς καὶ νύκτα εἰς ἀνάπαυσιν τῆς ἀσθενείας ἡμῶν· σὴ γάρ ἐστιν ἡ ἡμέρα καὶ σή ἐστιν ἡ νύξ, σὺ κατηρτίσω φαῦσιν καὶ ἥλιον· αὐτὸς καὶ νῦν, δέσποτα φιλάνθρωπε καὶ πανάγαθε, εὐμενῶς πρόσδεξαι τὴν ἑσπερινὴν εὐχαριστίαν ἡμῶν ταύτην. 3. ὁ διαγαγὼν ἡμᾶς τὸ μῆκος τῆς ἡμέρας καὶ ἀγαγὼν ἐπὶ τὰς ἀρχὰς τῆς νυκτός, φύλαξον ἡμᾶς διὰ τοῦ Χριστοῦ σου· εἰρηνικὴν παράσχου τὴν ἑσπέραν καὶ τὴν νύκτα ἀναμάρτητον, καὶ καταξίωσον ἡμᾶς τῆς αἰωνίου ζωῆς διὰ τοῦ Χριστοῦ σου, δι' οὗ σοι δόξα, τιμὴ καὶ σέβας ἐν ἁγίῳ πνεύματι εἰς τοὺς αἰῶνας· ἀμήν. 4. καὶ ὁ διάκονος λεγέτω· Κλίνατε τῇ χειροθεσίᾳ.

8.37.1-4

1. And let the bishop pray and say: 2. O God, without beginning and without end, Maker of the universe through Christ, and Preservor, and above all things its God and Father, the Lord of the spirit[1] and king of the intelligible and perceptible things,[2] who made day for works of light and night for rest of our infirmity; for the day is yours and the night is yours; you fashioned[3] the illumination and the sun. You yourself also now,[4] Master, Lover of mankind and All-good, accept kindly this our evening thanksgiving. 3. You who have led us through the length of the day and led us to the beginnings of night, guard us through your Christ. Grant (that) the evening be peaceful and the night free from sin, and permit us (to have)[5] eternal life through your Christ, through whom be glory to you, honor and reverence in the Holy Spirit forever. Amen.

4. And let the deacon say: Bow for the laying on of hands.

---

[1]The same expression is found throughout the similitudes of Enoch (e.g. 1 En 38:2f).

[2]See the note on 8.12.7.

[3]The word usually meant "repair," but later came to mean also "fashion" (Lampe).

[4]This same phrase is found in 7.26.4, 7.37.1, 8.9.9, 8.16.4, 8.37.6, 8.38.4, 8.39.4 and 8.41.5.

[5]Or "vouchsafe." The word implies that something is granted from a superior to an inferior (LSJM).

8.37.5-7

5. καὶ ὁ ἐπίσκοπος λεγέτω· Θεὲ πατέρων καὶ κύριε τοῦ ἐλέους, ὁ τῇ σοφίᾳ σου κατασκευάσας ἄνθρωπον, τὸ λογικὸν ζῶον τὸ θεοφιλὲς τῶν ἐπὶ γῆς, καὶ δοὺς αὐτῷ τῶν ἐπὶ τῆς χθονὸς ἄρχειν, καὶ καταστήσας γνώμῃ σῇ ἄρχοντας καὶ ἱερεῖς, τοὺς μὲν πρὸς ἀσφάλειαν τῆς ζωῆς, τοὺς δὲ πρὸς λατρείαν ἔννομον· 6. αὐτὸς καὶ νῦν ἐπικάμφθητι, κύριε παντοκράτορ, καὶ ἐπίφανον τὸ πρόσωπόν σου ἐπὶ τὸν λαόν σου, τοὺς κάμψαντας αὐχένα καρδίας αὐτῶν, καὶ εὐλόγησον αὐτοὺς διὰ Χριστοῦ, δι' οὗ ἐφώτισας ἡμᾶς φῶς γνώσεως καὶ ἀπεκάλυψας ἡμῖν σαυτόν, μεθ' οὗ σοὶ καὶ ἡ ἐπάξιος ὀφείλεται προσκύνησις παρὰ πάσης λογικῆς καὶ ἁγίας φύσεως καὶ πνεύματι τῷ παρακλήτῳ εἰς τοὺς αἰῶνας· ἀμήν. 7. καὶ ὁ διάκονος λεγέτω· Προέλθετε ἐν εἰρήνῃ.

8.37.5-7

5. And let the bishop say: O God, of the fathers and Lord of mercy, who by your Wisdom[1] prepared man, the rational creature, loved of God (more than)[2] the (creatures) on the earth, and who granted him to rule the mundane (creatures), and you set up by your will rulers and priests, the one for security of life, the other for rightful worship; 6. you yourself also now[3] incline (toward us), O Lord almighty, and cause your face to shine on your people who bend the neck of their heart,[4] and bless them through Christ, through whom you enlightened us with the light of knowledge and revealed yourself to us, with whom also due worship is owed to you from every rational and holy nature and to the Spirit, the Paraclete forever. Amen. 7. And let the deacon say: Depart in peace.

---

[1]"Wisdom" is personified here and thus is capitalized.

[2]There is no comparative in the text.

[3]See the note on 8.37.2.

[4]Ps 31:17. MS d reads "servants" instead of "people," but this is merely in imitation of Ps 31:17 which is partially quoted here. This phrase from the psalter occurs elsewhere in 8.9.8 and 8.15.8.

8.38.4-5

4. Ὁ θεὸς τῶν πνευμάτων καὶ πάσης σαρκός, ὁ ἀσύγκριτος καὶ ἀπροσδεής, ὁ δοὺς τὸν ἥλιον εἰς ἐξουσίαν τῆς ἡμέρας, τὴν δὲ σελήνην καὶ τὰ ἄστρα εἰς ἐξουσίαν τῆς νυκτός· αὐτὸς καὶ νῦν ἔπιδε ἐφ᾽ ἡμᾶς εὐμενέσιν ὀφθαλμοῖς καὶ πρόσδεξαι τὰς ἑωθινὰς ἡμῶν εὐχαριστίας καὶ ἐλέησον ἡμᾶς· οὐ γὰρ διεπετάσαμεν τὰς χεῖρας ἡμῶν πρὸς θεὸν ἀλλότριον. 5. οὐ γὰρ ἔστιν ἐν ἡμῖν θεὸς πρόσφατος, ἀλλὰ σὺ ὁ αἰώνιος καὶ ἀτελεύτητος· ὁ τὸ εἶναι ἡμῖν διὰ Χριστοῦ παρασχόμενος καὶ τὸ εὖ εἶναι δι᾽ αὐτοῦ δωρησάμενος, αὐτὸς ἡμᾶς δι᾽ αὐτοῦ καταξίωσον καὶ τῆς αἰωνίου ζωῆς, μεθ᾽ οὗ σοὶ δόξα καὶ τιμὴ καὶ σέβας καὶ τῷ ἁγίῳ πνεύματι εἰς τοὺς αἰῶνας· ἀμήν.

8.38.4-5

4. God of the spirits and of all flesh, incomparable and without need, who gives the sun for authority over the day and the moon and stars for authority over the night. You yourself also now look down[1] upon us with kindly eyes and accept our morning thanksgiving and have mercy on us for we have not spread out our hands to another[2] God. 5. For there is no new God among us, but you the eternal and unending; who have granted us being through Christ, and have presented us well-being through him. You yourself permit us (to have)[3] eternal life, with whom to you be glory and honor and reverence and to the Holy Spirit forever. Amen.

---

[1] See the note on 8.37.2.

[2] Or a "foreign" God.

[3] Or "vouchsafe." The same phrase is found in 8.37.3.

8.39.3-4

3. Ὁ θεὸς ὁ πιστὸς καὶ ἀληθινός, ὁ ποιῶν ἔλεος εἰς χιλιάδας καὶ μυριάδας τοῖς ἀγαπῶσίν σε, ὁ φίλος ταπεινῶν καὶ πενήτων προστάτης, οὗ πάντα ἐν χρείᾳ καθέστηκεν, ὅτι τὰ σύμπαντα δοῦλά σου· 4. ἔπιδε ἐπὶ τὸν λαόν σου τοῦτον, τοὺς κεκλικότας σοι τὰς ἑαυτῶν κεφαλάς, καὶ εὐλόγησον αὐτοὺς εὐλογίαν πνευματικήν, φύλαξον αὐτοὺς ὡς κόρην ὀφθαλμοῦ, διατήρησον αὐτοὺς ἐν εὐσεβείᾳ καὶ δικαιοσύνῃ, καὶ καταξίωσον αὐτοὺς τῆς αἰωνίου ζωῆς ἐν Χριστῷ Ἰησοῦ τῷ ἠγαπημένῳ σου παιδί, μεθ᾽ οὗ σοὶ δόξα, τιμὴ καὶ σέβας καὶ τῷ ἁγίῳ πνεύματι νῦν καὶ ἀεὶ καὶ εἰς τοὺς αἰῶνας τῶν αἰώνων· ἀμήν.

8.39.3-4

3. God the faithful and true, who does mercifully to the thousands and ten thousands of them that love you,[1] the friend of the humble and protector of the poor, of whom all things stand in need, because all things are subject to you;[2] 4. look down now upon this your people,[3] who have bowed their heads to you,[4] and bless them with a spiritual blessing,[5] guard them as the pupil of the eye, keep them in piety and righteousness, and permit them (to have)[6] eternal life in Christ Jesus your beloved child, with whom be glory to you and honor and reverence and to the Holy Spirit now and always and forever and ever. Amen.

---

[1]Exod 20:6.

[2]As Lampe points out the adjective δοῦλος takes a genitive complement.

[3]See the note on 8.37.2.

[4]This phrase is similar to the one occurring elsewhere in the prayers of AC 8. See the note on 8.37.6.

[5]A cognate accusative (Smyth, *Greek Grammar*, §1564).

[6]The phrase is found elsewhere in the prayers. See the note on 8.37.3.

8.40.2-4

2. Εὐχαριστοῦμέν σοι, κύριε παντοκράτορ, δημιουργὲ τῶν ὅλων καὶ προνοητά, διὰ τοῦ μονογενοῦς σου παιδὸς Ἰησοῦ Χριστοῦ, τοῦ κυρίου ἡμῶν, ἐπὶ ταῖς προσενεχθείσαις σοι ἀπαρχαῖς, οὐχ ὅσον ὀφείλομεν, ἀλλ᾽ ὅσον δυνάμεθα. 3. τίς γὰρ ἀνθρώπων ἐπαξίως εὐχαριστῆσαί σοι δύναται ὑπὲρ ὧν δέδωκας αὐτοῖς εἰς μετάληψιν; ὁ θεὸς Ἀβραὰμ καὶ Ἰσαὰκ καὶ Ἰακὼβ καὶ πάντων τῶν ἁγίων, ὁ πάντα τελεσφορήσας διὰ τοῦ λόγου σου καὶ κελεύσας τῇ γῇ παντοδαποὺς ἐκφῦσαι καρποὺς εἰς εὐφροσύνην καὶ τροφὴν ἡμετέραν, ὁ δοὺς τοῖς νωθεστέροις καὶ βληχώδεσιν χιλόν, ποηφάγοις χλόην, καὶ τοῖς μὲν κρέα, τοῖς δὲ σπέρματα, ἡμῖν δὲ σῖτον τὴν πρόσφορον καὶ κατάλληλον τροφὴν καὶ ἕτερα διάφορα, τὰ μὲν πρὸς χρῆσιν, τὰ δὲ πρὸς ὑγείαν, τὰ δὲ πρὸς τέρψιν. 4. ἐπὶ τούτοις οὖν ἅπασιν ὑμνητὸς ὑπάρχεις τῆς εἰς πάντας εὐεργεσίας διὰ Χριστοῦ, μεθ᾽ οὗ σοὶ δόξα, τιμὴ καὶ σέβας καὶ πνεύματι τῷ ἁγίῳ εἰς τοὺς αἰῶνας· ἀμήν.

8.40.2-4[1]

2. We give you thanks, O Lord almighty, Creator of the universe and Supervisor through your only begotten child Jesus Christ our Lord, for the first fruits which are offered to you, not such as we should, but such as we can. 3. For what man can give thanks to you worthily for the things which you have given them to partake of? God of Abraham and Isaac and Jacob, and all the holy ones, who brings all things to full growth[2] through your word and commands the earth to bring forth all kinds of fruits for our enjoyment and our nourishment, who gives fodder to the more sluggish (creatures) and the bleating ones, sprouts to the grass-eaters, to some flesh, to others seeds, but to us grain, the fitting and appropriate nourishment and various other things, the things that are useful, the things for health, and those for delight.

4. Therefore, for all these things you are hymned for[3] your well-doing through Christ for all, with whom be to you glory, honor and reverence and to the Holy Spirit forever. Amen.

---

[1]This prayer is based on Apostolic Tradition 28. See Chapter II.

[2]τελεσφορέω, "to bring (fruit) to perfection" (LSJM).

[3]Lit. "hymned of the well-doing."

8.41.2-5

2. Καὶ ὑπὲρ τῶν ἀναπαυσαμένων ἐν Χριστῷ ἀδελφῶν ἡμῶν δεηθῶμεν, ὑπὲρ τῆς κοιμήσεως τοῦδε ἢ τῆσδε δεηθῶμεν, ὅπως ὁ φιλάνθρωπος θεὸς προσδεξάμενος αὐτοῦ τὴν ψυχὴν ἀφήσῃ αὐτῷ πᾶν ἁμάρτημα ἑκούσιον καὶ ἀκούσιον, καὶ ἵλεως καὶ εὐμενὴς γενόμενος κατατάξῃ εἰς χώραν εὐσεβῶν ἀνειμένων εἰς κόλπους Ἀβραὰμ καὶ Ἰσαὰκ καὶ Ἰακὼβ μετὰ πάντων τῶν ἀπ' αἰῶνος εὐαρεστησάντων καὶ ποιησάντων τὸ θέλημα αὐτοῦ, ἔνθα ἀπέδρα ὀδύνη καὶ λύπη καὶ στεναγμός. ἐγειρώμεθα· ἑαυτοὺς καὶ ἀλλήλους τῷ ἀϊδίῳ θεῷ διὰ τοῦ ἐν ἀρχῇ λόγου παραθώμεθα. 3. καὶ ὁ ἐπίσκοπος λεγέτω·
4. Ὁ τῇ φύσει ἀθάνατος καὶ ἀτελεύτητος, παρ' οὗ πᾶν ἀθάνατον καὶ θνητὸν γέγονεν, ὁ τὸ λογικὸν τοῦτο ζῷον τὸν ἄνθρωπον τὸν κοσμοπολίτην θνητὸν ἐκ κατασκευῆς ποιήσας καὶ ἀνάστασιν ἐπαγγειλάμενος, ὁ τὸν Ἐνὼχ καὶ τὸν Ἠλίαν θανάτου πεῖραν μὴ ἐάσας λαβεῖν· ὁ θεὸς Ἀβραὰμ καὶ Ἰσαὰκ καὶ Ἰακὼβ οὐχ ὡς νεκρῶν, ἀλλ' ὡς ζώντων θεὸς εἶ· ὅτι πάντων αἱ ψυχαὶ παρὰ σοὶ ζῶσιν καὶ τῶν δικαίων τὰ πνεύματα ἐν τῇ χειρί σού εἰσιν, ὧν οὐ μὴ ἅψηται βάσανος· πάντες γὰρ οἱ ἡγιασμένοι ὑπὸ τὰς χεῖράς σού εἰσιν.

8.41.2-5[1]

2. And on behalf of our brethren who are at rest in Christ, let us entreat, on behalf of the repose of this (man) or this (woman) let us entreat that God the lover of mankind may receive his soul and forgive his every sin, willing and unwilling, and that he being gracious and kindly may appoint[2] (him) to the land of the reverent ones who are sent to the bosom of Abraham and Isaac and Jacob[3] with all those of old[4] who were well-pleasing and did his will, from which sorrow, grief and groaning have fled.[5] Let us arise; let us entrust ourselves and one another to the eternal God through the Word (which was) in the beginning.

3. And let the bishop say: 4. You who are by nature immortal and unending, by whom everything immortal and mortal has come to be, who made this rational creature, man, the cosmopolitan, mortal from constitution,[6] and promised the resurrection, who did not allow Enoch and Elijah to experience[7] the trial of death, the God of Abraham, Isaac and Jacob, you are not the God of the dead, but of the living,[8] because the souls of all live in your presence,[9] and the spirits of the righteous are in your hand, whom anguish shall not[10] touch. For all of them are sanctified by your hands.

---

[1]For the Latin fragment (see the introduction to this chapter) of this prayer, see Turner, "A Fragment," 492-94.

[2]LSJM define κατατάσσω, "appoint to do" or "pay into the treasury." Lampe defines it, "appoint to an office." Latin, "connumero," to "number with."

[3]Cf. Luke 16:22. A similar phrase was found in Greek on a Lumbrosian grave stone. See F. Preisigke, *Sammelbuch griechischer Urkunden aus Ägypten* (Strassburg: Trübner, 1915) vol. 1, no. 2034. See also the Jewish prayer for the dead quoted in Warren (*Liturgy*, 219-21) which contains a similar phrase.

[4]For this idiom see LSJM.

[5]Isa 35:10.

[6]See Lampe for this definition. For "cosmopolitan," see the note on 7.34.6.

[7]Lit. "to receive."

[8]Matt 22:32.

[9]For παρὰ σοί, see LSJM. Or this phrase may be a paraphrase of Luke 20:18 αὐτῷ "by him" which would mean here: "the souls of all live by you." See Lampe for the latter usage of παρά.

[10]Emphatic negative. See Smyth, *Greek Grammar*, §2755.

5. αὐτὸς καὶ νῦν ἔπιδε ἐπὶ τὸν δοῦλόν σου τόνδε, ὃν ἐξελέξω καὶ προσελάβου εἰς ἑτέραν λῆξιν, καὶ συγχώρησον αὐτῷ, εἴ τι ἄκων ἢ ἑκὼν ἐξήμαρτεν, καὶ ἀγγέλους εὐμενεῖς παράστησον αὐτῷ· καὶ κατάταξον αὐτὸν ἐν τῷ κόλπῳ τῶν πατριαρχῶν καὶ τῶν προφητῶν καὶ τῶν ἀποστόλων καὶ πάντων τῶν ἀπ᾿ αἰῶνός σοι εὐαρεστησάντων, ὅπου οὐκ ἔνι λύπη καὶ ὀδύνη καὶ στεναγμός, ἀλλὰ χῶρος εὐσεβῶν ἀνειμένος καὶ γῆ εὐθέων σοὶ ἀνακειμένη καὶ τῶν ἐν αὐτῇ ὁρώντων τὴν δόξαν τοῦ Χριστοῦ σου, μεθ᾿ οὗ σοὶ δόξα, τιμὴ καὶ σέβας, εὐχαριστία καὶ προσκύνησις καὶ τῷ ἁγίῳ πνεύματι εἰς τοὺς αἰῶνας· ἀμήν.

5. You yourself also now look down upon this your servant,[11] whom you elected and received into another lot, and forgive[12] him if he has sinned in any way (whether) unwillingly or willingly, and station kindly angels beside him, and appoint him (a place) in the bosom of the patriarchs and prophets and apostles and all of them from of old who were well-pleasing to you, where there is[13] no grief and sorrow and groaning, but the quiet region of the reverent ones, and the land[14] of the upright ones which is dedicated to you and of those in it who see the glory of your Christ, with whom be to you glory, honor, reverence, thanks and worship, and to the Holy Spirit forever. Amen.

---

[11]See the note on 8.37.2.

[12]This meaning is not found in classical and hellenistic Greek. See Lampe.

[13]Lit. "where there is no...in (it)."

[14]MS d reads χορός, "chorus," instead of χῶρος, "land," as in the other MSS. But the Latin here agrees with the other MSS: "locus," "place."

CHAPTER IV

THE ARGUMENTS FOR ORIGINALLY JEWISH PRAYERS IN AC

This chapter will answer some of the questions of Chapter I: Are any of the prayers alleged to be Jewish really from a Jewish source? Have Kohler, Bousset and others proved their contention? We shall argue below that Kohler was essentially correct in saying that AC 7.33-38 is a version of the Seven Benedictions, but that Bousset--though he possessed a fine sensitivity in recognizing that AC 7.33-38 is Jewish--used an inadequate methodology in arguing for his thesis, and that this methodology led him to suggest incorrectly that other prayers in AC books seven and eight are Jewish as well.

The Prayer Collection of AC 7.33-38

Kohler[1] asserted in 1905 that the prayers in AC 7.33-38 are the "Essene version" of the synagogal Seven Benedictions (ברכת שבע). Though Kohler may have misunderstood the milieu of the prayers--and this must be examined later--his recognition of the Jewish Seven Benedictions in AC 7.33-38 was correct. The Seven Benedictions for Sabbaths and festivals consist of the first three and last three benedictions of the Eighteen Benedictions for daily recitation, plus the middle benediction, that for sanctification of the day.[2] Although the earliest texts date from the Gaonic era, there is a consensus among scholars that the content and order--though not the wording[3]--of the Eighteen Benedictions was standardized at least by the Mishnaic period--if not before--probably at the time of Gamaliel II,[4] and that the Seven Benedictions were also fixed at least by this time.[5] The implication of this conclusion for dating the prayers in AC 7.33-38 will be analyzed later. The important fact now is that the Seven Benedictions antedate the compilation of AC by at least three hundred years and thus some form of it could be a source of the AC.

Kohler's publication in 1905 and the subsequent one in 1924 were little more than translations of his reconstructed text of the prayers with some notes. He left it to the reader to find the points of similarity between the prayers, therefore it is necessary here to point out the resemblances in general content, and secondly, the correspondences in wording. The prayers in AC 7.33-38 follow closely the contents of the first six of the Seven Benedictions (the seventh is omitted) and in the same order. AC 7.33 is similar in content to the first benediction, the אבות[6] ("fathers"). Both prayers praise the God of the fathers Abraham, Isaac and Jacob (Exod 3:16) for his might and his protection. Both prayers echo Genesis 15: מגן אברהם and ὑπερμάχος ἀβραάμ (Gen 15:1).[7]

AC 7.34 is similar to the second benediction, the גבורות ("powers"). Both prayers speak of God's power and end with the blessing of God who revives the dead.

AC 7.35.8f corresponds to the קדושת השם ("sanctification of the Name"), the third benediction. In addition, AC 7.35.4 has incorporated the Kedusha (see Chapter III) which was recited just before the third benediction, precisely where it is placed in AC 7.35.

AC 7.36 is the fourth benediction, the קדושת היום ("sanctification of the day") recited on Sabbaths. Both prayers exalt the seventh day as a day of rest and refer to the study of Torah on the Sabbath.

AC 7.37 corresponds to the fifth benediction[8] the עבודה ("service"). Both the Abodah and AC 7.37 are petitions to accept the prayers of the people,[9] but the Abodah also requests that the (temple) service be restored in Jerusalem.

AC 7.38 is very much like the הודאה ("thanksgiving") prayer of the sixth benediction.[10] The theme of both prayers is thanksgiving for God's deeds in history.

The seventh[11] benediction ברכת כהנים ("priest's blessing") is omitted in AC 7.33-38. This omission is perhaps because the prayer was only supposed to be recited in Hebrew, while the other prayers could be recited in any other language.[12]

The main content of the Seven Benedictions and AC 7.33-38 is very similar, though the corresponding prayers may add or omit subordinate themes. What makes this evidence compelling is that: (1) These prayers are collected or grouped together, and not scattered throughout the AC. (2) The prayer collection follows immediately in the AC, as a source, after the Didache is used as a source. Thus, it appears that the compiler used three sources in succession in his work: the Didascalia (books one through six), the Didache (7.1-32), and the prayer collection (7.33-38). (3) This prayer collection exactly corresponds both in general content and in the order of the prayers to a Jewish prayer collection, the Hebrew Seven Benedictions. To find such a prayer collection which contains six prayers treating the same themes and in the same order as the first six of the Seven Benedictions is unbelievably coincidental. Thus, the third source in the AC is a Jewish Greek version of the Seven Benedictions.

Even more striking evidence exists, however, that a form of the Seven Benedictions stands behind the present text of AC 7.33-38. There are verbal Greek equivalents in AC 7.33-38 to phrases in the Hebrew Seven Benedictions. Since the prayers of the synagogue were probably improvised orally, with only the general content and order becoming fixed by the end of the first century A.D. --as Heinemann said--we would not expect to find many verbal parallels between AC 7.33-38 and the Seven Benedictions, especially since one exists in Greek and the other in Hebrew. Heinemann maintained:

> Therefore, we must lay down as a fundamental axiom...that from the first no single "original" text of any particular prayer was created, but that originally numerous diverse texts and versions existed side by side...we are dealing with materials which originated as part of an oral tradition and hence by their very nature were not phrased in any fixed uniform formulation--which at a later stage came to be "revised" and expanded--but rather were improvised on the spot; and, subsequently, "reimprovised" and reworded in many different formulations in an equally spontaneous fashion....[13]

Nevertheless, there are a few verbal similarities, and these similarities only serve to support the argument that behind AC 7.33-38 lies a Greek version--or a formulation in Greek--of the Seven.

Chart C presents the Hebrew Seven Benedictions with the verbal parallels to the Greek equivalents in AC 7.33-38 underlined. Before we analyze these parallels in order we must note that virtually every benediction has at least one verbal parallel. To find such impressive verbal similarities with the Seven is incredible unless we conclude that a form of the Seven actually stands behind AC 7. 33-38. We shall compare the prayers of AC 7.33-38 with the Palestinian version of the Seven, represented by the Geniza fragments, and the Babylonian version, represented by R. Amram's text.[14]

The first of the Hebrew benedictions begins with the standard formula, ברוך אתה '' ("Blessed are you O Lord."). This formula is absent from the beginning AC 7.33, either from being edited out by the compiler or from its absence from the Jewish source. The formula does appear in 7.34 which corresponds to the second benediction. In the Hebrew versions, benediction two does not begin with this formula, but ends with it. AC 7.34 begins with the formula, but does not end with it. Thus, the placement of the formula, which became fixed at least in the early Gaonic era (since the text of these two Hebrew rites dates from this era) and probably in the late Amoraic era if Heinemann is correct, was perhaps not fixed at the time Christians appropriated these Jewish prayers. But perhaps the text was rearranged by the compiler and thus the formula was moved. The appearance of this formula at all, however, is a striking parallel.

Benediction one continues to describe God as the "God of our fathers, God of Abraham, Isaac and Jacob." This same description appears in AC 7.33: "God of our holy and blameless fathers and of those before us; God of Abraham, Isaac and Jacob...." Perhaps the compiler has interpolated, "holy and blameless" and "and of those before us" (as we shall argue in Chapter V), or this particular version of the Seven may have included those words. At any rate, the occurrence at the beginning of AC 7.33 of the same description of God as the first benediction,can hardly be coincidental.

The first benediction concludes with "Blessed are you, O Lord, Shield of Abraham." AC 7.33 concludes: "O Defender of the offspring of Abraham, blessed are you forever." The first benediction apparently alludes to Gen 15:1 where God states that he is Abraham's "shield" (מגן). The Septuagint renders this expression, ὑπερασπίζω. The AC, however, as "protector" of Abraham (ὑπέρμαχος). But can ὑπέρμαχος be a translation of מגן? Symmachus translates מגן at Gen 15:1 as ὑπερμάχομαι. Thus, there is precedent for rendering מגן as a form of ὑπέρμαχος.[15] The clause in AC 7.33 is so near that in the Hebrew benediction that the clause in AC must be a Greek version of the same thing. Again, that the first prayer in the collection of AC 7.33-38 concludes with such a clause must be more than coincidence.

AC 7.34 ends with a striking parallel to the second benediction: "O Quickener of the dead" (AC); "Who quickens the dead" (Heb.). Although we can find no instance where the hiphil participle of חיה is translated ζωόποιος, as it is in AC 7.34, the Septuagint renders it ζωοποίησις (Ezra 9:8f) which is very close.[16] Again, both clauses come at the end of the second prayer of a collection. The similar pattern suggests a similar origin.

The only verbal equivalents in the two versions of the Kedushah are the scripture quotations (Isa 6:3, Ezek 3:12). Each version (i.e. the Hebrew of Amram[17] and the Greek of AC) introduces the scriptures differently. Again, though, it is more than coincidental that the juxtaposition of these two scriptures comes at this point in the prayer collection of AC 7.33-38.

AC 7.35.9, "For there is no God except you alone, no holy one but you..." parallels differing phrases in the Babylonian and Palestinian rites. Amram's rite reads: "he alone is high and holy." The Geniza version is: "there is no God beside you." The Babylonian rite emphasizes the holiness of God, while the Palestinian stresses the unity of God. Yet AC 7.35.9 catches both of these themes!

AC 7.36, the prayer for Sabbath, contains the obvious verbal parallels already mentioned: the seventh day and the Law. Again, the appearance of these elements at this point in the prayer collection suggests commonality with the Seven.

The fifth benediction begins: "accept (רצה) O Lord, our God, your people Israel and their prayer" (Babylonian), "Accept (us), O Lord our God, and dwell in Zion, and may your servants serve you in Jerusalem" (Palestinian). AC 7.37 may have been recast by the compiler. It begins:

> You who have fulfilled the promises of the prophets and had mercy on Jerusalem by exalting the throne of David your servant in its midst, by the birth of Christ who was born of his seed according to the flesh from a virgin only, you yourself also now, O Master, God, accept the entreaties from the lips of your people...."

This section requests that God accept the entreaties of his people as in the Babylonian rite, and speaks of God's mercy on Zion and Jerusalem as in the Palestinian rite. Perhaps the compiler has changed a request, regarding Zion and Jerusalem, to a fulfillment (see Chapter V below). At any rate, the mention in a prayer, of Zion and Jerusalem, in connection with a request to accept the prayers[18] of the people would, even if the prayer stood isolated from any collection, cause us to conclude that it was based upon the Hebrew fifth (of the Seven) benediction. And since the prayer stands in this position in the prayer collection of AC 7.33-38, we can hardly doubt such a connection.

Finally, AC 7.38 begins exactly as the Hebrew sixth benediction: "We give thanks to you." The hiphil participle of ידה is not rendered in the Septuagint as εὐχαριστεῖν as we have it in AC 7.38, but Aquila rendered תודה, the noun form, as εὐχαριστία.[19] Thus there is precedent for translating a form of ידה with a form of εὐχαριστεῖν. There is another phrase in AC 7.38 which is a Semiticism and which occurs in the sixth benediction: γενεὰν καὶ γενεάν ("every generation") equals the Hebrew דור ודור which appears in the Babylonian rite.[20]

These verbal similarities and equivalents would be striking enough if they appeared in isolated prayers. But, coming as they do in a prayer collection, and appearing for the most part in their proper order, they constitute a convincing corpus of evidence to suggest that AC 7.33-38 is a Greek version of the Hebrew Seven Benedictions.

Bousset's Method of Argument

Kohler had perceptively recognized a Greek version of the Seven Benedictions in AC 7.33-38, though he had not developed the argument as fully as possible. Ten years after Kohler's publication in the Jewish Encyclopedia another distinguished scholar, Bousset, produced a work on the prayers of AC. Bousset was so sensitive to Jewish thought that he recognized the Jewishness of AC 7.33-38. Yet his methodology, which was considerably different from Kohler's, led him to suggest that other prayers in AC books seven and eight were originally Jewish as well. We shall first summarize Bousset's handling of AC 7.33-38, then his treatment of the other alleged Jewish prayers (see Chart A, above, p. 11).

Bousset apparently was not aware of Kohler's publications and he also evidently did not know about the parallels to the Seven Benedictions. Rather than comparing one prayer collection with the other, he argued for the Jewishness of each prayer individually--and not in their order of appearance in AC--a more difficult task and a more suspect methodology than Kohler's, as we shall see.

Bousset first appealed to the parallel in Jewish liturgy which is found in AC 7.35.3, the Kedusha. He argued correctly that the juxtaposition of Isa 6:3 with Ezek 3:12 cannot be coincidental and must be the result of Jewish influence.[21] Yet Bousset did not demonstrate that the remainder of AC 7.35 is similarly influenced by Judaism. Perhaps a Christian--the compiler or someone before him--composed a Christian prayer using the Jewish Kedusha which he had heard recited by Jews. Therefore, the prayer in AC 7.35 is not necessarily a Jewish prayer, though it does contain a Jewish expression.

Bousset's treatment of his first alleged Jewish prayer indicates the weakness of his methodology. Merely finding a Jewish expression--or later on, Jewish ideas--in a prayer which is now Christian does not mean that a Jewish stratum lies underneath. It might just as easily have happened that the expression or idea was picked up by a Christian and used in his prayer. The weakness in Bousset's method is that he treated each prayer individually and failed to discover the larger context of the prayers. He argued with respect to AC 7.35 on the basis of the Jewish element in that prayer alone. Kohler's argument is more convincing, however, because he not only found Jewish parallels to individual elements of AC 7.35, but could place the whole of AC 7.35 in a prayer collection, 7.33-38, the structure, ideas and arrangement of which are also paralleled in Jewish liturgy.

Next Bousset turned to AC 7.36, the *Sabbatgebet*. One would assume that any prayer which extols the Sabbath in similar fashion to the Sabbath Kiddush prayer has originated in Judaism. The emphasis on Sunday at the end of the prayer only confirmed that conclusion for Bousset. In brilliant fashion he argued that no one would extol Sabbath observance for two-thirds of a prayer, then weakly assert the superiority of Sunday observance at the very end. Bousset concluded then that the emphasis on Sunday at the end of the prayer was abrupt and contradictory, and thus a Christian interpolation.[22]

Bousset is certainly correct that the latter part of the prayer is interpolated, but it is also possible that the original prayer was a Christian prayer and not a Jewish prayer, since many Christians may have observed the Sabbath as well as Sunday. Dugmore asserts: "...the general practice of the East seems to have been to regard Saturday as a day of festival rejoicings."[23] He cites several passages in Christian literature which refer to Sabbath observance.[24] One of the citations is from John Chrysostom, the contemporary of the compiler of AC and also a Syrian, who complained that Christians could not find time to give up a part of both days (Sabbath and Sunday) to attend church.[25] Thus Sabbath observance seems to have been practiced in the compiler's community and during his time.

This conclusion is necessary anyway, since the compiler included the prayer in his constitutions, for if Sabbath observance were so foreign to the compiler, why did he incorporate a prayer which extolled it? One would assume that the compiler also observed the Sabbath, but revered Sunday more and, hence, appended a reference to Sunday to the end of this prayer. There are several other references in the AC to the Sabbath which are in redactional material: 2.36.2, 2.59.3, 5.20.19, 7.23.3f. The compiler not only observed the Sabbath, but urged his community to do so as well: "Keep the Sabbath on account of the one who rested from his work" (2.36.2).

Thus, though we agree with Bousset that this prayer was originally Jewish, his methodology only discovers two possibilities. It is equally possible--using his method of argument--that the compiler took an older Christian prayer which extolled the Sabbath. Considered as an individual unit, in isolation from its broader context, the prayer could have been Jewish originally; but from what is known of Christian practice regarding the Sabbath, it could also have been an old Christian prayer which the compiler edited. According to Kohler's methodology, however, standing as it does exactly where the Kedushat ha-Yom stands in the Seven Benedictions, and containing similar ideas, the prayer very probably was a Jewish prayer.

A second error in Bousset's methodology comes to view with respect to his treatment of AC 7.37 and 7.38. He continued to handle the prayers as individual units and argued that the lists of OT heroes in these prayers indicate that they are Jewish prayers. Both prayers contain lists of heroes which end with the Maccabeans. The first list (in AC 7.37) contains no reference to Jesus Christ or to other NT heroes. Bousset maintained--arguing from silence--that a Christian composing such a list would have at least mentioned Christ. Thus, concluded Bousset, AC 7.37 must be a Jewish prayer. In 7.38, in a similar list, Jesus is included, but Bousset claimed that this was an interpolation since what is said about Jesus ("he rescued us even from the sword and removed us from hunger," 7.38.3) fits Judas Maccabeus better, who is listed just before Jesus.

To argue from silence is often precarious. Bousset only assumed that a Christian would have mentioned Jesus in 7.37. The NT itself demonstrates that this assumption is not always valid. Hebrews 11 and Jas 5:11, 17 cite only OT heroes as illustrations of faith, patience, and effective prayer. Further, it is not uncommon in non-canonical Christian literature to cite examples only from the OT. Clement of Rome, for example, wrote a long section exhorting the Corinthians to imitate the heroes of the past and did not cite one NT character.[26] Such lists of heroes occur also in other liturgies, e.g. the liturgy of James.[27] But the most damaging evidence to Bousset's argument is that several such lists appear in the AC: 2.55.1, 5.7.12, 6.12.13, 7.5.5, 7.39.3, 8.5.3f, 8.12.21-27. The first four passages appear in unquestionably redactional sections (since we can compare them with the sources). We cannot determine with assurance that the other passages are redactional, though it seems likely that they are as well since the compiler obviously favored such lists. Thus it is also likely that the lists in AC 7.37 and 38 are redactional.

Here the second error of Bousset's methodology arises. He failed to consider the theological tendencies and linguistic and literary conventions of the compiler. We saw in Chapter II that the compiler has freely edited, rearranged, recast, and interpolated his sources, even when the source contained a prayer (see Chart B, above, pp. 28-35). This discovery led us to wonder about the extent of redaction of any Jewish prayers which the compiler may have incorporated into his work. Bousset did not consider this problem. Although Kohler as well failed to consider it in a thorough manner, his method was still valid. When one argues that a certain element in an individual prayer is Jewish and, therefore, that the prayer was originally Jewish, and does not consider the tendencies and conventions of the redactor of the prayer, one's argument is incomplete and may therefore be invalid. Perhaps the redactor of the prayer himself has been influenced by such ideas. With Kohler's method--based upon the structure of the prayers--one may incorrectly identify various elements or passages as being Jewish--as we believe he did, ignore the redactor's handling of his sources, and still have a valid argument.

The prayer in AC 7.38 is unlike that of AC 7.37, however, in that the list of heroes in the former contains a reference to Jesus. Bousset maintained as we said above, that this reference is an interpolation, since what is said about Jesus more appropriately describes Judas Maccabeus who is listed just before Jesus. One need not, however, regard the mention of Jesus here as an interpolation. We might assume that the deeds attributed to Jesus (saving from the sword, famine, disease and an evil tongue) are more properly attributed to Judas Maccabeus, but could not the compiler have believed that in some way Christ had done these things? If he interpolated a reference to Jesus, he must have understood these deeds to refer to Jesus in some fashion. If the compiler could thus have understood the prayer, why could he not have written it?

Bousset next argued that in 7.34 and 8.12.9-20 we find two different redactions of the same source (*Grundlage*), a hellenistic (Stoic)-Jewish source.[28] This thesis must be addressed in Chapter V, but even conceding it for the moment, Bousset failed to prove that his hypothetical source was Jewish. He pointed out that many of the specifically Christian elements could easily be separated from the text (e.g. "through Christ"). But it is an indefensible assumption that everything else in the prayers, then, is Jewish.

Bousset also pointed to two passages in Philo (*Spec. Leg*. 1.97, 210) which parallel AC 7.34 and 8.12.9-20 in content: one should thank God for his creation, listing the individual parts, i.e. stars, earth, planets, seas etc. Philo also mentions cosmopolitan man as do AC 7.34 and 8.12.9-20, though in a different passage (*Op*. 3, *Conf*. 106). Bousset assumed that Philo's admonition to thank God for his creation reflects a dim recollection of the diaspora synagogue.

It is also possible, however, that Philo's admonition to list the wonders of God's creation reflects his Stoic influence. In our note in Chapter III on 7.34.5, we summarized the lengthy section in Cicero (*de. Nat. De*. 2.39f) where the creation is also extolled by a Stoic by listing its various parts. Cicero's passage bears striking similarity not only to Philo, but to AC 7.34 and 8.12.9-20 as well. Furthermore, man as the cosmopolitan is also a common Stoic teaching (see the note in Chapter III on 7.34.6). Why then must the hypothetical *Grundlage* of these prayers be Jewish if the only argument for this contention can also be used to show a purely Stoic influence? Why could not a Christian influenced by Stoicism have composed this *Grundlage* or both prayers in AC 7.34 and 8.12 using OT imagery? Either alternative is possible from the above evidence alone.

Additional evidence, however, makes Christian authorship more likely. Such prayers are rather common in Eastern Christian liturgy, occuring before the participation of the eucharist as in AC 8.12. They begin with "It is meet and right" as in AC 8.12.6 and end with the tersanctus as in AC 8.12.27. Between these two points is usually mention of the wonders of creation. The Liturgies of James (Palestinian), Adai and Mari (East Syrian), and John Chrysostom (Antiochian) all have such prayers.

> Liturgy of James: Verily it is becoming and right, proper and due to praise Thee, to sing of Thee, to bless Thee, to worship Thee, to glorify Thee, to give Thee thanks, Maker of every creature visible and invisible, the treasure of eternal good things, the fountain of life and immortality, God and Lord of all:
>
> Whom the heavens praise, and all the host of them; the sun, and the moon, and all the choir of the stars (ὁ τῶν ἄστρων χορός, cf. AC 8.12.9); earth, sea, and all that is in them....[29]
>
> Adai and Mari: Worthy of glory from every mouth, and of thanksgiving from all tongues, and of adoration and exaltation from all creatures is the adorable and glorious name of Father, Son, and Holy Ghost, who created the world through His grace, and its inhabitants through His clemency....[30]

> Liturgy of John Chrysostom: It is meet and right to praise Thee, to glorify Thee, to bless Thee, to give thanks to Thee, to worship Thee, in all places of Thy dominion, for Thou art God...Thou hast bought us from nothingness (ἐκ τοῦ μὲ ὄντος, cf. AC 7.34.6, 8.12.17).[31]

Cyril of Jerusalem the contemporary of the compiler (d. c. A.D. 386) who wrote a treatise on the liturgy, also mentioned this practice. Cyril stated that after the "meet and right" is said:

> we make mention of heaven, and earth and sea; of sun and moon, of stars and all the creation, rational and irrational, visible and invisible....[32]

Justin Martyr wrote that in the eucharistic prayer they not only remembered the suffering of Christ, but they "at the same time thank God for having created the world, with all things therein...."[33]

This convention in the liturgy may reach back to the time of Clement of Rome (late 1st cent.) since he wrote a passage in his epistle reminiscent of this (1 Clement 20).

> 1. The heavens moving at his appointment are subject to him in peace; 2. day and night follow the course allotted by him without hindering each other. 3. Sun and moon and the companies of the stars (ἀστέρων χοροί, cf. AC 8.12.9) roll on.... 4. The earth teems according to his will at its proper seasons, and puts forth food in full abundance for men and beasts and all the living things that are on it... 6. the hollow (κύτος, cf. AC 8.12.13) of the boundless sea is gathered by his working into its allotted places, and does not pass the barriers placed around it, but does even as he enjoined on it; 7. for he said "Thus far shalt thou come and thy waves shall be broken within thee" (Job 38:11, cf. AC 7.34.3, 8.12.13).... 9. The seasons of spring, summer, autumn, and winter give place to one another in peace. 10. The stations of the winds fulfil their service without hindrance at the proper time. The everlasting springs (ἀέναοι πηγαί, cf. AC 8.12.14) created for enjoyment and health, supply sustenance for the life of man without fail; and the smallest of animals meet together in concord and peace.[34]

The same practice seems to be reflected in the treatise of Theophilus of Antioch 1.6f (c. A.D. 180). R. M. Grant[35] has pointed out the parallels in this work to the Christian anaphora, and especially the verbal similarities in Theophilus to AC 8.12.9-20. We shall indicate only the most important verbal similarities. As Grant explains, at 1:6 of *Ad Autolycum*, "Theophilus' style abruptly changes. His writing takes on a liturgical tone."[36] Grant thinks that Theophilus alluded to the Christian eucharistic prayer at this point. The passage is as follows:

> Consider his works, O man: the periodic alternation of the seasons and the changes of winds, the orderly course of

> the stars, the orderly succession of days and nights and months and years (cf. AC 8.12.15), the diversified beauty of seeds and plants and fruits, the variegated offspring of quadrupeds and birds and reptiles and fishes in rivers and seas...the flow of fresh springs and ever-flowing rivers (ποταμῶν ἀενάων, cf. AC 8.12.14)...and the chorus of the other stars (ἄστρων χορείαν, cf. AC 8.12.9) to all of which the manifold Sophia of God...gave individual names....
>
> It is this God alone who made light from darkness...who brought light out of his treasuries (ἐκ θησαυρῶν, cf. AC 8.12.9)...and the limits of the seas (Job 38:10; cf. AC 7.34.3, 8.12.13)....
>
> This is my God, Lord of the universe, who...stirs up the deep of the sea (τὸ κύτος τῆς θαλάσσης, cf. AC 8.12.13)....
>
> You speak of him, O man; you breathe his breath...God made everything through Logos and Sophia...His Sophia is most powerful... (cf. AC 7.34.6, 8.12.16).[37]

Thus, AC 8.12.9-20 which is the ante-sanctus of the CL merely repeats the common Christian practice of extolling God's power as creator in a prayer before the participation of the eucharist. AC 7.34 reflects the themes and language of this liturgical tradition even though it does not appear in connection with the eucharist. If AC 8.12.9-20 and 7.34 are redactions of a common source, this source was probably Christian liturgical tradition. Perhaps the theme of God's power (גבורות), which is the theme of the second benediction, led the compiler to recast the prayer of 7.34 using his liturgical tradition.

Bousset's argument, then, carries little weight. Bousset's third error comes to light in his handling of these two prayers. He failed to consider the Christian liturgical tradition which was available to the compiler. Before one can safely argue that a convention, such as praising God by listing his acts of creation, is Jewish he must demonstrate that such a practice did not obtain in Christianity. Bousset's argument is also suspect because it depends upon his correct identification of a hypothetical *Grundlage*. Kohler's argument did not require basing the hypothesis upon another hypothesis. One did not have to argue about a supposed *Grundlage* or a recollection of a hypothetical practice in the synagogue to employ his method. We have an actual, existing parallel text (the Hebrew Seven) which represents a form of the source we are maintaining was originally Jewish.

Further on in his article Bousset argued that AC 8.12.31-37 was also based upon a Jewish original, since here there appears another list of OT heroes.[38] The discussion above, however, has already explained that such lists are common in the AC and almost certainly originate from the compiler himself.

Although Bousset[39] was doubtful that AC 8.12.6-8 was Jewish, Goodenough[40] and Lietzmann[41] were inclined to regard this section along with 8.12.9-27 as a Jewish prayer. But AC 8.12.6-8 is not particularly Jewish, while it does present some peculiarly Christian emphases. In the first place, paragraph six and much of seven consist of descriptions of God based upon negative attributes (usually in the form of alpha privatives). The discussion below on AC 8.15.7-9 will explain that such descriptions are common in AC (see 6.10.2, 8.5.1, 8.6.11, 8.37.2). The rest of paragraph seven consists of: descriptions of God's "only begotten son" (cf. John 1:14), an obvious reference to the Christ; an apparent quotation from Col 1:15 ("first born of all creation"); and finally, an allusion to Col 1:17 ("the one before all things, through whom are all things"). Paragraph eight begins with a reference to providence, which is also a common theme in AC. Every place in which the word πρόνοια is found in AC, it stands in a redactional passage (see below on AC 7.39.2-4). The paragraph concludes with a reference to the heavenly orders which appears to quote Col 1:16. Thus there are themes and expressions throughout these paragraphs that are reminiscent of both the NT and the rest of AC. We should conclude that this section is not Jewish.

Last of all, Bousset turned to AC 7.33 in which he believed he found strong evidence to support his thesis. Ralfs had discovered in 7.33.4 a word manufactured by Aquila in his attempt to produce a literal translation of the OT (ὀραματισμός, see the note on 7.33.4 in Chapter III) and Bousset believed he had found three more words from Aquila's version. AC 7.33.3 reads: "you guided (Abraham) in a vision (ὀραματισμός)...and the covenant (συνθήκη) was the follower of faith." συνθήκη is Aquila's translation of ברית, but the usual Septuagint translation is διαθήκη (though it does also use συνθήκη). As Bousset maintained, it appears that the author of the prayer was referring to the events of chapter 15 of Genesis where God gave a vision to Abraham (Gen 15:1) and later made a covenant with Abraham (Gen 15:18). But the author had read the story in Aquila's version and thus used his vocabulary.[42]

AC 7.37.3 reads ("you accepted the sacrifice...) of Josiah at Phassa" (φασσᾶ). As Bousset explained, if this means "at Passover" it is a strange spelling, for the Septuagint transliterates פסח as πάσχα or φασέκ. Aquila, however, transliterates פסח as φασέ or φεσά. Thus this word φασσᾶ may have come from Aquila as well.[43]

Thirdly, Bousset claimed that the Greek spelling of Sinai (σιναί) in AC 7.35.4 reflects Aquila's spelling of the word since Aquila spelled it identically. The Septuagint spelling of Sinai is normally σινᾶ.[44] Bousset suggested that the composer of the Jewish prayers quoted scripture from Aquila's version. Later, the Christian redactor replaced these quotations with the Septuagint quotations which stand now in the prayers. These words, however, the redactor overlooked since they are not in quotations. Thus they are vestigial evidence that Aquila's version was used. Since Aquila's version was intended to rival the Septuagint used by Christians, Bousset was convinced that a Jew must have composed these prayers.[45]

Nevertheless Bousset's evidence is not convincing. In the first place the word συνθήκη is employed by the compiler elsewhere in the AC: 5.16.9 and 7.22.2, both in redactional sections (in the plural). But when he uses διαθήκη he refers only to the canon of the Old or New Testaments: 8.47.85 (διαθήκη παλαία); 8.5.7, 8.12.36, 8.47.85 (διαθήκη καινή). Thus the compiler's word for "covenant" in general appears to be συνθήκη. Again, Bousset failed to consider the compiler's own vocabulary. His argument that the word συνθήκη is a vestige from the use of Aquila's version by the author of the prayers, is suspect.

Secondly, the word φασσᾶ as a word from Aquila presents us with several problems: (1) In the note on AC 7.37.3 in Chapter III above we pointed out that textual problem here. Readings range from φάσκα to σάφφα. The original of MS d has the last, but the margin corrects this to φάσσα. As we indicated above, one could understand σάφφα in this context as Shaphan the scribe of Josiah (2 Kgs 22:3-20=2 Chr 34:8-28) who played a prominent role at the time the book of Law was found. Thus, although the meaning "Passover" for φασσᾶ seems more likely in the context (i.e. God accepted Josiah's gift at the passover) one could make sense of the meaning "Shaphan" (i.e. Josiah made a gift of thanks to God *with* Shaphan his scribe when the book of Law was found). (2) Aquila's spelling of passover is φασέ or φεσά, not quite what appears in AC 7.37.3 (φασσᾶ, if we accept this MS reading). (3) Finally, we have already determined that the lists of OT heroes such as we find in AC 7.37.2-4 is redactional. As we explained above, such lists are common in the AC, and whenever they occur--where we can check the AC with its source--they are redactional. Thus Bousset's assertion that φασσᾶ is a vestige of Aquila's version is also unacceptable.

Thirdly, the MSS vary on the spelling of the word Sinai at AC 7.35.4: σιναεί, σιναῆ, σινᾶ ἦν. Most MSS (including MS d), however, spell it σιναί. Bousset, however, did not explain how this spelling of the word was interpolated into a Septuagint quotation, for the word is found in AC 7.35.4 in a Septuagint quotation of Psa 68:18. It is difficult to imagine a Christian redactor assiduously replacing every scripture quotation of the prayers with Septuagint readings, but preferring Aquila's spelling of Sinai.

Probably, however, ὁραματισμός is from Aquila's version. As we explained in Chapter III above (note on AC 7.33.4), Aquila used different Greek words to translate each Hebrew word. If this was impossible, he sometimes manufactured Greek words. Thus he created the verb ὁραματίζεσθαι to translate חזה, and the corresponding noun form ὁραματισμός for מחזה. These Greek words--as far as one can tell--are found no where else but in Aquila's version of the OT.[46]

The word seems to be from Aquila, then, but does this conclusion mean that a Jew must have written AC 7.33? The compiler himself may have picked this word up from Aquila's version. He lived two-hundred and fifty years after Aquila; thus, he probably knew about the version and may have read it. If Origen of Caesarea was interested in versions of the OT other than the Septuagint, might not the compiler of the AC have been similarly interested? Indeed, we shall argue in the next chapter that the section of AC 7.33 in which this word appears is largely redactional. It is precarious, therefore, to affirm too much on the basis of only one word. Bousset's conclusion, therefore, regarding AC 7.33 is an overstatement: "Therefore, we have received confirmation anew of our main thesis." This evidence does not confirm the thesis that the prayers of AC 7.33-38 are Jewish.

Although it is likely, therefore, that the prayers of AC 7.33-38 were originally Jewish prayers, Bousset's arguments for this position are not convincing. He argued for this thesis by treating each prayer individually, and pointing out both elements within the prayers which could be found in Jewish literature and the scarcity of Christian elements. But this methodology depends upon the essential integrity of the text, except for the obvious Christian elements (e.g. "through Christ"). One must assume that the Christian redactor only interpolated a few scattered references to Christ or to Sunday worship. Bousset largely ignored the question of whether any of the themes or ideas in those prayers which are "Jewish" are found elsewhere in the AC. We saw above that answering this question often leads to the conclusion that the "Jewish" elements are actually favorite themes or literary conventions of the compiler of AC. The emphasis upon Sabbath worship and the listing of OT heroes are examples. Bousset also failed to consider the liturgical tradition of Eastern Christianity, and in arguing that AC 7.34 and 8.12.9-20 were based upon a Jewish prayer because the theme of these prayers is similar to a section in Philo, he seemed unaware of the fact that most of the Eastern liturgies have a similar prayer at the same location in the Mass as AC 8.12.9-20. What Bousset believed to be a Jewish practice (praising God the creator by naming various parts of creation) is actually, by the time of the compiler of AC, an indubitably Christian practice. Regarding his argument for 7.35--that the Jewish Kedusha is quoted here--he is certainly correct. But using his methodology, one cannot say that the whole prayer is Jewish. His argument in reference to AC 7.33--that evidence that Aquila's version was used in the prayer indicates that this prayer was originally Jewish, since he has really only one word which is certainly from Aquila--is not as convincing as Bousset thought.

The Other Alleged Jewish Prayers

Bousset's methodology led him to believe that other prayers in the AC were Jewish as well. But while it seems clear that AC 7.33-38 is Jewish--for reasons other than those given by Bousset--it is not clear that all of these prayers are Jewish, though some may be. It can even be demonstrated that many of these prayers were probably composed by the compiler of the AC.

Bousset knew that the evidence for the original Jewishness of these other prayers was weak, for he usually only suggested that these might be Jewish, often admitting that this suggestion was no more than mere conjecture. Such was his handling of AC 7.39.2-4, the instruction for the catechumens. He was hesitant to argue strongly, but maintained (*argumentum ex silentio*) that since little is said in this section about Christian doctrinal concerns--such as remission of sins by Christ--in speaking to the initiates, the passage looked more like Jewish proselyte instruction.[47]

That AC 7.39.2-4 is originally Jewish is unlikely, however. The section begins with a trinitarian statement which is obviously Christian. Next it admonishes the initiates to learn: "the order of a diverse creation, the sequence of Providence, the judgment seats of different legislation, why the world came to be and why man was appointed a cosmopolitan." Of these five themes, three are definitely the compiler's own interests and the remaining two appear as well to have been favored themes.

First of all the phrase διάφορος δημιουργία, "diverse creation," which is found in this section of 7.39, also appears in a redactional section in AC 2.36.2 with the admonition, "know the diverse creation," very similar to the admonition in our section. A similar phrase, διάφορος κτίσις, is found in 6.11.3 in a redactional passage. That the compiler was very interested in the theme of creation is obvious from reading the prayers of AC books seven and eight, but also in the numerous references to creation (3.2.3, 3.9.2, 5.14.20, 6.4.1, 6.14.1, 6.16.3, 6.23.3, 7.23.3,4, 8.33.2) and to God as creator (1.8.2, 3.9.4, 5.7.25, 5.12.2, 5.14.20, 6.10.1, 6.11.1,3, 7.23.4, 7.27.2, 7.41.4, 8.20.1, 8.31.3) which occur throughout the AC, always--where we can tell--in redactional passages. There is little doubt that the compiler was polemicizing against the Gnostics in his emphasis on the beauty and goodness of creation, and in his emphasis on learning about and remembering creation. In AC 6.16.3 he reproves the "heretics" for "reproaching creation." Thus it is not unusual that the compiler would want Christian initiates to know about creation and, secondly, that he would want them to know: "why the world came to be."

Moreover, the emphasis on providence is also found in numerous places in the AC, especially in association with creation. Every place in which the word πρόνοια is found in AC, it stands--where one can determine it--in a redactional passage (2.24.3, 2.57.4, 3.3.2, 4.1.2, 4.5.4, 6.4.1, 6.6.4, 6.10.1, 6.14.4, 6.16.3, 6.23.3, 6.28.8).[48] Thus three of the elements of the instruction for catechumens in AC 7.39.2 were definitely of great importance to the compiler.

A fourth theme, man as cosmopolitan, is also found in 7.34.6, 8.12.16 and 8.41.4. All of these sections were alleged to be Jewish by Bousset and Goodenough. We shall maintain below that 8.41 is probably not a Jewish prayer and in Chapter V, we shall maintain that these sections of 7.34 and 8.12 are redactional. Nevertheless, without yet demonstrating these positions, we may say that when a phrase or theme is found in four different sections, scattered throughout books seven and eight of AC, with no apparent connection with one another, we would assume that the theme has come from the compiler.

Finally, the phrase "judgment seats of different legislation" may refer to the Law as written and as implanted as Goodenough suggested. This same emphasis is found more clearly in 7.33.3, 8.6.5, 8.12.18 and 8.12.25 where the notion is expressed as νόμος ἔμφυτος καὶ γραπτός. Again one cannot state with certainty that these passages are redactional, but their frequency and distribution at least make one suspect that they are.

The section of AC 7.39 which Bousset thought might be Jewish proselyte instruction ends with a list of OT heroes (par. 3). We have seen above, however, that such lists are common in AC and seem to have been a favorite with the compiler. Thus most of AC 7.39. 2-4 can be paralleled with the compiler's favorite themes and literary conventions, and we, therefore, conclude that the compiler authored this section, or so much of it that it is impossible to argue that it was originally instruction for Jewish proselytes.

Next Bousset suggested that AC 8.5.3f was originally Jewish, because it contained a list of heroes similar to that of AC 7.39.3. Again, however, we have shown that such lists are more likely to have been composed by the compiler.[49]

Bousset next suggested that AC 8.6.5, the prayer for the catechumens, might be Jewish, since again little is said which could not pertain to Jewish proselytes. Nevertheless, he refused to draw a firm conclusion about this prayer or about AC 8.9.8f, a prayer for repentance, which he also believed might be Jewish. Though Bousset said very little about the AC 8.9.8f, he seemed to suggest that it could be Jewish because it contained expressions similar to prayers he had already concluded were Jewish (κόσμου κόσμος in 7.34.6, 8.12.16 and νόμος ἔμφυτος καί γράπτος in 7.33.3, 8.12.18, 25).[50] We cannot demonstrate, as in the two previous cases, that these two prayers are probably from the compiler's own hand, but we would argue that Bousset's evidence is not sufficient to cause us to conclude that they are Jewish. Whenever prayers appear in a document believed to have been composed (or compiled) by a Christian author, the burden of proof is on those who would assert that those prayers are from Judaism. One should not argue that there is little which could *not* pertain to Judaism, but that there is little which *could* pertain to Christianity.

Goodenough, who followed Bousset's suggestion regarding 8.6.5, maintained that the whole prayer in this section is Jewish (i.e. 8.6.5-8) and not just paragraph five as Bousset had suggested. But either way, it is difficult to maintain that AC 8.6 contains a Jewish prayer with Christian interpolations. There are three references to Christ (par. 5,6,8); a plea for Christian death (par. 8), two quotations from the NT (par. 6), two phrases which also appear in the Christian liturgy of John Chrysostom ("washing of regeneration, of the garment of incorruption,"[51] [par. 6]), and emphasis on the "mysteries" and "initiation" (par. 7) which is common both in Christian literature in general[52] and the AC in particular (5.14.7, 7.40.1, 8.1.1, 8.5.7, 8.8.2, and see especially Chapter II, Chart B on AC 7.26.6; cf. Didache 9). The rest of the prayer consists of four quotations from the Psalms (par. 5, 6). There is mention of studying the Law day and night, which one might think is a Jewish element, but this is a quotation of Ps 1:2. The compiler was interested in studying the Law anyway (see 2.61.4, 6.19.3 and 6.20 where the compiler again polemicizes against the Gnostics who denigrate the OT and the Law). Thus, nothing in this prayer is particularly Jewish; much is peculiarly Christian. We see no reason for affirming that AC 8.6.5 or 8.6.5-8 was originally Jewish.

The same conclusion holds true for 8.9.8f. We have discussed the prayers of 7.34 and 8.12.9-20 sufficiently to make us suspicious about arguments for Jewish prayers based upon phrases found therein. We shall argue in Chapter V that much of the phrasing of these prayers is redactional. Thus the phrase κόσμου κόσμος is not sufficient to argue for the Jewishness of AC 8.9.8f. Further, the emphasis on Law as implanted and written is not particularly a Jewish notion. In the note on 7.33.3 in Chapter III, we listed Christian authors who had similar notions (Clement, *Paid.* 3.3, Origen, *Contra Cels.* 5.37, cf. Rom 2:14, Jas 1:21). Again the idea is found in sections which we shall argue are redactional in Chapter V, but a passage in AC 7.26.3 will demonstrate for now that this notion is redactional. The compiler interpolated into Didache 9 where the Didache mentioned the creation: "and you implanted a law in our souls...." Further, two phrases appear to be formulaic for the compiler: "look down upon those who have bowed the neck of soul and body to you...," is similar to Psa 31:17 and is repeated in AC 8.15.8 and 8.37.6. The same formula occurs in the liturgies of James and Chrysostom.[53] The phrase, "you yourself also now" is repeated in AC 7.26.4 (in a redactional section), 7.37.1, 8.8.5, 8.16.4, 8.20.2, 8.21.4, 8.22.3, 8.37.6, 8.38.4, 8.39.4 and 8.40.5. In addition, the mention of the son "who dissolutely consumed his livelihood" is evidently a reference to the parable in Luke 15:11-32. Again much here is Christian or conventional and thematic to the compiler, but nothing is particularly Jewish in AC 8.9.8f.

Bousset argued that AC 8.15.7-9 is Jewish because of its similarity to 7.35.9 (which he assumed he had already shown was Jewish). Both sections contain a similar list of adjectives describing the magnificence of God using negative or especially alpha privatives: e.g. ὁ γενέσει μὴ ὑποκείμενος, "not subject to beginning";

ὁ τροπῆς ἀνεπίδεκτος, "does not admit of change"; ὁ τῇ φύσει ἀόρατος, "invisible by nature" (8.15.7). Bousset concluded that the passages were a twofold redaction of an old text.[54] Nevertheless, he again failed to consider the literary convention of the compiler. It appears that he was fond of such constructions in describing God, since they appear several times: 6.10.2, 8.5.1, 8.6.11, 8.12.6f, 8.37.2.[55] We shall argue in Chapter V that the passage in 7.35.9 which Bousset referred to is redactional. It is true that only AC 6.10.2 is a definitely redactional section, but since the alpha privatives which describe God's character do appear there and at 8.6.11--which no one claims is a Jewish passage--one should assume that the other sections which contain such constructions are redactional as well. Thus, this prayer, far from being a separate redaction of a Jewish text, is quite likely the compiler's composition.

Bousset went on to suggest that AC 8.37-41 contained five prayers which possibly were Jewish. He gave no reasons for suggesting this, however. We shall discuss this suggestion below.

Goodenough's Treatment of the Prayers

Goodenough saw in these prayers a striking similarity to Philonic thought. Thus he concluded that they offered an example of "mystic liturgy." Goodenough was convinced that Bousset had demonstrated that these prayers were Jewish.[56] In contrast to the cautious Bousset, Goodenough did not hesitate to affirm that all of Bousset's suggested Jewish prayers were really Jewish,[57] and he even added a few prayers to Bousset's list (see Chart A above): 7.26.1-3, 8.16.3 and 8.40. We cannot, however, consider a prayer which appears in a known source of the AC. Such an investigation would lead us too far afield. Our problem is alleged Jewish prayers in the AC, not prayers appearing in the known sources of AC which may be Jewish. Thus, the prayers in AC 7.26 and 8.40 cannot be considered, though they may have been originally Jewish, since these sections are based upon Didache 10 and Apostolic Tradition 9 respectively (see Chapter II). Apparently Goodenough was unaware of this fact.

Goodenough suggested that AC 8.16.3 reads "perfectly as a Jewish prayer *if* one supplies 'Logos' in place of the 'Christ'" (italics mine).[58] But he did not demonstrate why one should do this. Why should one believe that this prayer originally read "Logos"? The prayer only emphasizes the favorite themes of the compiler that we have mentioned above. It begins with a reference to God as creator ("our God who created all things") which was an important theological notion for the compiler, due to his anti-Gnostic polemic. Next the prayer moves to the concept of God's providence, which was also important to the compiler as we explained above, and develops this theme to the end of paragraph three. Thus paragraph three of AC 8.16 looks like the compiler's work.[59]

Bousset had suggested, as we mentioned above, that 8.41.2-5, the prayer for the dead, is Jewish, but gave no reason for this suggestion. Goodenough was also convinced that the prayer is "thoroughly Jewish," since there is a reference, he believed, to "voluntary and involuntary offences against the law...."[60] But as a matter of fact, there is no mention of law, but of voluntary and involuntary sin (εἴ τι ἄκων ἢ ἐξήμαρτεν, "if he unwillingly or willingly has sinned"). Furthermore, his claim that only Judaism made a distinction between willing and unwilling offenses is untrue. Pagan authors refer to unintentional sin (Plato, *Republic* 336E, Dio Chrysostom 17, 13) as well as Christian authors (1 Clem 2:3, John Chrysostom's liturgy) and the notion is found in the Septuagint (Job 14:17 LXX).[61] This same notion occurs also at AC 8.9.3. Furthermore, there are at least three themes in paragraph four of the prayer which betray the compiler's hand. The theme, already familiar to us, of man the cosmopolitan that occurs here is not only found at 7.34.6 and 8.12.16--two sections which we shall argue in Chapter V have been heavily edited by the compiler--but also in 7.39.1, the section that we demonstrated above was probably composed by the compiler.

Secondly, the notion of man as the "rational creature" (τὸν λογικὸν...ζῷον) in paragraph four is repeated throughout the AC always--where we can determine--in redactional passages (2.19.2, 2.25.7, 6.10.2, 6.11.7, 6.23.5, 6.30.10, 7.34.6, 7.35.10, 7.38.5, 8.9.8, 8.12.17, 8.15.7, 8.37.5, 8.37.6).

Thirdly, the clause "who did not allow Enoch and Elijah to experience the trial of death" in paragraph four is found almost verbatim in AC 5.7.8 in a redactional section. The remainder of paragraph four seems to be based upon Matt 22:32 and Luke 20:18.

Paragraph five begins with the formula that we maintained above is typical of the compiler: "You yourself also now look down upon this your servant" (see Chapter III, note on 8.37.2). The rest of paragraph five repeats (though not word for word) what was said in paragraph two: a plea for forgiveness of every sin, willing and unwilling; a plea to appoint the deceased a place in the bosom of the patriarchs (Abraham, Isaac, and Jacob in par. 2); the allusion to Isa 35:10, "from which sorrow and grief have fled."

Why does paragraph five repeat paragraph two? It may be that paragraphs four and five, the bishop's prayer, are the compiler's repetition and redaction of a Jewish prayer for the dead represented by paragraph two. Nevertheless, there is no reason to conclude that paragraph two is Jewish. The first element (forgiveness of willing and unwilling sin) is not particularly Jewish as we explained above. The second main element of paragraph two (the bosom of Abraham, etc.) sounds reminiscent of Luke 16:22, though there are other places where a similar clause occurs (see Chapter III, note on AC 8.41.2). Warren[62] quoted a prayer for the dead, which he found in a Jewish service manual, which contained a reference to the bosom of Abraham, Isaac and Jacob. The final main element is a verbatim quotation of Isa 35:10 (LXX). None of these elements are particularly Jewish, though, the second element could be Jewish.

But these three main elements appear in a prayer for the dead in Serapion's liturgy (mid-fourth cent. in Egypt). This liturgy requests God's forgiveness of sins; asks God to give rest to the soul of the departed "in chambers of rest with Abraham and Isaac and Jacob and all thy saints"; and requests God to "heal the griefs" of the departed (but does not quote Isa 35:10).[63] This prayer is so similar to the one in AC 8.41 that a common tradition should be assumed. Perhaps the tradition goes back to Judaism, but nothing argues convincingly for this conclusion.

Further, though Warren[64] believed that Judaism was the source for the Christian practice of praying for the dead, I. Levi[65] maintained that Judaism obtained the practice from Christianity. But even if Warren is correct, it is a different matter to admit that AC 8.41 has come ultimately from Jewish practice, than to say that AC 8.41 is based upon a Jewish prayer. Thus we cannot demonstrate that all of AC 8.41.2 has come from the compiler, but we see no good reason for believing that it was originally Jewish either.

Summary of Results Thus Far

We have argued that AC 7.33-38 was originally Jewish, and that this section of AC represents a form of the Seven Benedictions. Secondly, we have ruled out of consideration several prayers as either improbably Jewish (AC 7.39.2-4, 8.5.1-4, 8.6.5-8, 8.9.8f, 8.15.7-9, 8.16.3), beyond the scope of our investigation (AC 7.26.1-3, 8.40.2-4), or those for which there is simply inadequate evidence for affirming that the prayer is Jewish (8.41.2-5).

Prayers in Book Eight of AC Which are Difficult to Judge

There are four other prayers which were quite possibly originally Jewish. The evidence for the Jewishness of these prayers, however, is scanty.

AC 8.37.1-4, an evening prayer, may correspond to the Jewish Maariv prayer, said before the Ahabah in the evening. AC 8.37.5-7 may correspond to the Ahabah, said just after the Maariv and before the Shema. Both the Ahabah ("with abounding love") and AC 8.37.5-7 ("God...prepared man...loved of God") mention God's love. AC 8.38.4f ("who gives the sun"), a morning prayer, may correspond to the Yotzer ("who formest light"), said just before the morning Ahabah. Both prayers mention God's giving of light. AC 8.39.3f may correspond to the Ahabah said after the Yotzer and before the morning Shema, since again the notion of love is introduced (8.39.2), though here it is in a scripture (Exod 20:6) and refers to man's love of God ("who does mercifully to...them that love you"). Thus this series of evening and morning prayers which Bousset had suggested might be Jewish--without giving any reasons--may have been based upon the prayers accompanying the Shema.

These similarities are spare, but the striking thing is that these themes come in their proper order; the Ahabah theme follows the evening and morning themes. As in the case of the prayer collection of AC 7.33-38, these prayers contain ideas corresponding to prayers in an existing Hebrew text, and they correspond to the order of these prayers in the Hebrew text.

Nevertheless problems exist in believing that these prayers were originally Jewish. Unlike the prayer collection of AC 7.33-38, there are no verbal parallels and the main themes or central themes of the corresponding prayers are different. AC 8.37.1-4 is essentially a request for God's protection throughout the night, but the Maariv in Amram's rite[66] is praise of the Lord of hosts who has power over day and night. In addition 8.37.1-4 contains phrases which betray the compiler's hand: "the intelligible and perceptable things" (8.12.7, 8.12.49); the formula, "you yourself also now" which we commented on above; the formula "permit us (to have) eternal life" which occurs two other times in the prayers in this section (8.38.5, 8.39.4), and in another place (8.11.6).

AC 8.37.5-7 is a second request for God's blessing, but the Ahabah is a statement about God's love of Israel as shown by his giving of Torah, and a pledge to meditate upon that Torah "when we lie down and when we rise up." There is no mention of Law in AC 8.37.5-7 and one cannot justify this as an editorial exclusion, since the compiler believed in some sense in keeping the Law (2.61.4, 6.19.3, 6.20, see Chapter V below). Secondly, this prayer also has several redactional elements: Man as "rational (λογικός) creature" as we explained above is a favorite theme in AC; the formula "you yourself also now"; and the formula "your people who bend the neck of their heart" which also occurs in AC 8.9.8 and 8.15.8.

AC 8.38.4f is a request for God's mercy throughout the day, but the Yotzer praises God for his power in creation. AC 8.38.4f also contains two recurrent formulas: "you yourself also now"; and "permit us (to have) eternal life."

AC 8.39.3f continues to request God's protection throughout the day, but the Ahabah after the Yotzer, in Amram's prayer book, requests God's enlightenment to understand Torah. Further, the reference to love in AC 8.39.3f ("God...who does mercifully to... them that love you") is, as we said above, only very vaguely parallel to "with abounding love hast thou loved us..." in the Ahabah. AC 8.39.3f also contains redactional elements: the formula "look down now upon this your people" (8.16.4, 8.37.6, 8.38.4, 8.41.5, Chrysostom in Brightman, *Liturgies*, p. 373); and "permit them (to have) eternal life."

Each prayer in this section of AC not only has a different main theme from its possible corresponding prayer in the Hebrew liturgy, but the prayers in AC also contain several obvious redactional elements. In addition each prayer in AC ends with a stock trinitarian formula.

Thus, we conclude that if these evening and morning prayers were based upon the Hebrew liturgy accompanying the Shema, the original form has been so edited as to be now irretrievable. We cannot discern whether all of this editing was done by the compiler or whether some of it took place before he received the prayers. Although the prayers may have been Jewish, we cannot be as definite about this conclusion as we were about AC 7.33-38, and we cannot reconstruct the original form of the prayers as we shall attempt to do in Chapter V for AC 7.33-38.

Finally, although Bousset's reasons for arguing that AC 8.12.9-27 was originally Jewish are not adequate, it may have been Jewish nonetheless. As Kohler, Heinemann, and Price suggested,[67] this prayer may be based upon the Yotzer. As we stated above, the Yotzer essentially praises God for his power in creation and concludes with the Kedusha. AC 8.12.9-27 does likewise, except that the Kedusha in AC 8.12.27 contains only the passage from Isa 6:3 and not the passage from Ezek 3:12 as well (contrast AC 7.35).

There are two main problems with this view, however. First, there are no verbal parallels, while many of the minor themes and much of the vocabulary and phraseology are typical of the compiler. Thus, this text too has been heavily edited. Chapter V will evaluate the redactional activity in AC 8.12, since it must be considered in relation to AC 7.34. Secondly, most Christian prayers coming just before the eucharist in the liturgy contain the same elements: praise of God for his power in creation (as we explained above) concluding with the *tersanctus* (Isa 6:3). We find such prayers in the liturgies of Serapion, Mark (with no creation theme, however), James, Adai and Mari, and Chrysostom (see above). Furthermore, Justin Martyr (*Dial.* 41) and Cyril (*De Catech.* 23.4f) allude to such a prayer before the eucharist, and Clement of Rome (34.5f) and Tertullian (*De Oratione* 3) may also have had this prayer in mind. Thus, if this prayer, which is recited in all the above liturgies, was based upon the Yotzer, it probably was adapted very early and spread to most of the churches in the East (and West if Clement of Rome and Tertullian of Carthage alluded to such a prayer). The prayer in AC 8.12.9-27, then, is more likely based upon a Christian liturgical tradition which very early may have appropriated and adapted the Yotzer for its worship. AC 8.12, however, has developed the creation theme in much more detail than the other liturgies present it. This detail indicates more editorial activity by the compiler, as Chapter V will explain. Such emphasis on creation is expected, since the compiler was polemicizing against the Gnostics who denigrated both creation and the creator.

Conclusion

First, it is highly probable that AC 7.33-38 is a Jewish Greek version of the Hebrew Seven Benedictions. Secondly, many of the additional prayers that Bousset suggested might be Jewish probably are the work of the compiler of AC. Goodenough's additional suggested Jewish prayers are either beyond our present scope, or probably also the work of the compiler. We shall not consider any of those additional alleged Jewish prayers further. Thirdly, the evening and morning prayers in AC 8.37-39 are curiously reminiscent of the prayers accompanying the Shema, but different enough from those prayers and edited sufficiently, that their original Jewishness is far less likely than in the case of AC 7.33-38. Even if we conclude that they were originally Jewish, we could not get at the original form of these prayers. We shall, therefore, no longer consider these prayers. Last of all, AC 8.12.9-20 is reminiscent of the Yotzer prayer, but probably stands in a Christian liturgical tradition which may have appropriated the Yotzer. We shall evaluate the compiler's redaction of AC 8.12.9-20 in Chapter V as well as his redaction of AC 7.33-38.

CHART C

The Text of the Babylonian and Palestinian Seven Benedictions*

Babylonian Text	*Palestinian Text*
ברוך אתה ה' אלהינו ואלהי אבותינו אלהי אברהם אלהי יצחק ואלהי יעקב האל הגדול הגבור והנורא אל עליון גומל חסדים טובים וקונה הכל וזוכר חסדי אבות ומביא גואל לבני בניהם למען שמו באהבה מלך עוזר ומושיע ומגן ברוך אתה ה' מגן אברהם	ברוך אתה יי אלהינו ואלהי אבותינו אלהי אברהם אלהי יצחק ואלהי יעקב האל הגדול הגבור והנורא אל עליון קונה שמים וארץ מגנינו ומגן אבותינו מבטחינו בכל דור ודור ברוך אתה יי מגן אברהם
אתה גבור לעולם ה' מחיה מתים בימות הגשמים אומר משיב הרוח ומוריד הגשם מכלכל חיים בחסד ובימות החמה אינו צריך אלא אומר מכלכל חיים בחסד מחיה מתים ברחמים רבים סומך נופלים רופא חולים מתיר אסירים ומקיים אמונתו לישני עפר מי כמוך בעל גבורות ומי דומה לך מלך ממית ומחיה ומצמיח ישועה בקרוב ונאמן אתה להחיות מתים ברוך אתה ה' מחיה המתים	אתה גבור משפיל גאים חזק ומדין עריצים חי עולמים מקים מתים משיב הרוח ומודים הטל מכלכל חיים מחיה המתים כהרף עין ישועה לנו תצמיח ברוך אתה יי מחיה המתים
קדושה... כתר יתנו לך המוני מעלה עם קבוצי מטה יחד כלם קדושה לך ישלשו כמה שנ' על ידי נביאך וקרא זה אל זה ואמר קדוש קדוש קדוש ה' צבאות מלא כל הארץ כבודו אז בקול רעש גדול אדיר וחזק	
משמיעם ומתנשאים לעומתם ברוך יאמרו ברוך כבוד ה' ממקומו	
לדור ודור המליכו לאל כי הוא לבדו מרום וקדוש ושבחך אלהינו מפינו לא ימוש לעולם	קדוש אתה ונורא שמך ואין אלוה מבלעדיך ברוך אתה יי האל הקדוש

*The Hebrew texts are from R. Amram in Hedegard, *Seder R. Amram* (Babylonian) and Schechter, "Geniza Specimens," 656-58 (Palestinian). The text for the fourth benediction in R. Amram is from T. Kronholm, *Seder R. Amram Gaon, Part II* (Lund: Gleerup, 1974) 22.

Babylonian Text	*Palestinian Text*
ומאהבתך יי אלהינו שאהבת את עמך ישראל ומחמלתך מלכנו שחמלת על בני בריתך נתת לנו יי אלהינו את יום השביעי הגדול והקדוש הזה באהבה לגדולה לקדושה למנוחה ולהודאה ולאות ברית ולתת לנו ברכת ושלום מאתך אלהינו ואלהי אבותינו רצה נא במנוחתנו וקדשנו במצותיך ותן חלקנו בתורתך ושבענו מטובך ושמח לבנו בישועתך וטהר לבנו לעבדך והנחילנו יי אלהינו באהבה וברצון את שבת קדשך וישמחו בך כל אוהבי שמך ברוך אתה יי מקדש השבת	
רצה ה' אלהינו בעמך ישראל ותפלתם שעה והשב עבודה לדביר ביתך ואשי ישראל ותפלתם מהרה תקבל ברצון ותהי לרצון תמיד עבודת ישראל עמך ותחזינה עינינו בשובך לרצון ברחמים ברוך אתה ה' המחזיר שכינתו לציון	רצה יי אלהינו ושכון בציון ויעבדוך עבדיך בירושלם ברוך אתה יי שאותך ביראה נעבוד
מודים אנחנו לך שאתה הוא ה' אלהינו צור חיינו מגן ישענו לדור ודור נורה לך ונספר תהלתך על חיינו המסורים בידך ועל נשמותינו הפקודות לך הטוב כי לא כלו רחמיך המרחם כי לא תמו חסדיך כי מעולם קוינו לך לא הכלמתנו ה' אלהינו ולא עזבתנו ולא הסתרת פניך ממנו ועל כלם יתברך ויתרומם תמיה שמך מלכנו לעולם ועד כל החיים יודוך סלה ויהללו לשמך הטוב באמת ברוך אתה ה' הטוב שמך ולך נאה להודות	מודים אנחנו לך אתה הוא יי אלהינו ואלהי אבותינו על כל הטובה החסד והרחמים שגמלתנו ושעשיתה עמנו ועם אבותינו מלפנינו ואם אמרנו מטה רגלינו חסדך יי יסעדינו ברוך אבה יי הטוב לך להודות

Translation*

Babylonian Text

1. Blessed are you, O Lord, our God and God of our fathers, God of Abraham, Isaac and Jacob, the Great, mighty and revered God, God most high, who bestows loving kindness and who created all things, and who remembers the pious deeds of the fathers, and who brings a redeemer to their descendants on account of his name in love. King, Helper, Savior, and Shield. Blessed are you, O Lord, Shield of Abraham.

2. You are mighty forever, O Lord, who quickens the dead. (and in the rainy season one says: Who causes the wind to blow and sends down the rain, who sustains the living in kindness. But in the summer one does not recite this but only: Who sustains the living in loving kindness.) Who quickens the dead in great compassion, who supports the falling, heals the sick, loosens the bound, keeps faith with them that sleep in the earth. Who is like you, Lord of mighty acts, and who is similar to you, King, who kills and quickens and causes salvation to spring forth quickly. And you are faithful to quicken the dead. Blessed are you, O Lord, who quickens the dead.

Kedusha....The multitudes above will give a crown to you along with the congregation below, all of them as one will three times repeat the Kedusha to you as it is written by your prophet: one said to the other, Holy, holy, holy, Lord of Hosts, all the earth is full of your glory.

Palestinian Text

1. Blessed are you, O Lord our God and God of our fathers, God of Abraham, God of Isaac, and God of Jacob, the Great, mighty, and revered God, God most high, Creator of heaven and earth, our Shield and Shield of our fathers, our confidence in every generation. Blessed are you, O Lord, Shield of Abraham.

2. You are mighty, who humbles the proud, strong, and judges the ruthless, who lives forever, who raises the dead, who makes the wind to blow and sends down the dew, who sustains the living, who quickens the dead. As a blink of an eye you cause salvation to spring forth to us. Blessed are you, O Lord, who quickens the dead.

*The translation of the Babylonian version is adapted from that of Hedegard and Kronholm, *Seder R. Amram, Parts I, II*; and the translation of the Palestinian version is adapted from that in Dugmore, *Influence*.

Babylonian Text	*Palestinian Text*
Then with a noise of a great rushing, forceful and strong, they cause themselves to be heard and lift themselves toward them, and say: Blessed, blessed be the glory of the Lord from his place.	
3. From generation to generation give homage to God, because he alone is high and holy, and your praise, our God, will not depart from our mouth forever and ever, because you are a great and holy King. Blessed are you, O Lord, holy God.	3. You are holy, and your name is revered, and there is no God beside you. Blessed are you, O Lord, the holy God.
4. And out of your love, O Lord, our God, with which you have loved your people Israel, and out of thy compassion, our King, with which you are compassionate over the people of thy covenant, you have given us, O Lord our God, this great and holy seventh day in love, for greatness, for holiness, for rest and for thanksgiving, and for a sign of the covenant, and to give us blessing and peace from thee. Our God and God of our fathers, accept our rest, and sanctify us by your commandments, and grant us our lot in your Law; and satisfy us with your goodness, and gladden our heart with your salvation, and purify our heart to serve you; and let us inherit, O Lord our God, in love and in favor, your holy Sabbath; and let all who love your name rejoice in you. Blessed are you, O Lord our God, who sanctifies the Sabbath.	
5. Accept, O Lord our God, your people Israel and their prayer and restore the service to the Holy of Holies of your house, and receive quickly in love and favour the fire offerings of Israel and their prayer, and may the service of your people Israel ever be	5. Accept (us), O Lord our God, and dwell in Zion, and let your servants serve you in Jerusalem. Blessed are you, O Lord, whom we serve in reverence.

Babylonian Text

acceptable, and let our eyes behold your return in mercy to Zion. Blessed are you, O Lord, who restores your presence to Zion.

6. We give thanks unto you, because you are the Lord our God, the Rock of our lives, the Shield of our salvation are you through every generation. We will give thanks unto you and declare your praise, for our lives which are committed unto you, and for our souls which are in your charge. You are all-good, for your mercies fail not, you are merciful, for your loving-kindnesses never cease, for we have always hoped in you. Let us not come to shame, O Lord, our God, and do not abandon us and do not hide your face from us. And for all these things your name, our King, will be blessed and exalted forever and ever. And everything that lives will give thanks unto you. Selah, and will praise your name, you All-good, in truth. Blessed are you, O Lord, whose name is All-good, and unto whom it is becoming to give thanks.

Palestinian Text

6. We give thanks unto you, who are the Lord our God, and God of our fathers, for all the good things, the kindness, and mercy which you have wrought, and done with us, and with our fathers before us. And if we said, "our feet slip," your kindness, O Lord, would secure us. Blessed are you, O Lord, to whom it is good to give thanks.

NOTES

CHAPTER IV

[1]Kohler, "Essenes," 224-31, and later, "The Essene Version," 410-25.

[2]See Birnbaum, *Daily Prayer Book*, 81-95, 265-71.

[3]Though Finkelstein ("The Development of the Amidah," 1-43) has been followed by a few scholars (namely F. C. Grant, "The Modern Study of the Jewish Liturgy," *ZAW* 65 [1953] 59-77 and Dugmore, *Influence*), most scholars recently have denied his thesis that there was one original fixed text. See, e.g., Elbogen, *Der jüdische gottesdienst*, 41f; E. J. Bickermann, "The Civic Prayer for Jerusalem," 164; H. Avenary, "Amidah," *Encyclopedia Judaica*, ed. C. Roth and G. Wigoder (Jerusalem: MacMillan, 1971) vol. 2, col. 840; M. Liber, "Structure and History of the Tefillah," 332; A. E. Milgrom, *Jewish Worship* (Philadelphia: Jewish Publication Society of America, 1971) 104; and Finkelstein was especially and decisively refuted by Heinemann, *Prayer in the Talmud*, 43f; Heinemann is followed by L. A. Hoffman, *The Canonization of the Synagogue Service* (Notre Dame: University of Notre Dame, 1979) 4, 50.

[4]Zunz, *Die gottesdienstliche Vorträge der Juden* (Berlin: Asher, 1832) 367f; E. G. Hirsch, "Shemoneh Esreh," *JE*, vol. 11, 276; E. Schürer, *History of the Jewish People* (Edinburgh: Clark, 1924) Pt. 2, vol. 2, 77f; G. F. Moore, *Judaism in the First Centuries of the Christian Era, the Age of the Tannaim* (Cambridge: Harvard University, 1946) vol. 1, 177f; Elbogen, *Der jüdische Gottesdienst*, 31-35, 245-50; Bickerman, "The Civic Prayer," 164; Avenary, "Amidah," col. 839; Liber, "Structure and History," 342-56; Milgrom, *Jewish Worship*, 104; Finkelstein, "Development of the Amidah," 91-177; Grant, "The Modern Study," 59-77; J. Schirmann, "Hebrew Liturgical Poetry and Christian Hymnology," *JQR* 44 (1953/54) 137; Kohler, "The Essene Version," 390f; J. Heinemann and J. J. Petuchowski, *Literature of the Synagogue* (New York: Behrman, 1975) 31f; Heinemann, *Prayer in the Talmud*, 224; Idlesohn, *Jewish Liturgy*, 109f; Hoffman, *Canonization*, 50f. See Ber 28b-29a which speaks of the editing of the Amidah at the time of R. Gamaliel II; Meg 17b, Ber 33a.

[5]Heinemann, *Prayer in the Talmud*, 226f; Kohler, "The Essene Version," 391; Avenary, "Amidah," col. 839; Bickerman, "The Civic Prayer," 174. See T.Ber 3:13 which says the Seven Benedictions were accepted as the norm by the schools of Hillel and Shammai. Heinemann (226) pointed out that the tradition (j. Shab 11:15b) is incorrect which states that the Seven Benedictions for Sabbath are derived from the Eighteen (actually nineteen) minus the twelve middle benedictions. The tradition says that no petitions (i.e. the twelve middle benedictions) could be uttered on the Sabbath. But, argued Heinemann, we recite other petitions on the Sabbath (e.g. ברכת המזון "grace after meals").

[6]See RHS 4:5 for the earliest list of the names of the Seven Benedictions.

[7]The Hebrew is the reading of both the Palestinian and Babylonian texts. See S. Schechter, "Geniza Specimens," *JQR* O.S. 10 (1898) 656; D. Hedegard, *Seder R. Amram Gaon, Part I* (Motala: Broderna, 1951) Hebrew text 38a.

[8]Or, in the Eighteen Benedictions for daily recitation to the seventeenth benediction of the Babylonian Amidah and sixteenth of the Palestinian. In the Babylonian prayer book there are nineteen benedictions. The Babylonian fourteenth and fifteenth are combined in the Palestinian.

[9]In the Babylonian Amidah but not in the Palestinian.

[10]Or the eighteenth benediction of the Babylonian and seventeenth of the Palestinian Amidah for daily recitation.

[11]Or nineteenth benediction of the Babylonian and eighteenth of the Palestinian Amidah for daily recitation.

[12]See Sota 7:2, b. Sota 38a, b. Ber 13a, T. Sota 7:7 and Idlesohn, *Jewish Liturgy*, 107.

[13]Heinemann, *Prayer in the Talmud*, 43.

[14]The Hebrew texts are from R. Amram in Hedegard, *Seder R. Amram* (Babylonian) and Schechter, "Geniza Specimens," 656-58 (Palestinian).

[15]See F. Field, *Origenis Hexaplorum* (Hildesheim: Olms, 1964) 32. The word ὑπέρμαχος does not occur in the LXX translation of the OT. It is found in Wisdom of Solomon 10:20, 16:17, 2 Macc 8:36, 14:34. See E. Hatch and H. A. Redpath, *A Concordance to the Septuagint and Other Greek Versions of the Old Testament*, vol. 2, 1415 and vol. 3, 243.

[16]See Hatch and Redpath, *Concordance*, vol. 1, 601.

[17]The Geniza fragments have apparently not preserved the Kedusha. Schechter ("Geniza Specimens," 656-58) did not print the Kedusha or the Sabbath prayer.

[18]The LXX usually renders תחנה as δεήσις (Hatch and Redpath, *Concordance*, vol. 1, 285), rarely תפלה (vol. 2, 1214f). Aquila renders תחנה also as δεήσις (Reider and Turner, *Index*, 51). But see AC 7.37.5 where προσευχή is found, the ordinary word for תפלה in Aquila (Reider and Turner, *Index*, 204) and LXX (Hatch and Redpath, *Concordance*).

[19]ידה hiphil is usually rendered in LXX as αἰνεῖν or ἐξομολογεῖν (Hatch and Redpath, *Concordance*, vol. 1, 33, 499) and never as εὐχαριστεῖν. This verb is only found in Jdt 8:25, Wis 18:2, 2 Macc 1:11, 10:7, 12:31, 3 Macc 7:16. Aquila renders תודה as εὐχαριστία, e.g. Lev 7:12. See Reider and Turner, *Index*, 102.

[20]For the Hebrew idiom, see Brown, Driver and Briggs, *Hebrew Lexicon*, 189f.

[21]Bousset, *Nachrichten*, 435-39.

[22]Ibid., 443-45.

[23]Dugmore, *Influence of the Synagogue*, 31.

[24]Statues of the Apostles 66; Acts of Peter 15, 16; Egyptian Church Order 24; Testament of our Lord 1.22; Gregory of Nyssa, *De Castig.* 2; Augustine, *In Joannis Evang. Tract.* 3.19; Origen, *Hom. in Num.* 23.4. See Dugmore, *Influence*, 28-37.

[25]*In Matt. Hom.*

[26]1 Clement 9-12. For Syrian Christian prayers containing lists of this sort, see A. Moberg, *Book of the Himyarites* (Lund: Gleerup, 1924) cxxxvi. This work was composed in Syriac in A.D. 525 in South Arabia (xxiii). It is especially interesting in this connection that B. Capelle thought he had proven that the text of the *gloria in excelsis* (AC 7.47f) in AC was not the original form of the hymn, as used to be thought, but that the compiler had adapted the original and turned the prayer to Christ into a prayer addressed to the Father only! Thus the compiler may tend to delete Christ's name, not add it. See "Le text du 'gloria in excelsis,'" *Revue d'histoire ecclesiastique* 44 (1949) 439-57. Also see A. Baumstark, "Eine Parallele zur commendatio animae in griechischer Kirchenpoesie," *Origens Christianus* N.S. 4 (1915) 298-305.

[27]See ANF, vol. 7, 548, 540, 543.

[28]Bousset, *Nachrichten*, 455-57.

[29]Translation from W. Macdonald in ANF, vol. 7, 543. Greek text in Brightman, *Liturgies*, 50.

[30]Translation from the Syriac by J. Donaldson in ANF, vol. 7, 564.

[31]Translation from *The Divine Liturgy of St. John Chrysostom* (London: Faith, 1951) 38. Greek text in Brightman, *Liturgies*, 384.

[32]*Catech.* 23.6. Translation by E. H. Gifford in *A Select Library of Nicene and Post-Nicene Fathers*, ed. P. Schaff and H. Wace (New York: Christian Literature, 1894) vol. 7, 154.

[33]*Dial.* 41. Translation from Dods and Reith, ANF, vol. 1, 215.

[34]Translation and Greek text in K. Lake, *The Apostolic Fathers* (LCL; Cambridge: Harvard, 1970) 42-45.

[35]R. M. Grant, "The Early Antiochene Anaphora," *Anglican Theological Review* 30 (1948) 91-94.

[36]Idem, *After the New Testament* (Philadelphia: Fortress, 1967) 131.

[37]Translation and text in R. M. Grant, *Theophilus of Antioch, Ad Autolycum* (Oxford: Clarendon, 1970) 8-11.

[38]Bousset, *Nachrichten*, 473.

[39]Ibid., 472.

[40]Goodenough, *By Light, Light*, 310.

[41]Lietzmann, *Mass and the Lord's Supper*, 102-105.

[42]Bousset, *Nachrichten*, 465.

[43]Ibid., 466.

[44]Ibid.

[45]Ibid., 465.

[46]See LSJM and J. Reider, "Prolegomena to a Greek-Hebrew and Hebrew-Greek Index to Aquila I, II and III," *JQR* 4 (1913/14) 321-56, 577-620; *JQR* 7 (1916/17) 287-364.

[47]Bousset, *Nachrichten*, 470.

[48]Brightman (*Liturgies*, xxv) also mentions this characteristic.

[49]Bousset, *Nachrichten*, 480f.

[50]Ibid., 482f.

[51]See Brightman, *Liturgies*, 374.

[52]See Lampe.

[53]See ANF, vol. 7, 541; Brightman, *Liturgies*, 374.

[54]Bousset, *Nachrichten*, 479.

[55]Brightman also noted this characteristic in AC (*Liturgies*, xxiv).

[56]"The Jewish origin of these Fragments was made certain by Bousset's analysis..." (*By Light, Light*, 336). Cf. Simon's assessment: "Bousset...en a établi de façon irrefutable l'origine et le caractère authentiquement juifs" (*Verus Israel*, 74).

[57]E.g. "certainly no Christian ever wrote" AC 7.39.2-4. Christian authorship for this passage is "unthinkable" (Goodenough, *By Light, Light*, 327). "Certainly we are presented with a formula for introducing Jewish legalism..." in AC 8.6.5-8 (ibid., 328, 332).

[58]Ibid., 335.

[59]The rest of the prayer beginning at 8.16.4 is based on Apostolic Tradition 8.

[60]Goodenough, *By Light, Light*, 333.

[61]Arndt and Gingrich, *Greek Lexicon*, 33 (see article, ἄκων). For Chrysostom's liturgy, see Brightman, *Liturgies*, 360.

[62]Warren, *Liturgy*, 219-21.

[63]See the introduction and translation in J. Wordsworth, *Bishop Serapion's Prayer-Book* (London: SPCK, 1923) 13, 79f.

[64]Warren, *Liturgy*, 19-21.

[65]I. Levi, "La commemoration des Ames dans le judaisme," *REJ* 29 (1894) 43-60.

[66]Hedegard, *Seder*, 46-51, 163f.

[67]Kohler, "Ueber die Ursprünge," 447; Heinemann, *Prayer in the Talmud*, 231; Price, "Jewish Morning Prayers," 153-68.

CHAPTER V

RECONSTRUCTING THE ORIGINAL SOURCE

In his publications on the prayers of AC 7.33-38, Kohler spoke of "the few Christian interpolations"[1] as if the prayers had been edited only slightly. Baumstark referred to the Christian redaction of the prayers as "the light veneer of a somewhat superficial Christian revision."[2] Goodenough maintained:

> The general method of the Christian redactor is obvious and clumsy enough. There is no attempt to alter the fundamental Judaism of the prayers by any method other than the crudest sort of casual insertion of references to Christ or bits of Christian creed.[3]

All of these scholars appear to have assumed that the sum of the Christian redaction consists of explicit references to Christ or the New Testament. Bousset also implied such a view, for he wrote of the dearth of Christian elements in the prayers except for some loosely connected phrases (e.g. "through Christ").[4]

Nevertheless, in light of what we saw in Chapter II, it is unwise to suppose that the compiler has altered his source only where there is peculiarly Christian content (e.g. the mention of Christ). Chapter II demonstrated that the compiler, in handling the prayers in his other sources (Didache, Apostolic Tradition) remolded prayers adding numerous scriptural embellishments and favorite themes and phrases; quoted a prayer almost verbatim except for the necessary interpolations for the sake of contemporaneity; and freely composed a prayer which only faintly echoes the original. In other words, the compiler's manipulation of his sources ranged from simple interpolation to thorough redactional activity. Therefore, it is important to examine the prayers in AC 7.33-38 to attempt to discern the extent of the compiler's editorial activity.

This undertaking is of course considerably more difficult than our examination in Chapter II of the compiler's editorial method, since in the case of AC 7.33-38 we do not possess the original source. However, we do possess partial parallels to the original source of this section of AC, in the Babylonian and Palestinian versions of the Seven Benedictions. Where there exist close similarities with these Benedictions, we should conslude that the compiler probably has faithfully represented his source. Where there are only vague resemblances to portions of the Seven Benedictions, and at the same time evidence of the compiler's vocabulary and theological interests, it is probable that he has recast his source at that point. In other places it will appear that the compiler has added interpolations to the source.

We should perceive editorial activity in:

1) Material containing peculiarly Christian elements. References to Christ and Christian practice, and New Testament quotations were obviously not in the original source, the Seven Benedictions.

2) Material containing words, phrases or themes which were apparently favored by the compiler. By comparing the sources of AC, the Didascalia, the Didache, and the Apostolic Tradition (incorporated into books 1-6, 7.1-32, and various parts of book 8 respectively), with the compiler's redaction of those sources, definite stock expressions and literary conventions, as well as certain theological themes, are evident. If these elements appear in AC 7.33-38 we should assume that they are redactional in that section as well, though we must admit that it is remotely possible that the Jewish source could have furnished the compiler with a theme or expression which he favored.

3) Material in which we find recurrent words, phrases or themes which only appear elsewhere in books seven and eight of AC, in those portions where the source (if any) is unknown. We cannot demonstrate as conclusively in this case that the material is redactional--since we cannot compare the AC with a source--but repeated appearance of these elements in scattered portions of books seven and eight of AC certainly suggests that the material is redactional.

4) Material discordant with the rest of the text; i.e. extraneous to the context; disrupting the flow of thought, or otherwise self-contained.[5]

5) Material strongly reminiscent of Pseudo-Ignatius in expression or idea. Without deciding whether or not Pseudo-Ignatius compiled the AC, we may repeat what was written in Chapter II: If there are strong resemblances in language and thought to Pseudo-Ignatius in any of the phrases of the alleged Jewish prayers, it should cause us to suspect that at least that particular phrase has come from the pen of the compiler; for no one denies that the compiler at least shared many ideas and expressions with Pseudo-Ignatius (see above, pp. 26-27).

6) Material which has parallels in other Christian liturgies. Expressions in AC 7.33-38 which appear elsewhere in Christian

liturgies suggest that a liturgical tradition is the source of the expression.

The main tools for this investigation consist of the index of Greek words in Funk's edition, the linguistic and theological analysis of AC in Brightman's *Liturgies*, and the linguistic and theological analysis of Pseudo-Ignatius by M. P. Brown.[6]

The method employed here assumes that what material cannot be demonstrated to have come from the compiler is from his source. *When we cannot show that material in AC 7.33-38 meets the six criteria above, we assume that it was in the original.* The great mistake of everyone who has treated the redaction of AC 7.33-38 is that they all failed to proceed beyond our first criterion. Thus, much material which we believe is redactional, previous scholars attributed to the source.

There are two problems with this methodology which are not solvable in light of the nature of the evidence. Obviously, there must be a great deal of material in AC composed by the compiler which could not stand this test. He did not use stock expressions, we would assume, and refer to the same themes in all of his redactional work. We may then occasionally assign to the source what is really redactional. Secondly, the compiler may have at times so heavily edited the source by recasting the ideas of the prayer in his own vocabulary that it will be impossible to determine what was in the source. We may, then, occasionally assign to the compiler material which was in the source but has been recast by the compiler.

At the end of this chapter the results will be presented in the form of a reconstructed Greek text and translation (Chart E).

AC 7.33

"Our eternal savior...." Σώτηρ is used of God as opposed to Jesus only twice in AC: here and at AC 7.35.1. This is in striking contrast to its numerous references to Christ[7] (and see Chart B on AC 7.26.2 and Didache 10). This suggests that the appellation "savior" stood in the source.

We next read in the text "king of the gods," a quotation from Esth 4:17.[8] Since this expression is found no where else in AC and Esther is only quoted one other time (5.20.16), we can discern no conventionalism on the part of the compiler, and thus assume that this phrase was in the source.

Next the text reads "the one alone who is almighty and Lord, God of all that is." The title παντοκράτωρ is used very often in

AC (though not only by the compiler)[9] and it appears that this entire phrase is his addition. As Brightman pointed out, excessive emphasis on the pre-eminence of the father by such phrases as this is typical of the compiler.[10] Moreover, it is also typical of Pseudo-Ignatius to stress the supremacy of the father by the repeated use of παντοκράτωρ.[11]

The phrase "God of our holy and blameless fathers and of those before us, God of Abraham, Isaac and Jacob" seems to have been edited by the compiler. First of all ἀμέμπτος is a favorite term of the compiler.[12] Second, the phrase "and of those before us" is a needless repetition and looks like a later addition (by someone not racially connected to Abraham?). The phrase "God of our fathers" would appear to be original since it is only in one other place in AC which is clearly authored by the compiler (7.26.3) that the patriarchs are referred to as "our fathers." Kohler thought that only a Jew could make such a statement. At any rate its rarity in AC may argue that its appearance here is from a source.[13]

The phrase "God of Abraham, Isaac and Jacob" which is a quotation of Exod 3:16 appears five other times in AC. It is found in the Prayer of Manasses which is in the Didascalia (AC 2.22.12,13) and twice it appears as a quotation of Matt 22:32 (AC 6.30.4, 8.41.4). Once it is found inserted into the Didache at AC 7.26.3 and once it is inserted in Apostolic Tradition 28 at AC 8.40.3. But this same phrase appears in the Hebrew first benediction (see Chart C). Thus this phrase may have been quoted from the source or supplied by the compiler. It is impossible to decide which is the case from this evidence alone, and thus we assume that the phrase was in the source.

Joel 2:13 ("the merciful and compassionate, the patient and very merciful") follows next. This is the only quotation of this scripture in AC. This phrase could be the compiler's scriptural embellishment,[14] but nothing has been said previous to this scripture about God's mercy, so this passage appears to be part of the source.

The next series of clauses demonstrates nothing which is peculiar to the compiler ("the one to whom every heart is seen as naked and to whom every hidden thought is revealed; to you the souls of the righteous cry out, upon you the hopes of the righteous rely"). The vocabulary in this section is atypical of the compiler. γυμνοφανής is not listed in Funk's index (which must mean the word is rarely or never used elsewhere) nor is κρύφιον. The only citation for ἐνθύμημα is for this section. βοάω is not listed. Therefore, we assume that this section was in the source.

The phrase which follows ("father of the blameless") is based upon the favorite term mentioned above (ἀμέμπτος) and thus has probably come from the compiler's pen.

The clause ("the one who listens to those with uprightness who summon you, the one who even knows the petitions which are kept silent") is repeated word for word at AC 8.15.2. This makes it probable that this was a stock expression, perhaps one used in the compiler's church. Thus, we shall assume that the passage is redactional.

It follows then that the subsequent clause which is intended to explain the clause previously mentioned is also from the compiler. The clause ("for your providence reaches even to the inward parts of men and you search out the thought of each through the conscience") makes no sense without the preceding clause which we have already decided is probably an addition. In addition, the compiler appears to have been fascinated with the idea of πρόνοια ("providence"). In every case where the word occurs in AC, where we can compare the AC with its source, the word has come from the compiler.[15]

However, the clause which follows ("and in every region of the inhabited earth incense is sent up to you through prayer and words") clashes with the preceding clause. The preceding clause ("for your providence" etc.) explained how God could know petitions that were kept silent, but this clause declares that men lift up audible prayers to God all over the world. This fits better with the phrase further above "to you the souls of the righteous cry out." Vocabularly alone in this clause leads us to no firm conclusion since κλίμα is a hapax, while θυμίαμα and οἰκουμένη are used more often.[16] Thus we conclude that this clause was in the source.

Paragraph three of AC 7.33 also appears to have been worked over by the compiler. The origin of the clause ("the one who began the present world as a race course of righteousness") is difficult to determine. The compiler used this metaphor in 2.14.6 to illustrate that good often mingles with bad, as in athletic competition. These are the only two appearances of this word, however. A clue to the origin of this clause is in its structure. The whole clause is encased between an article and a participle, a structure which was seen above in the passage identical to 8.15.2. This structure is a common stylistic trait of the compiler. God's deeds are listed in a series of clauses encased in participial constructions: "you are the one who...." See AC 6.23.2,3, 7.34, and 8.12.9-20 for a series of such clauses. Therefore, this clause is probably redactional.

The next two clauses ("and opened to all the gate of mercy, and showed to all mankind") are impossible to judge by vocabulary, since the words are so ordinary. The clauses present us with no reason for claiming the compiler as its author, and therefore we must accept this clause as originally in the Jewish stratum. It can easily be understood without the preceeding clause (i.e. "the one who began the present world" etc.).

The clause which follows ("through implanted knowledge, and natural judgment and from the exhortation of the law") is probably the compiler's work. These are recurring themes in AC. ἔμφυτος is used elsewhere of the implanted law given to man at creation (AC 8.9.8, 8.12.18, cf. *7.26.3*) while φυσικός is also repeatedly used with reference to an innate law in each man.[17] Further, the emphasis upon the written Law or Old Testament is not rare in AC. Kohler and Goodenough assumed that references to law, especially the Law were irrefutable evidence of Jewish authorship.[18] Yet at least 87 references to law of any kind appear in AC, of which 57 refer to the Pentateuch. At least 21 of the latter are from the compiler's own hand. The most significant references are the following: 2.61.4, Christians practice the Laws of God; 6.19.3 where the Didascalia reads "he did not destroy the Law but taught what the Law is and what the second Law is." AC reads "he did not destroy the Law as Simon thinks but he fulfilled it." The apparently anti-Jewish polemic in Didascalia where the first Law is praised (i.e. the ten commandments, see Didascalia 6.15 in Funk) and second (ceremonial) Law is denigrated, becomes an anti-Gnostic polemic in AC where the Law in general is upheld. At 6.20 the same distinction is found. Thus, emphasis on the Law, whether natural or written, does not at all prove that a Jew is the author of the statement. On the other hand, the "implanted knowledge" and "natural judgment" which apparently are synonymous with the natural and implanted law emphasized elsewhere indicate that the phrases are interpolated.

"How the possession of wealth is not eternal, the beauty of comeliness is not everlasting, the strength of power is easily dissolved." Since no conclusion can be drawn regarding the author of this passage on the basis of vocabulary,[19] and there is nothing here to cause us to believe that the compiler has composed it, we should accept it as part of the Jewish stratum. Further, if we accept the passage above ("and showed to all" etc.) there must be an object for it.

In the next phrase ("though all is vapor and entirely vain"), the vocabulary looks suspiciously like the compiler's,[20] and the last line is reminiscent of Jas 4:14. These considerations argue that it has come from the compiler's hand. In addition, the phrase is grammatically connected with the next clause which is probably redactional.

"Only the undisguised consciousness of faith traverses through the midst of the heavens and returning with truth receives the right hand of the impending joy; at the same time also before the promise of rebirth is fulfilled the soul itself exalts in hope and rejoices." This obscure passage (see Chapter III, note on 7.33.3) appears to be the work of the compiler. In the first place, if we review our results so far (see Chart E for the reconstructed text), it is obvious that this entire prayer is centered upon petitioning God to hear the prayers of his people just as he did with the fathers. This passage which seems to describe a mystical experience is out of place in such a prayer. Second, the key concept in this passage, παλιγγενεσία, appears to be a favorite one of the compiler. The other words in this passage are either too common or rare to lead to any conclusions.[21] On the whole, however, it would seem that this passage was not in the Jewish source.[22]

Paragraphs four through six of AC 7.33 list specific examples of the mystical experience described above. The compiler lists three examples of mystic visions (as he interprets it) in the OT: Abraham in Genesis 15, Jacob at Bethel in Genesis 28, and Moses at the burning bush in Exodus 3. He could not omit mentioning Isaac, but--since the OT does not attribute a vision to him--can only say that God found Isaac to be just like Abraham. These three paragraphs so perfectly illustrate what was said at the end of paragraph three that, if we conclude that the end of that paragraph is the product of the compiler, we must also conclude that paragraphs four through six are his composition.

Furthermore, there may be an anti-Gnostic polemic in paragraph four ("and faith traveled before his knowledge, and the covenant was the follower of faith").[23] Faith is elevated above knowledge. Gnoticism is maligned in at least four passages (AC 2.61.4, 6.16.3, 6.20, 7.19) and thus was probably a problem for the compiler's community.

The closing sentence ("O Defender of the offspring of Abraham, blessed are you forever") gives no indication of being composed by the compiler and is parallel to the ending of the first benediction (see Chart C). Therefore it stood in the source.

AC 7.34

The striking thing about this prayer, which Bousset pointed out, is that it is so similar to a section of AC 8.12 (8.12.9-20). The prayer opens with the formula of a synagogal benediction ("Blessed are you, O Lord"), then adds a title ("king of the ages"), and then strikes the theme of the prayer ("who through Christ made the universe"). None of this appears to be the compiler's work, except for the interpolation "through Christ." The title (king of the ages) is similar to one in 1 Tim 1:17, but is only found here in AC and is not a particularly Christian title. The clause "who *through Christ* made the universe" has been adapted to introduce Christ's role in creation by a simple prepositional phrase. This technique is not uncommon in Christian adaptations of Jewish works.[24] It is also worth noting that, although the structure of this clause consists of the article and participle with its object, the object is not placed between the article and participle as the compiler appears often to have done (see above on 7.33.3, and throughout the rest of 7.34), but after the participle. The only words between the article and participle are those of the prepositional phrase which we have maintained is from the compiler's pen.

At this point, however, the prayer begins to enumerate God's power in the creation of the celestial bodies, the plants and animals and finally man. Using the language of the Septuagint of Genesis 1, the prayer describes how God "brought order to the unformed." Next the firmament was made and heaven was arched. At this point also the parallels to 8.12.9-20 begin (see Chart D). The sequence of creational events shows that both prayers are roughly patterned on Genesis 1, but a great deal of liberty has been taken with the order of creation.

7.34	8.12
1. order (day one)	1. heaven arched, firmament (day two)
2. firmament, heaven arched (day two)	2. night, day light, darkness, sun, moon, stars (day four)
3. stars, light, sun, moon, night, day (day four)	3. water, air, fire
4. dry land (day three)	4. dry land (day three)
5. sea described (Job 38:11)	5. animals in the sea and on land (days five and six)
6. earth became green, plants (day three)	6. plants (day three)

7. luminaries for signs, seasons, and years (day four)	7. abyss and seas (Job 38:8)
8. animals (day six)	8. rivers, herbs, living creatures, circuits of years and winds described
9. man (day six)	9. man (day six)
10. weather described	10. resurrection promised
11. resurrection promised	

The comparison of this sequence with the sequence in Genesis 1 (see above for the day on which each was created in Genesis) reveals great dissimilarity. The two prayers only roughly follow Genesis 1. Furthermore, we can see from the synopsis above that there are vague similarities of sequence between the two prayers, while Chart D points out occasional verbal parallels.

Bousset argued that 7.34 and 8.12.9-20 were different redactions of the same Jewish text. Each prayer contains a web of Stoic ideas woven into the Genesis account and follows a common line of thought. The stars are also created out of place in both prayers compared with Genesis, and thus there must have been a common source besides Genesis. In addition Job 38 has been used at the same point, when mentioning the sea. Finally, both prayers emphasize that man was created by God and Wisdom.

Further, the redactor of 7.34 shows that he was not the redactor of 8.12 wrote Bousset, since he first followed his source to list the creation of the stars out of place (in comparison to Genesis), then listed the stars again to parallel Genesis (nos. 3 and 7). Bousset concluded that the relationship of 7.34 and 8.12 was not one of dependence of one upon the other or of a free invention of both, rather, they used a common source. He also maintained that it is doubtful, even improbable, that the same compiler of AC could have worked over the common source (*Grundlage*) twice in such a different way.[25] Goodenough agreed with Bousset but stressed that both redactions of the common source were Jewish redactions.[26]

Bousset's four explanations, then, for the relationship of these two prayers are: (1) his own explanation that they were separate redactions of a common source; (2) that one prayer is dependent upon another; (3) that both are free inventions by different authors; (4) that the same redactor filled out both prayers based upon the common source. Bousset was correct in maintaining that the second and third explanations are not probable, since the two prayers are too different for one to be dependent upon another, and too similar for independent composition by different authors. Thus, a common source does seem to stand behind the two prayers, but as we maintained in Chapter IV, Bousset did not convincingly demonstrate that the *Grundlage* is Jewish. It rather seems that the common source was Christian liturgical tradition.

Bousset also did not establish that the two prayers had different redactors. Whenever two such similar passages occur in the same document, which is believed to have been compiled and edited by the same person, the burden of proof lies with whomever would assert anything other than that the same redactor edited them both. Bousset maintained that a single redactor would not have worked over a common source twice in such different ways. But how many weeks, or even months, separated his compilation and redaction of books seven and eight of the AC? Although there are not many verbal parallels between 7.34 and 8.12.9-20, there are some (see Chart D), and the general outline of the prayers is similar. One should not expect near verbal equivalency in two redactions of a source separated by weeks or months.

Bousset contended that the redactor of AC 7.34 is different from the redactor of 8.12.9-20 because in the first redaction, the creation of the stars is mentioned twice; the first time to harmonize with his source, and the second time out of conformity with Genesis. In 8.12.9-20 there is no attempt to harmonize with Genesis. But did the redactor of 7.34 reintroduce the creation of the stars or luminaries (no. 7) to parallel Genesis after he had already followed his source (no. 3)? This conclusion does not follow, since he may have only mentioned the stars (no. 3) the first time as a natural course in describing the vault of heaven. The redactor has taken poetic license with the Genesis account and the order of events does not seem to have been important to him.

Furthermore, some common themes and stock expressions of AC that appear also in AC 7.34 and 8.12.9-20 indicate that the same person--viz. the compiler--redacted both prayers. The theme of providence (7.34.5) was very important to the compiler, especially in connection with creation, as we explained above.[27] Man as λόγικος (7.34.6, 8.12.17) was also a favorite theme to the compiler. Every passage in which this word appears--where one can determine it--is redactional.[28] Man as κοσμοπολίτης also appears to have been a notion important to the compiler (7.34.6, 8.12.16). The notion occurs two other times outside of the two prayers in question (7.39.1, 8.41.4). The rather rare usage of χορηγία as "abundance" and χόρηγος as "supplier of" or "abundant in" (LSJM) may have been a literary convention of the compiler (see note in Chapter III on 7.35.10): χορηγία: *2.48.1*, *4.2.2*, 7.34.7. χόρηγος: 7.35.1,10, 8.12.6,22, 8.29.3. The word θεογνωσία (8.12.18) and its meaning "knowledge of God" seems to have been important to the compiler. At *2.26.7* he instructs that the presbyters must be the teachers of the knowledge of God. At 8.6.5 his prayer for the catechumens requests for them "knowledge of God." The word τρυφή, "pleasure," may also have been a conventional word for the compiler, especially when referring to paradise or Eden. The word first occurs in 5.5.3 in a redactional section, but probably not in this sense. At 7.33.3, however, in a section which we have already determined is redactional, the word occurs in connection with the paradise of the end of the age. At 7.43.4, the word is used in connection with the garden of Eden. The word in 8.12.19 also describes Eden. The idea of "rebirth" or "regeneration" was also a favorite theme in AC (7.34.8, 8.12.20). The word παλιγγενεσία also appears in *5.7.14*, 7.33.3 (in a passage we decided above is redactional), 7.39.4, 7.43.3, and 8.6.6. Finally, AC 8.12.18,25 contain references to the implanted Law. That this theme was important to the compiler is evident from his interpolation (at AC 7.26.3) into Didache 9, "and you implanted a law in our souls." See also the similar notion φυσικὸς νόμος: *1.6.8*, *6.12.13*, *6.20.4*, *6.22.5*, *6.23.1*, 8.12.30.

Furthermore, in addition to the parallels with the rest of AC, both prayers share a parallel with Pseudo-Ignatius. The prayers speak of God creating man from the four elements (7.34.6, ἐκ τῶν τεσσάρων σωμάτων; 8.12.17 ἐκ τῶν τεσσάρων στοιχείων). This parallels the spurious Ignatian letter to Hero 4 where it is said that God created Adam ἐκ τῶν τεσσάρων στοιχείων.[29]

Therefore, since no one has given a valid reason for concluding that different redactors edited 7.34 and 8.12.9-20, and since the two prayers exhibit parallel ideas and expressions with other parts of AC, and at least one parallel with Pseudo-Ignatius, the same redactor--the compiler of AC--has edited both prayers.

As we explained in Chapter IV, the common source for these two prayers was probably a Christian liturgical tradition. This tradition the compiler has expanded with much detail in his zeal to extoll both creator and creation. Motivated by his anti-Gnostic polemic, the compiler believed it necessary to explain "the diverse creation" (see AC 2.36.2, 6.11.3, 7.39.2 and the discussion on AC 7.39 in Chapter IV). Thus, we assume that where 7.34 becomes similar to 8.12.9-20 (at 7.34.1 ἐν ἀρχῇ) until the end of their similarities (7.34.8 ὅρον θανάτου ἔλυσας; see Chart D), the content of both of these prayers is either based on the Christian liturgical tradition, or the compiler's redaction of that tradition. The bulk of AC 7.34, then, contains none of the material of the second benediction.

But while we have concluded that much of 7.34 (as 8.12) is a free redaction by the compiler based upon Christian eucharist liturgy, it does not mean that he has failed to reflect the theme of the second benediction. We saw in Chapter II that the compiler could freely compose a prayer, expressing in his vocabulary the same theme as his source. It is not unreasonable to suggest that something similar to this has happened with respect to 7.34. The Hebrew word גבורות ("powers"), which is the title of the second benediction (RHS 4:5), suggests that a theme such as this one--God's power in creation--was in the compiler's source of the Seven Benedictions. AT least something, it is likely, was in the source to bring to the compiler's mind one of his favorite themes: creation of the world. But when the compiler began to expound upon God's power as creator and to explain the "diverse creation," he naturally drew upon his liturgical tradition, the same tradition which stands behind the ante-sanctus prayer in CL.

Paragraph eight ends with "O you Quickener of the dead through Jesus Christ our hope." The prepositional phrase may be from 1 Tim 1:1. The beginning of the phrase just as the entire theme about resurrection is parallel to the second benediction and thus was probably in the source (see Chapter IV, Chart C).

AC 7.35

This prayer begins with a quotation from Psa 146:5 (LXX): "Great are you O Lord almighty and great is your strength, and of your understanding there is no measure, Creator, Savior." The word "almighty" has been inserted into the scripture. We have already seen that this was a favorite appellation of the compiler. It is impossible to tell, however, whether the compiler has prefaced the prayer with this verse or the verse stood in the source. For the appellation "Savior" see above under 7.33.

The rest of paragraph one, however, speaks of God's mercy. The evidence from the vocabulary for this section is inconclusive and thus a judgment based upon it is impossible. Nevertheless, we shall see that this section is out of place with the theme of the prayer and therefore probably added by the compiler.

Paragraph two reintroduces one of the compiler's favorite themes: God's greatness in creation. We saw how he emphasized--though probably did not originate--this idea in 7.34 and 8.12 (see also Chapter II and Chart B). Here he returns to his old expression of God's might by recalling the greatness of the sea which is bounded by the sandy shore (7.34.3, 8.12.13).

He reiterates the creation theme again in paragraph five. Here we have even closer parallels to 7.34 and 8.12: Heaven as a vault (καμαρόω, 7.34.2, 8.12.9) is mentioned; fire as the "consolation in darkness" (σκότους παραμυθία, 7.34.2, 8.12.11); and the "chorus of stars" (χόρος ἀστέρων, 8.12.9). Undoubtedly, paragraphs two and five are the compiler's work.

In paragraphs three and four the theme changes and it is here that we find God's holiness emphasized in terms parallel to the prayers of the synagogue. The Kedusha, which was recited between the second and third benedictions, is reproduced at this point. Apart from some interpolations in this section, very little of the vocabulary[30] is typical of the compiler.

The passage, "The flaming army of angels and the intellectual spirits say to Phelmuni, 'There is one holy one,'" is probably an interpolation. The quotation from Dan 8:13 based on Theodotion's version betrays the compiler's hand. By the fourth century A.D., Theodotion's version of Daniel seems to have supplanted the Septuagint in Christian circles. Jerome[31] witnesses to this development as does the appearance of Theodotion as the Daniel text of Codex Vaticanus. S. Jellicoe[32] was inclined to date the transition from the Septuagint text of Daniel to Theodotion to the second half of the third century, since Chester Beatty X contains the Septuagint text of Daniel. At any rate, when the compiler of AC quoted Daniel he usually quoted Theodotion: 5.20.11, 3.4.6, 5.4.1, 5.20.15. Sometimes the two versions are so similar that it is impossible from a single quotation to determine its origin: 5.7.23, 7.24.2, 8.12.27, 8.9.3. The other quotations of Daniel are in the sources. Thus, clearly--where one can determine it--the compiler used Theodotion's version of Daniel, and therefore, one should conclude that this quotation of Dan 8:13 (Theodotion) is an interpolation.

The seraphim and cherubim are said to be "singing the victory ode." This phrase may be a replacement for another expression--the Hebrew version reads אמר "to say" (Chart C)--because these words almost never appear anywhere but in the compiler's material in AC.[33] In addition this phrase appears in the liturgies of James and Chrysostom in connection with the *tersanctus*.[34]

The passage from Isa 6:3 does not correspond exactly to the Hebrew, the Septuagint or any other extant Greek version of the OT. This quotation reads, "heaven and earth are full of your glory." The reading "heaven and earth" eventually became standard for Christian liturgies (see the liturgies of Chrysostom, James, Mark, Adai and Mari, and Serapion[35]). But this does not mean that the phrase "heaven and earth" betrays a Christian hand. As D. Flusser[36] has demonstrated, this change of the wording of Isa 6:3 is very ancient and appears in several Jewish sources. The Dead Sea Scrolls (1QH 16:3), the targum on Isaiah, and the Kedusha de Sidra (which is based on the targum)[37] witness to this reading of Isa 6:3. Flusser even believes that Luke 2:14 reflects this reading ("glory to God in the highest, peace on earth"). Be that as it may, Flusser has demonstrated that the emendation of Isa 6:3 to "heaven and earth" originated in Judaism. Thus, no sign of Christian redaction is evident in the quotation of Isa 6:3 in AC 7.35.4.

After the seraphim and cherubim sing about God's holiness, they are answered by "angels, archangels, thrones, dominions, rulers, authorities and powers." "Archangels" may be an addition since elsewhere it is found only in the compiler's material in AC.[38] Certainly "thrones, dominions, rulers and authorities" are interpolated since this is an exact quotation from Col 1:16. Bousset and Goodenough[39] were reluctant to admit that this is an interpolation. Bousset pointed out that similar orders of angels are found in 1 Enoch 61:10 and 2 Enoch 20, and thus the passage could have been in the Jewish source. Nevertheless, these passages are only similar to AC 7.35.3; Col 1:16 is identical with it. Goodenough maintained that since AC 7.35.3 adds "archangels" and "powers" to the list in Col 1:16, the two lists must be independent of each other. But why could not the compiler have simply inserted Col 1:16 between "archangels" and "powers" (or, if we are correct, have added "archangels" to the list and slipped it between "angels" and "powers")? In paragraph four Israel sings[40] "with full heart and willing soul (cf. 2 Macc 1:3). This looks like a stock phrase since it appears in 8.6.12 and 8.16.5.

We pass over paragraph five, which we discussed above, to come to paragraph six. Apart from the phrase "through Christ," which could easily be interpolated (see above on 7.34.1), the paragraph appears to belong to the source. It would follow smoothly after paragraph four in which Israel says "the chariot of God" etc. The fitting conclusion is that everyone should join in praise of God as paragraph six says: "Wherefore, also every man ought to send up a hymn...."[41]

The first part of paragraph seven offers no clues as to origin apart from the compiler's stock phrase "the only almighty,"[42] and the unharmonious emphasis on God's mercy: "For you are beneficial in kindness and bountiful in mercies, the only almighty." As with the bulk of paragraph one, we shall reject it as part of our source since neither of these sections seems to harmonize well with the theme of sanctification of God.

The origin of the last part of paragraph seven is difficult to determine. The vocabulary is not typical of the compiler[43] and this section follows smoothly after paragraph six ("on account of you he has power over all things...for your power both cools the flame," to the end). Thus we should assume that this section was in the source. The only cause to doubt this conclusion is that there is a vague parallel between the end of paragraph seven and Heb 11:33f. The differences, however, are as striking as the similarities: AC 7.35.7, "for your eternal power cools the flame, muzzles the lions, pacifies sea monsters, raises up those who are sick, turns back powers and lays low the army of enemies and the people numbered with those who behave arrogantly"; Heb 11:33f, "who through faith...stopped the mouths of lions, quenched raging fire, escaped the edge of the sword, won strength out of weakness, became mighty in war, put foreign armies to flight" (RSV). The differences in vocabulary also argue against a dependence here.

AC 7.35.7	Heb 11:33f
φλόγα καταψύχει	ἔφραξον στόματα λεόντων
λέοντας φιμεῖ	ἔσβεσον δύναμιν πυρός
. . .	. . .
νοσοῦντας ἐγείρει	ἐδυναμώθησαν ἀπο ἀσθενείας
δυνάμεις μετατρέπει	ἐγενήθησαν ἰσχυροὶ ἐν πολεμῷ
καὶ στρατὸν ἐχθρῶν	παρεμβολὰς ἔκλιναν ἀλλοτρίων

It is interesting, however, that O. Michel believed that Heb 11:33f contained a poetic structure of three tristichs:

1) conquered kingdoms,
   enforced justice,
   received promises,

2) stopped the mouths of lions,
   quenched raging fire,
   escaped the edge of the sword,

3) won strength out of weakness,
   became mighty in war,
   put foreign armies to flight. (RSV)

Michel thought the passage may once have been a separate unit.[44] Thus, Heb 11:33f and AC 7.35.7 may witness to an old Jewish hymn, and reflect, then, a common tradition.

Paragraph eight and the first part of nine appear to be from the source. At precisely this point, that is, in the third benediction, in the Palestinian and Babylonian rites we find this same emphasis: "there is no God beside you" (see Chart C). This notion is expressed in AC 7.35.8 by quoting Deut 4:39 and followed by an affirmation of this scripture in 7.35.9 that God is holy. This passage was most likely in the original source.[45] But the three clauses at the very beginning of paragraph eight may have been edited somewhat: "you are the one in heaven, on earth, in the sea, the one among those delimited who is delimited by nothing, for of your magnitude there is no limit...." The emphasis on God not being delimited is also found in AC 8.15.7. Thus the clause "the one among those delimited" etc. may be an interpolation.

After the affirmation of God's singularity and holiness in 7. 35.9, which we have determined was in the source ("for there is no God except you alone, no holy one but you, Lord God of knowledge, God of holy ones, holy above all holy ones; for they are sanctified by your hands") the text, beginning with "Glorious and exceedingly exalted," becomes a series of alpha privatives which extoll God's attributes. Such constructions, a favorite with the compiler, are also found listed in *6.10.2*, 8.5.1, 8.6.11, 8.12.6f, 8.15.7 and 8.37.2,[46] and are thus redactional.

At paragraph ten the alpha privatives cease momentarily: "you are the father of Wisdom, the craftsman of the creation as cause, through a mediator, the supplier of providence, the giver of law, the provider in want, the avenger of the impious ones, and rewarder of the righteous ones, the God of Christ and father, and Lord of those who act reverently toward him...." The reference to Christ is obviously redactional. Here we once again meet familiar themes: creation coupled with providence, creation and Wisdom, the giving of laws. Thus, this too is almost certainly a product of the compiler's redaction.

Kohler,[47] who agreed that the above passage was from the Christian redactor, maintained that this passage was in contradiction to paragraph nine (the section of alpha privatives) since here God is creator "through a mediator" while in paragraph nine God's "work is without mediation." This contradiction, Kohler claimed, proves that paragraph nine is from the Jewish source.[48] Yet, as we have seen, both passages are so typical of the compiler's style of expression and theological emphasis that we are led to conclude that the compiler composed both of these sections, in spite of the apparent contradiction. Although the compiler is in the habit of stating that God created the world through Christ (7.34.1, 8.12.7, 14,18) he is also used to emphasizing the pre-eminence of the father (e.g. "the one and only true God" *2.6.9, 2.56.1, 5.6.7*, 8.1.1, cg. Ps-Ignatius Magn 11, Ant 2:4). Paragraph nine is nothing more than a lavishing of praise upon God. One must not hold the compiler to strict consistency when he succumbs to such eulogistic inclinations.

After this interruption, the alpha privatives continue until the closing formula. Surely then, most of paragraph nine and all of ten is the composition of the compiler.

AC 7.36

The prayer for the Sabbath is not peculiar to Judaism, as Bousset also admitted.[49] What argues for its Jewish origin here is that this is precisely the point at which the prayer for the Sabbath occurs in the Seven Benedictions. But the compiler also practiced Sabbath observance and urged his community to do so.[50] Thus we might reasonably expect the compiler to edit this prayer to fit his need.

"Lord, almighty, you created the world through Christ and set apart the Sabbath to remember this--because on it you rested from (your) works--for meditation on your laws...." This passage not only contains the favorite appellation "almighty" and the obvious interpolation "through Christ," but the less obvious addition "for meditation on your laws." This same expression is found in AC 2. 36.2 (in the compiler's editorial work) and Pseudo-Ignatius *Magnesians* 9. If this phrase is deleted the awkward syntax is removed.

"And you ordained feasts for the gladdening of our souls, so that we may be reminded of the Wisdom created by you...." We saw in AC 7.35.10 that God is said to be the father of Wisdom. But no where else in AC is Wisdom created.[51] Since the compiler immediately in paragraph two identifies Wisdom with Christ this would have been a heretical statement. Although the compiler has been accused of Arianism (see Chapter II), such a blatant statement is out of harmony with his usual descriptions of Christ. The element of his theology which has caused many to doubt his "orthodoxy" is his *repeated emphasis* of the pre-eminence of the father as "the one and only true God" (2.69, 2.56.1, 5.6.7, 5.16.3). The compiler describes Christ as θεὸς μονογενής (3.17, 5.20.5) θεὸς λόγος (2.24.2, 5.16.1, 6.11.3) though clearly subordinate to the Father (2.26.2, 30.2, 5.7.12, 20.6). Christ is called the πρωτότοκος πάσης κτίσεως (2.61.4, 6.11.1), but there is also a definite anti-psilanthropic polemic (6.10f, 6.26.1).

Of course whether or not the compiler wrote these words, he must have accepted them in some sense, else he would have removed them. It is unwise to suppose with Goodenough[52] that the compiler simply did not notice this heretical statement. It is very difficult to decide on the source of this statement "so that we may be reminded of the Wisdom created by you," but in light of the compiler's tendency to associate creation of the world with Wisdom (7.34.6, 8.12.16), it is likely that he has done so here as well. The mention of the creation of the world at the beginning caused him to introduce a reference to Wisdom. Nevertheless, the description does seem somewhat uncharacteristic.

Paragraph two is obviously interpolated. It tells the story of the earthly Wisdom, that is Jesus, from his birth to his death and resurrection. The paragraph closes with "for through him you brought the Gentiles to yourself for a special people, the true Israel, the beloved of God, the one who sees God." Goodenough, following Bousset, wanted to emend the text to read "for through *her* (Wisdom) he has led *us* to Himself to be a peculiar people, the true Israel, that is the group that is beloved by God and sees God."[53] Kohler and Bouyer claimed the interpolation should include this passage as well.[54] Obviously, even if the reference "through him (or her)" refers to Wisdom in the last clause of paragraph one this reference is an interpolation, since we have decided that the clause in paragraph one is also from the compiler's pen. Goodenough was convinced of the Jewishness of the last clause of paragraph two largely because the phrase "the one who sees God" is so common in Philo.[55] Yet, this phrase is also a commonplace in Christian literature.[56]

Paragraph three, which recounts the Exodus event, contains none of the language or themes which we can identify as the compiler's. In addition, the words "our fathers" may indicate a Jewish source.[57] Thus, we assume that the whole of this paragraph was in the source.

Paragraph four appears to contain an interpolation. The paragraph begins: "You gave them the law of ten oracles clearly expressed by your voice and written by your hand. You commanded them to keep the Sabbath...." So far there are no stock words or themes which might indicate the compiler's work. Indeed, he seemed unwilling to talk about the "ten oracles" in books 1-6 where the Didascalia discussed them (see esp. 6.19f and above under 7.33).

Yet, the next series of phrases ("not giving a pretext for idleness but an opportunity for piety, for the knowledge of your power, for prevention of evil...") is reminiscent of a familiar theme in AC (AC 2.36.2 and 6.23.3; and cf. Ps-Ignatius, *Magn* 9) which reiterates the idea that the Sabbath is no excuse for idleness. Here it may be a polemic against the Jews--one should not rest on the Sabbath but use it to study--as it certainly is in Pseudo-Ignatius, *Magnesians* 9. Since the phrases which follow this ("an opportunity for piety" etc.) seem to be connected in thought to the first phrase, we assume that the entire passage is interpolated. The rest of paragraph four, however ("Therefore you confined [them] in the holy circuit for the sake of teaching, for exultation in the number seven. On account of this there is one seven and seven sevens and a seventh month and a seventh year and according to this cycle the fiftieth year is for remission.") is devoid of the compiler's themes and expressions. The emphasis on the number seven is found no where else in AC.[58] Thus this section, we conclude, was in the source.

Paragraph five begins with: "(This is) so that men may have no excuse to plead ignorance. On account of this you entrusted (them) to keep every Sabbath that no one may desire to send forth a word from his mouth in anger on the day of the Sabbath." Here again we find no clues that the compiler has composed this material. However, the end of paragraph five appears to have been added by the compiler: "For the Sabbath is rest from creation, the completion of the world, the seeking of laws, thankful praise to God for (those things) which were given to men." The phrase "rest from creation is also found in reference to the Sabbath in AC 5.14.20, and Pseudo-Ignatius, *Magnesians* 9; while similar statements are made in AC 7. 23.3f. The "seeking of laws" we have already seen above as "meditation on your law." The "thankful praise to God" may be simply the addition of the compiler or a re-statement of the eulogy of the fourth benediction: "Blessed art thou, O Lord, who hallowest the Sabbath."[59]

Paragraph six is obviously the work of the compiler since it states the superiority of the "Lord's day" and stands in tension with the rest of the prayer. Paragraph seven appears to be the compiler's, since it is the fitting conclusion to paragraph six.

AC 7.37

"You who have fulfilled the promises of the prophets and had mercy on Zion and compassion on Jerusalem by exalting the throne of David your servant in its midst...." This passage appears to have been recast by the compiler. Neither the Babylonian or Palestinian rites speak of these things as if they had happened (see Chart C). Only a Christian could say that they had happened, that is, in a symbolic way, by the Christ event. In the Babylonian version the prayer reads, "Be pleased, O Lord our God with thy people Israel and with their prayer, restore the worship to thy holy sanctuary; accept Israel's offerings and prayer with gracious love. May the worship of thy people be ever pleasing to thee. May our eyes behold thy return in mercy to Zion."[60] There is no mention of Jerusalem in the Babylonian version as it is extant today, and neither version mentions the throne of David. The Palestinian reads, "Accept us, O Lord our God and dwell in Zion; and may Thy servants serve Thee in Jerusalem."[61] Both of these versions look forward to a return to Jerusalem or Zion, while the prayer in AC 7.37 proclaims the request granted.

We should probably recast this back into a petition: "Fulfill the promises of the prophets and have mercy on Zion and compassion on Jerusalem, and exalt the throne of David your servant in its midst."[62] There is no reason to suppose, however, that the compiler composed this passage originally.[63] Thus it looks like he has remolded the source in favor of contemporaneity.

This same phenomenon appears in the NT in Jude 15 where the author of the epistle quoted from the Greek text of 1 Enoch 1:9. 1 Enoch speaks of the Lord coming with his myriads to bring judgment and places the event in the future (ἔρχεται,[64] "he is coming," present tense with future significance)[65] but the author of Jude recast the event and put it in the past (ἦλθον). For Jude this prophecy had been fulfilled in the Christ event.

"By the birth of Christ who was born of his seed according to the flesh from a virgin only." This obvious interpolation explains how God has had mercy on Zion and exalted the throne of David.

"You yourself also now" implies a previous statement about God in the past accepting mercifully the entreaties of his people. If we are right in concluding that the statement about God acting mercifully toward Zion in the past is from the compiler, then this phrase is as well. This conclusion is confirmed by the fact that this phrase is a stock expression in the AC, and thus redactional.[66]

"O Master, God accept the entreaties of your people." This petition is very similar to the wording of the Babylonian "accept Israel's offerings and prayer," and thus was probably in the source.

"From the lips of your people which are out of the gentiles, which call upon you in truth." The Babylonian version reads, again,

"*Israel's* offerings and prayer." Here the prayer comes from gentiles and thus looks like a Christian addition as Kohler maintained. Perhaps, as again Kohler suggested, only the words "out of the gentiles" were added.[67]

The end of paragraph one ("as you accepted the gifts of the righteous in their generations") serves as an introduction to paragraphs two through four in which the righteous are listed. Thus it must be included or excluded with paragraphs two through four. He seems to have had a fondness for listing the heroes of the OT: AC *2.55.1*, *5.7.12*, *6.12.13*, *6.30.6*, *7.5.5*, 7.37.2-4, 7.38.2, 7.39.3, 8.5.3f, 8.12.21-27.[68] Thus, paragraphs two through four are probably redactional.

Paragraph five ("and now, therefore, accept the prayers of your people which are offered in the spirit [and] with knowledge to you through Christ.") seems to be simply a restatement of the request of paragraph one ("accept the entreaties" etc.) and is probably additional.[69]

AC 7.38

Nothing in paragraph one of this prayer is reminiscent of the compiler's style or theological themes,[70] but in paragraph two we once again read a list of OT heroes which is followed in the first part of paragraph three with a reference to Christ. So far we can rather easily tell where the compiler has interpolated. However, in the middle of paragraph three we read: "For he rescued (us) from hunger and nourished (us), he healed (us) from disease, he protected (us) from an evil tongue." Does this section refer to Jesus who is mentioned just prior to this passage? Bousset and Goodenough[71]--both of whom believed that the list of heroes was in the Jewish source--argued that this passage referred to Judas Maccabeus, the last hero mentioned before Jesus, and that Jesus was obviously an interpolation. Kohler[72] claimed that originally this Jesus in the text referred to Jesus ben Phabi (Josephus *Ant.* 15.9.3f) a high priest in the reign of Herod the Great. Kohler's rather far-fetched suggestion requires little attention since anyone called Jesus in a Christian document is likely to have referred originally to Jesus of Nazareth. It might be tempting to accept Bousset's suggestion, if not for the fact that we have seen that the compiler had a fondness for listing heroes and thus has probably interpolated paragraph two. But would one have said that Judas "healed us from disease" anyway?

There are two alternatives: (1) this passage belongs with the interpolation which preceeds it. In this case Jesus is the one who rescues from the sword, hunger, disease and an evil tongue; (2) the passage is from the source and should follow immediately after paragraph one.[73] As Perles[74] pointed out, this passage is almost identical with a portion of the Nishmath prayer (see Chart F): "Thou hast nourished us in famine and provided us with plenty. Thou hast rescued us from the sword, made us escape the plague, and freed us from severe and lasting diseases."[75] The Nishmath prayer is in second person singular while the passage in AC 7.38 is third person singular. It is possible that the compiler recast the passage to fit with his new context, that is, Jesus the helper in distress.

If we recast the passage in second person and place it after paragraph one it flows smoothly: "in each and every generation you save, rescue, help (and) protect. For you rescued (us) even from the sword...." Furthermore, this theme is parallel to the content of the Babylonian and Palestinian sixth benedictions (see Chart C).

Paragraph four is also similar to the passage in the Nishmath which follows immediately after the one quoted above (see Chart F): "Therefore the limbs which thou hast apportioned in us, the spirit and soul which thou hast placed in our mouth, shall all thank and bless, praise and glorify, extol and revere, hallow and do homage to thy name, our King."[76] It is not as closely parallel to the Nishmath as paragraph three, but the similarity is striking: "For all things we give thanks to you through Christ, who also has given (us) an articulate voice for confessing (you) and who has added a harmonious tongue in the manner of a plectrum as an instrument; and useful taste, appropriate touch, sight for seeing, the hearing of a sound, the ability to smell vapors, hands for work and feet for walking." Apart from the obvious interpolation ("through Christ") nothing here is reminiscent of the compiler's themes and expressions. Perhaps he has rephrased the original prayer--it is now difficult to tell--or the difference in wording may be due to the different versions of the prayer which circulated.

The references to the human body led the compiler to return to one of his favorite themes. In paragraph five he speaks of the formation of man, this time not at the original creation but in the womb. The familiar terms and associated themes are present however: Man is a λογικὸν ζῷον (see AC 7.34.6, 8.12.17); death and resurrection are mentioned (see AC 7.34.8, 8.12.20). This paragraph is, then, the compiler's addition.

Paragraph six appears to be from the Jewish stratum. It expresses what both the Babylonian and Palestinian versions say at their conclusions: It is right to give thanks to God. Again, perhaps the compiler has recast this paragraph, but it is now impossible to say.

It would seem that the original Jewish prayer stopped with paragraph six. Paragraph seven begins, "For you saved (us) from the impiety of polytheism." This is a common expression in Pseudo-Ignatius.[77] Here begins another christological passage which recounts Christ's earthly life and describes his nature ("only begotten God"). The final passage in paragraph seven, though not christological, is again reminiscent. God is described as creator and provider in familiar terms.[78]

Paragraph eight is a closing formula which seems to go with paragraph seven. It too, then, is probably redactional.

Conclusion

The discussion above has indicated that at times the compiler has edited the prayers of AC 7.33-38 with a heavy hand. The redactional elements in the prayers can often be easily identified by using the six criteria listed at the beginning of this chapter.

Nevertheless, because of the nature of the evidence, we may have occasionally--as we warned above--omitted from our reconstructed source what was in the Jewish stratum, due to the compiler's recasting of an idea. This methodology also may have included some material which is redactional, but which fails to meet the six criteria presented above. We can, therefore, state with reasonable conviction that the verbal parallels to the Hebrew texts (see Charts C and F) are from the Jewish stratum. The remainder of the material in Chart E (the reconstructed source) is assumed to roughly represent the Jewish source, but does not carry with it the same degree of probability as the verbal parallels.

CHART D

A Synopsis of AC 7.34 and 8.12

AC 7.34	*AC 8.12*
1. ...ἐν ἀρχῇ κοσμήσας τὰ ἀκατασκεύαστα, ὁ διαχωρίσας ὕδατα ὑδάτων στερεώματι καὶ πνεῦμα ζωτικὸν τούτοις ἐμβαλών,	
ὁ γῆν ἑδράσας καὶ οὐρανὸν ἐκτείνος καὶ τὴν ἑκάστου τῶν κτισμάτων ἀκριβῆ διάταξιν κοσμήσας 2. σῇ γὰρ ἐνβυμήσει, δέσποτα, κόσμος πεφαίδρυται,	9. σὺ γὰρ εἶ (τὴν γῆν ἐπ᾽ οὐδενὸς ἱδρύσας) (ὡς δέρριν ἐκτείνας)
οὐρανὸς δὲ ὡς καμάρα	ὁ τὸν οὐρανὸν ὡς καμάραν στήσας καὶ ὡς δέρριν ἐκτείνας καὶ τὴν γῆν ἐπ᾽ οὐδενὸς ἱδρύσας γνώμῃ μόνῃ ὁ πήξας στερέωμα καὶ νύκτα καὶ ἡμέραν κατασκευάσας, ὁ ἐξαγαγὼν φῶς ἐκ θησαυρῶν καὶ τῇ τούτου συστολῇ ἐπαγαγὼν τὸ σκότος εἰς ἀνάπουλον τῶν ἐν τῷ κόσμῳ κινουμένων ζώων ὁ τὸν ἥλιον τάξας εἰς ἀρχὰς τῆς ἡμέρας ἐν οὐρανῷ καὶ τὴν σελήνην εἰς ἀρχὰς τῆς νυκτὸς καὶ τὸν χορὸν τῶν ἀστέρων ἐν οὐρανῷ καταγράψας εἰς αἶνον τῆς σῆς μεγαλοπρεπείας 10. ὁ ποιήσας ὕδωρ πρὸς πόσιν καὶ κάθαρσιν, ἀέρα ζωτικὸν πρὸς εἰσπνοὴν καὶ ἀναπνοὴν καὶ φωνῆς ἀπόδοσιν διὰ γλώττης πληττούσης τὸν ἀέρα καὶ ἀκοὴν συνεργουμένην ὑπ᾽ αὐτοῦ ὡς ἐπαίειν εἰσδεχομένην τὴν προσπίπτουσαν αὐτῇ λαλιάν. 11. ὁ ποιήσας πῦρ πρὸς σκότους παραμυθίαν, πρὸς ἐνδείας ἀναπλήρωσιν καὶ τὸ θερμαίνεσθαι ἡμᾶς καὶ φωτίζεσθαι ὑπ᾽ αὐτοῦ·
πεπηγμένος ἠγλάϊσται ἄστροις ἕνεκεν παραμυθίας τοῦ σκότους,	(πρὸς σκότους παραμυθίαν)
φῶς δὲ καὶ ἥλιος εἰς ἡμέρας καὶ καρπῶν γονὴν γεγένηνται, σελήνη δὲ εἰς καιρῶν τροπὴν αὔξουσα καὶ μειουμένη, καὶ νὺξ ὠνομάζετο καὶ ἡμέρα προσηγορεύετο, στερέωμα δὲ διὰ μέσων τῶν ἀβύσσων ἐδείκνυτο	(ὁ συστησάμενος ἄβυσσον)

AC 7.34

καὶ εἶπας συναχθῆναι τὰ ὕδατα καὶ ὀφθῆναι τὴν ξηράν. 3. αὐτὴν δὲ τὴν θάλασσαν πῶς ἄν τις ἐκφράσειεν; ἥτις ἔρχεται μὲν ἀπὸ πελάγους μαινομένη παλινδρομεῖ δὲ ἀπὸ ψάμμου τῇ σῇ προσταγῇ κωλουμένη· εἶπες γὰρ ἐν αὐτῇ συντριβήσεσθαι αὐτῆς τὰ κύματα [Job 38:11] ζώοις δὲ μικροῖς καὶ μεγάλοις καὶ πλοίοις πορευτὴν αὐτὴν ἐποίησας.

4. εἶτ' ἐχλοαίνετο γῆ, παντοίοις ἄνθεσι καταγραφομένη καὶ ποικιλίᾳ δένδρων διαφόρων· παμφαεῖς τε φωστῆρες τούτων τιθηνοί, ἀπαράβατον σώζοντες τὸν δόλιχον καὶ κατ' οὐδὲν παραλλάσσοντες τῆς σῆς προσταγῆς, ἀλλ' ὅπη ἂν κελεύτῃς, ταύτῃ ἀνίσχουσι καὶ δύουσιν εἰς σημεῖα καιρῶν καὶ ἐνιαυτῶν, ἀμειβόμενοι τὴν τῶν ἀνθρώπων ὑπηρεσίαν. 5. ἔπειτα διαφόρων ζώων κατεσκευάζετο γένη, χερσαίων, ἐνύδρων, ἀεροπόρων, ἀμφιβίων, καὶ τῆς σῆς προνοίας ἡ ἔντεχνος σοφία τὴν καταλληλὸν ἑκάστῳ πρόνοιαν δωρεῖται· ὥσπερ γὰρ διάφορα γένη οὐκ ἠτόνησεν παραγαγεῖν, οὕτως οὐδὲ διάφορον πρόνοιαν ἑκάστου ποιήσασθαι κατωλιγώρησεν.

AC 8.12

(καὶ ποτε μὲν ἐκμαίνων)
(περιφράξας δὲ αὐτὴν πύλαις ἄμμου λεπτοτάτης)

(ζώοις μικροῖς καὶ μεγάλοις)

12. ὁ τὴν μεγάλην θάλασσαν χωρίσας τῆς γῆς καὶ τὴν μὲν ἀναδείξας πλωτήν, τὴν δὲ ποσὶ βάσιμον ποιήσας, καὶ τὴν μὲν ζώοις μικροῖς καὶ μεγάλοις πληθύνας τὴν δὲ ἡμέροις καὶ ἀτιθάσσοις πληρώσας, φυτοῖς τε διαφόροις στρέψας καὶ βοτάναις στεφανώσας καὶ ἄνθεσι καλλύνας καὶ σπέρμασι πλουτίσας· 13. ὁ συστησάμενος ἄβυσσον καὶ μέγα κύτος αὐτῇ περιθείς, ἁλμυρῶν ὑδάτων σεσωρευμένα πελάγη, περιφράξας δὲ αὐτὴν πύλαις [Job 38:8] ἄμμου λεπτοτάτης· ὁ πνεύμασί ποτε μὲν αὐτὴν κορυφῶν εἰς ὀρέων μέγεθος, ποτὲ δὲ στρωννύων αὐτὴν εἰς πεδίον, καὶ ποτὲ μὲν ἐκμαίνων χειμῶνι, ποτὲ δὲ πραΰνων γαλήνῃ ὡς ναυσιπόροις πλωτῆρσιν εὔκολον εἶναι πρὸς πορείαν· 14. ὁ ποταμοῖς διαζώσας τὸν ὑπὸ σοῦ διὰ Χριστοῦ γενόμενον κόσμον καὶ χειμάρροις ἐπικλύσας καὶ πηγαῖς ἀενάοις μεθύσας ὄρεσιν δὲ περισφίγξας εἰς ἕδραν ἀτρεμῆ ἀσφαλεστάτην.

(καταγράψας)
(ποικιλῶν)

AC 7.34	*AC 8.12*
	15. ἐπλήρωσας γάρ σου τὸν κόσμον καὶ διεκόσησας αὐτὸν βοτάναις εὐόσμοις καὶ ἰασίμοις, ζώοις πολλοῖς καὶ διαφόροις, ἀλκίμοις καὶ ἀσθενεστέροις, ἐδωδίμοις καὶ ἐνεργοῖς, ἡμέροις καὶ ἀτιθάσσοις, ἑρπετῶν συριγμοῖς, πτηνῶν ποικίλων κλαγγαῖς, ἐνιαυτῶν κύκλοις, μηνῶν καὶ ἡμερῶν ἀριθμοῖς, τροπῶν τάξεσιν, νεφῶν ὀμβροτόκων διαδρομαῖς εἰς καρπῶν γονὰς καὶ ζώων σύσ- τασιν, σταθμὸν ἀνέμων, δια- πνεόντων ὅτε προσταχθῶσιν παρὰ σοῦ, τῶν φυτῶν καὶ τῶν βοτανῶν τὸ πλῆθος.
6. καὶ τέλος τῆς δημιουργίας τὸ λογικὸν ζῶον τὸν κοσμοπολίτην	(τὴν λογικὴν διάγνωσιν) (τὸν κοσμοπολίτην) 16. καὶ οὐ μόνον τὸν κόσμον ἐδημιούργησας, ἀλλὰ καὶ τὸν κοσμοπολίτην ἄνθρωπον ἐν αὐτῷ ἐποίησας, κόσμου κόσμον αὐτὸν ἀναδείξας εἶπας γὰρ τῇ σῇ σοφίᾳ.
τῇ σῇ σοφίᾳ διαταξάμενος κατεσκεύασας εἴπων ποιήσωμεν ἄνθρωπον κατ᾿ εἰκόνα καὶ καθ᾿ ὁμοίωσιν ἡμετέραν	ποιήσωμεν ἄνθρωπον κατ᾿ εἰκόνα ἡμετέραν καὶ καθ᾿ ὁμοίωσιν καὶ ἀρχέτωσαν τῶν ἰχθύων τῆς θαλάσσης καὶ τῶν πετεινῶν τοῦ οὐρανοῦ.
κόσμου κόσμον αὐτὸν ἀναδείξας ἐκ μὲν τῶν τεσσάρων σωμάτων	(κόσμου κόσμον αὐτον ἀναδείξας) (ἐκ τῶν τεσσάρων στοιχείων)
διαπλάσας αὐτῷ τὸ σῶμα κατα- σκευάσας δ᾿ αὐτῷ τὴν ψυχὴν ἐκ τοῦ μὴ ὄντος αἴσθησιν δὲ πένταθλον αὐτῷ χαρισάμενος καὶ νοῦν τὸν τῆς ψυχῆς ἡνίοχον ταῖς αἰσθήσεσιν ἐπιστήσας.	(ἐκ τοῦ μὴ ὄντος), (τὴν πένταθλον ἐχαρίσω αἴσθησιν)
	17. διὸ καὶ πεποίηκας αὐτὸν ἐκ ψυχῆς ἀθανάτου καὶ σώματος σκεδαστοῦ, τῆς μὲν ἐκ τοῦ μὴ ὄντος, τοῦ δὲ ἐκ τῶν τεσσάρων στοιχείων· καὶ δέδωκος αὐτῷ κατὰ μὲν τὴν ψυχὴν τὴν λογικὴν διάγνωσιν, εὐσεβείας καὶ ἀσεβείας διάκρισιν, δικαίου καὶ ἀδίκου παρατήρησιν, κατὰ δὲ τὸ σῶμα τὴν πένταθλον ἐχαρίσω αἴσθησιν καὶ τὴν μετα- βατικὴν κίνησιν.
7. καὶ ἐπὶ πᾶσι τούτοις, δέσποτα κύριε, τίς ἐπαξίως διηγήσεται νεφῶν ὀμβροτόκον φοράν, ἀστραπῆς ἔκλαμψιν, βροντῶν πάταγον, εἰς τροφῆς χορηγίαν καταλλήλου καὶ κρᾶσιν ἀέρων παναρμόνιον;	

AC 7.34

8. παρακούσαντα δὲ τὸν ἄνθρωπον ἐμμίσθου ζωῆς ἐστέρησας οὐκ εἰς τὸ παντελὲς ἀφανίσας

ἀλλα χρόνῳ πρὸς ὀλίγον κομίσας, ὅρκῳ εἰς παλιγγενεσίαν ἐκάλεσας ὅρον θανάτου ἔλυσας

ὁ ζωοποιὸς τῶν νεκρῶν διὰ Ἰησοῦ Χριστοῦ τῆς ἐλπίδος ἡμῶν

AC 8.12

18. σὺ γάρ, θεὲ παντοκράτορ, διὰ Χριστοῦ παράδεισον ἐν Ἐδὲμ κατὰ ἀνατολὰς ἐφύτευσας παντοίων φυτῶν ἐδωδίμων κόσμῳ καὶ ἐν αὐτῷ, ὡς ἂν ἐν ἑστίᾳ πολυτελεῖ, εἰσήγαγες αὐτόν, κἀν τῷ ποιεῖν νόμον δέδωκας αὐτῷ ἔμφυτον, ὅπως οἴκοθεν καὶ παρ' ἑαυτοῦ ἔχοι τὰ σπέρματα τῆς θεογνωσίας.

19. εἰσαγαγὼν δὲ εἰς τὸν τῆς τρυφῆς παράδεισον, πάντων μὲν ἀνῆκας αὐτῷ τὴν ἐξουσίαν πρὸς μετάληψιν, ἑνὸς δὲ μόνου τὴν γεῦσιν ἀπεῖπας ἐπ' ἐλπίδι κρειττόνων, ἵνα ἐὰν φυλάξῃ τὴν ἐντολήν, μισθὸν ταύτης τὴν ἀθανασίαν κομίσηται. 20. ἀμελήσαντα δὲ τῆς ἐντολῆς καὶ γευσάμενον ἀπηγορευμένου καρποῦ ἀπάτῃ ὄφεως καὶ συμβουλίᾳ γυναικὸς τοῦ μὲν παραδείσου δικαίως ἐξῶσας αὐτόν, ἀγαθότητι δὲ εἰς τὸ παντελὲς ἀπολλύμενον οὐχ ὑπερεῖδες, σὸν γὰρ ἦν δημιούργημα ἀλλὰ καθυποτάξας αὐτῷ τὴν κτίσιν δέδωκας αὐτῷ οἰκείοις ἱδρῶσιν καὶ πόνοις πορίζειν ἑαυτῷ τὴν τροφήν, σοῦ πάντα φύοντος καὶ αὔξοντος καὶ πεπαίνοντος χρόνῳ δὲ πρὸς ὀλίγον αὐτὸν κομίσας ὅρκῳ εἰς παλιγγενεσίαν ἐκάλεσας ὅρον θανάτου λύσας ζωὴν ἐξ ἀναστάσεως ἐπηγγείλω

Translation

AC 7.34

1. ...in the beginning brought order to the unformed (matter); who separated waters from waters by the firmament and put a living spirit in them;

who caused the earth to settle

and stretched out the heavens

and precisely arranged the disposition of each of the creatures. 2. By your resolution, O Master, the world has beamed (with joy) and heaven as a vault

has been fixed and adorned with the stars
for consolation in darkness; and light and sun have been created for the days and for the generation of fruit; and the moon waxing and waning for the change of seasons. Also night was named and day proclaimed and the firmament appeared in

AC 8.12.9-20

9. You are the one who (established the earth on nothing)
(who stretched it out like a curtain)

set up heaven as a vault, stretched it out like a curtain and established the earth upon nothing by (your) will alone who fixed the firmament and prepared night and day, who brought out light from the treasuries and brought forth darkness by its dimming for rest for living creatures that move on the earth, who arranged in heaven the sun for ruling of the day and the moon for ruling of the night and who inscribed the chorus of stars in heaven to praise your magnificence. 10. (You are the one) who made water for drinking and cleansing, living air for breathing in and out and rendering sound by the tongue striking the air and the sense of hearing which is helped by it so as to have perception when it receives the voice which falls upon it. 11. (You are the one) who made fire for consolation in darkness, for satisfying of want and to warm us and for us to be illuminated by it.

(for consolation in darkness)

AC 7.34	*AC 8.12*
the midst of the abyss, and you said, "Let the waters be collected and the dry land appear." 3. And how could anyone tell about even the sea?	(who set up the abyss)
She who comes from the ocean raging,	(and sometimes it rages)
and being hindered by your command, runs back from the shore. For you said, "In it its waves are shattered" but "you have made it a thoroughfare for small and large (creatures) and for boats."	(and you circumscribed it with the gates of the lightest sand)
	12. (You are the one) who separated the great sea from the land and showed one navigable and made the other passable on foot; and the one you made numerous with animals small and large and the other you filled with animals tame and wild, crowning it with various plants, wreathing it with herbs, beautifying it with flowers and enriching it with seeds. 13. (You are the one) who set up the abyss and surrounded it with a great cavity when the sea was heaped up with salty water. But you circumscribed it with the gates of the lightest sand. (You are the one) who by the winds sometimes arches it as high as mountains, while at other times you spread it out like a plain. Also sometimes it rages in a storm, while at other times it is meek and calm so as to be gentle for traveling for sea faring sailors. 14. (You are the one) who girds the world which was created by you through Christ with rivers and flooded (it) with torrents and drenched (it) with everlasting springs, and bound (it) round with mountains for a firm (and) very sure foundation.
4. Next the earth became green (and) was painted with all	(who painted)
kinds of flowers and with a multicolor of various trees; and the radiant luminaries are their nurses, who preserve the unalterable course and never	(multicolor)

AC 7.34	*AC 8.12*
vacillate from your command; but just as you order, so they rise up and they set, for signs of seasons and years, changing for the service of mankind. 5. Next kinds of different animals were prepared those on dry land, in the water, traversing the air (and) amphibians and the artful wisdom of your providence gives graciously the corresponding providence to each; for as he was not too weak to introduce different kinds (of animals) thus he did not neglect to make a different providence for each.	
	15. For you filled your world and adorned it with herbs, fragrant and healing, with many and varied animals, both strong and weak, for food and for working, tame and wild, with hissing of serpents, with flapping of various flying creatures, with cycles of years, with enumeration of months and days, with the order of seasons, with the procession of rain clouds for generating fruits and sustaining animals, for the station of winds which blow when commanded by you (and) for the multitude of plants and herbs.
6. And the end of the creation the rational being the cosmopolitan	(rational discernment) (cosmopolitan) 16. And not only did you create the world but you also made man in it the cosmopolitan, exhibiting him an ornament of the world.
	For you said
you ordained by your wisdom and prepared saying,	to your Wisdom
"Let us make man in our image and our likeness,"	"Let us make man in our image and likeness, and let them rule over the fish of the sea and the birds of the heaven."
presenting him an ornament of the world.	(presenting him an ornament of the world)
You formed his body from the four elements	(from the four elements)
but his soul you made from nothing;	(from nothing)
and you endowed	(you endowed

AC 7.34	*AC 8.12*
him with fivefold sense perception and you set the mind (as) the helmsman of the soul over the senses.	the fivefold sense perception)
	17. Wherefore also you have made him from an immortal soul and a dissoluble body, the one from nothing, the other from the four elements. You have given to him with respect to his soul rational discernment between piety and impiety, observation of justice and iniquity; but with respect to his body you have bestowed the five senses, motion and mobility.
7. And in all these things, O Lord Master, who will worthily recount the movement of the rain producing clouds, the flash of lightning, the clap of thunder; for the abundance of appropriate nourishment and the harmonious blending of air.	
	18. For you, O God almighty, planted through Christ a paradise in Eden to the East adorned with all sorts of edible plants and in it as if in a very costly home, you brought him. And when you made (him) you gave (him) a law implanted in him that originally he might have in himself the seeds of divine knowledge.
8. And you deprived wayward mankind of the reward of life, not removing it for all time	
	19. And when you brought (him) into the paradise of pleasure you allowed him the power to participate in everything except you forbade him to taste of one (tree) only, in hope of greater things, that if he keep the commandment he would receive immortality as the reward. 20. But when he ignored the commandment and tasted the forbidden fruit by the deceit of a serpent and counsel of his wife, you justly drove him out of paradise. But in (your) goodness you did not

AC 7.34

but making (mankind)
sleep for a little while,
you called them into rebirth
by an oath,
you loosed the bonds of death

O Quickener of the dead
through Jesus Christ our hope.

AC 8.12

completely overlook (him) when he was lost. For he was your creation. But subjecting creation to him, you have granted to him to provide food for his family by sweat and toil by himself, while you caused all things to grow and increase and become ripe.
Although you caused him
to sleep for a little while
you called him into rebirth
by an oath,
loosed the bond of death
and promised life by resurrection.

CHART E

A Reconstruction of the Original Source

7.33

Αἰώνιε σῶτερ ἡμῶν, ὁ βασιλεὺς τῶν θεῶν, θεὸς πατέρων ἡμῶν ὁ θεὸς Ἀβραὰμ καὶ Ἰσαὰκ καὶ Ἰακώβ, ὁ ἐλεήμων καὶ οἰκτίρμων ὁ μακρόθυμος καὶ πολυέλεος, ᾧ πᾶσα γυμνοφανὴς βλέπεται καρδία καὶ πᾶν κρύφιον ἐνθύμημα ἀποκαλύπτεται πρὸς σὲ βοῶσιν ψυχαὶ δικαίων, ἐπὶ σοὶ πεποίθασιν ἐλπίδες ὁσίων, καὶ κατὰ πᾶν κλίμα τῆς οἰκουμένης τὸ διὰ προσευχῆς καὶ λόγων ἀναπέμπεταί σοι θυμίαμα.

Πᾶσι δὲ ἀνέῳξας πύλην ἐλεημοσύνης ὑπεδείξας δὲ ἑκάστῳ τῶν ἀνθρώπων ὡς πλούτου οὐκ ἀΐδιον τὸ κτῆμα, εὐπρεπείας οὐκ ἀέναον τὸ κάλλος, δυνάμεως εὐδιάλυτος ἡ ἰσχύς.

ὑπέρμαχε γένους Ἀβραάμ, εὐλογητὸς εἶ εἰς τοὺς αἰῶνας.

7.34

Εὐλογητὸς εἶ κύριε, βασιλεῦ τῶν αἰώνων, ὁ ποιήσας τὰ ὅλα.

(Praise of God for his power)

Ὁ ζωοποιὸς τῶν νεκρῶν.

7.35

Μέγας εἶ, κύριε καὶ μεγάλη ἡ ἰσχύς σου καὶ τῆς συνέσεώς σου οὐκ ἔστιν ἀριθμός, κτίστα, σωτήρ, καὶ Σεραφὶμ ἅγια ἅμα τοῖς Χερουβὶμ τοῖς ἑξαπτερύγοις σοι λέγοντα ἀσιγήτοις φωναῖς βοῶσιν, Ἅγιος, ἅγιος, ἅγιος κύριος Σαβαώθ, πλήρης ὁ οὐρανὸς καὶ ἡ γῆ τῆς δόξης σου, καὶ τὰ ἕτερα τῶν ἀγγέλων πλήθη, ἐπιβοῶντα λέγουσιν, Εὐλογημένη ἡ δόξα κυρίου ἐκ τοῦ τόπου αὐτοῦ. Ἰσραὴλ δέ, ἡ ἐπίγειός σου ἐκκλησία ἡ ἐξ ἐθνῶν, ταῖς κατ᾽ οὐρανὸν δυνάμεσιν ἁμιλλωμένη νυκτὶ καὶ ἡμέρᾳ ψάλλει, Τὸ ἅρμα τοῦ θεοῦ μυριοπλάσιον χιλιάδες εὐθηνούτων κύριος ἐν αὐτοῖς ἐν Σιναῒ ἐν τῷ ἁγίῳ.

Διὸ καὶ ὀφείλει πᾶς ἄνθρωπος ἐξ αὐτῶν τῶν στέρνων σοὶ τὸν ὑπὲρ πάντων ὕμνον ἀναπέμπειν, διὰ σὲ τῶν ἁπάντων κρατῶν. τὸ γὰρ σὸν αἰώνιον κράτος καὶ φλόγα καταψύχει καὶ λέοντας φιμοῖ καὶ κήτη καταπραΰνει καὶ νοσοῦντας ἐγείρει καὶ δυνάμεις μετατρέπει καὶ στρατὸν ἐχθρῶν καὶ λαὸν ἀριθμούμενον ἐν τῷ ὑπερηφανεύεσθαι καταστώννυσιν. σὺ εἶ ὁ ἐν οὐρανῷ, ὁ ἐπὶ γῆς, ὁ ἐν θαλάσσῃ, τῆς γὰρ μεγαλοσύνης σου οὐκ ἔστιν πέρας. μὴ γὰρ ἡμέτερόν ἐστιν τοῦτο, δέσποτα, τοῦ θεράποντός σου λόγιόν ἐστιν φάσκοντος, καὶ γνώσῃ τῇ καρδίᾳ σου, ὅτι κύριος ὁ θεός σου, θεὸς ἐν οὐρανῷ ἄνω καὶ ἐπὶ γῆς κάτω, καὶ οὐκ ἔστιν ἔτι πλὴν αὐτοῦ. οὐδὲ γὰρ ἔστι θεὸς πλὴν σοῦ μόνου ἅγιος οὐκ ἔστι πλὴν σοῦ, κύριος θεὸς γνώσεων, θεὸς ἁγίων, ἅγιος ὑπὲρ πάντας ἁγίους, οἱ γὰρ ἡγιασμένοι ὑπὸ τὰς χεῖράς σού εἰσιν.

Translation

7.33

Our eternal Savior, the king of the gods, God of our fathers, God of Abraham, Isaac and Jacob, the merciful and compassionate, the patient and very merciful, the one to whom every heart is seen as naked and (to whom) every hidden thought is revealed; to you the souls of the righteous cry out, upon you the hopes of the pious rely, and in every region of the inhabited earth, incense is sent up to you through prayer and words.

(You) opened to all the gate of mercy and showed to all mankind how the possession of wealth is not eternal, the beauty of comeliness is not everlasting, the strength of power is easily dissolved.

O Defender of the offspring of Abraham, blessed are you forever.

7.34

Blessed are you O Lord, king of the ages, who made the universe.

(Praise of God for his power)

O Quickener of the dead.

7.35

Great are you, O Lord and great is your strength, and of your understanding there is no measure, Creator, Savior. And the holy Seraphim together with the six winged Cherubim say to you and cry out with never-ceasing voices, "Holy, holy, holy Lord Sabaoth, heaven and earth are full of your glory." And the other multitudes of angels cry out and say, "Blessed is the glory of the Lord from his place." But Israel your earthly assembly from the nations, competing night and day with the powers in heaven sings, 'The chariot of God is ten thousand fold thousands of flourishing ones. The Lord is among them on Sinai."

Wherefore everyman ought to send up the hymn to you from their breasts for all things, since on account of you he has power over all things; for your eternal power both cools the flame, muzzles the lions, pacifies sea monsters, raises up those who are sick, turns back powers and lays low the army of enemies and the people numbered with those who behave arrogantly.

You are the one in heaven, on the earth, in the sea, for of your magnitude there is no limit; for this is not our (oracle) Master, it is your servant's oracle who says, "And know in your heart that the Lord your God is God in heaven above, earth below and there is none except him." For there is no God except you alone, no holy one but you, Lord God of knowledge, God of holy ones, holy above all holy ones; for they are sanctified by your hands.

7.36

Κύριε παντοκράτορ, κόσμον ἔκτισας καὶ σάββατον ὥρισας εἰς μνήμην τούτου, ὅτι ἐν αὐτῷ κατέπαυσας ἀπὸ τῶν ἔργων καὶ ἑορτὰς διετάξω εἰς εὐφροσύνην τῶν ἡμετέρων ψυχῶν.

σύ γάρ, κύριε, καὶ τοὺς πατέρας ἡμῶν ἐξήγαγες ἐκ γῆς Αἰγύπτου καὶ ἐρρύσω ἐκ καμίνου σιδηρᾶς καὶ ἐκ πηλοῦ καὶ πλινθουργίας, ἐλυτρώσω ἐκ χειρὸς Φαραῶ καὶ τῶν ὑπ' αὐτὸν καὶ διὰ θαλάσσης ὡς διὰ ξηρᾶς αὐτοὺς παρήγαγες καὶ ἐτροποφόρησας αὐτοὺς ἐν τῇ ἐρήμῳ παντοίοις ἀγαθοῖς. νόμον αὐτοῖς ἐδωρήσω δέκα λογίων σῇ φωνῇ φθεγχθέντα καὶ χειρὶ σῇ καταγραφέντα. σαββατίζειν ἐνετείλω, οὐ πρόφασιν ἀργίας διδούς, ἀλλ' ἀφορμὴν εὐσεβείας, εἰς γνῶσιν τῆς σῆς δυνάμεως, εἰς κώλυσιν κακῶν ὡς ἐν ἱερῷ καθείρξας περιβόλῳ διδασκαλίας χάριν εἰς ἀγαλλίαμα ἑβδομάδος. διὰ τοῦτο ἑβδομὰς μία καὶ ἑβδομάδες ἑπτὰ καὶ μὴν ἕβδομος καὶ ἐνιαυτὸς ἕβδομος καὶ τούτου κατὰ ἀνακύκλησιν ἔτος πεντηκοστὸν εἰς ἄφεσιν. ὅπως μηδεμίαν ἔχωσιν πρόφασιν ἄνθρωποι ἄγνοιαν σκήψασθαι τούτου χάριν πᾶν σάββατον ἐπέτρεψας ἀργεῖν, ὅπως μηδὲ λόγον τις ἐν ὀργῇ ἐκ τοῦ στόματος αὐτοῦ προέσθαι θελήσῃ ἐν τῇ ἡμέρᾳ τῶν σαββάτων.

7.37

Πλήρωσον τὰς ἐπαγγελίας τὰς διὰ τῶν προφητῶν καὶ ἐλέησον τὴν Σιὼν καὶ οἰτείρησον τὴν Ἰερουσαλὴμ καὶ ἀνυψῶσον τὸν θρόνον Δαυὶδ τοῦ παιδός σου ἐν μέσῳ αὐτῆς. δέσποτα ὁ θεός, πρόσδεξαι τὰς διὰ χειλέων δεήσεις τοῦ λαοῦ σοῦ τοῦ ἐπικαλουμένου σε ἐν ἀληθείᾳ.

7.38

Εὐχαριστοῦμέν σοι περὶ πάντων, δέσποτα ὅτι οὐκ ἐγκατέλιπες τὰ ἐλέη σου καὶ τοὺς οἰκτιρμούς σου ἀφ' ἡμῶν, ἀλλὰ καθ' ἑκάστην γενεὰν καὶ γενεὰν σώζεις, ῥύῃ, ἀντιλαμβάνῃ, σκεπάζεις καὶ ἀπὸ μαχαίρας γὰρ ἐρρύσω καὶ ἐκ λιμοῦ ἐξείλω διαθρέψας, ἐκ νόσου ἰάσω, ἐκ γλώσσης πονηρᾶς ἐσκέπασας. περὶ πάντων σοι εὐχαριστοῦμεν, ὁ καὶ φωνὴν ἔναρθρον εἰς ἐξομολόγησιν δωρησάμενος καὶ γλῶσσαν εὐάρμοστον δίκην πλήκτρου ὡς ὄργανον ὑποθείς, καὶ γεῦσιν πρόσφορον καὶ ἁφὴν κατάλληλον καὶ ὅρασιν θέας καὶ ἀκοὴν φωνῆς καὶ ὄσφρησιν ἀτμῶν καὶ χεῖρας εἰς ἔργον καὶ πόδας πρὸς ὁδοιπορίαν. ποῖος τοιγαροῦν αὐτάρκης βίος, αἰώνων δὲ μῆκος πόσον διαρκέσει ἀνθρώποις πρὸς εὐχαριστίαν; ἢ τὸ μὲν πρὸς ἀξίαν ἀδύνατον, τὸ δὲ κατὰ δύναμιν εὐαγές.

7.36

Lord, you created the world and set apart the Sabbath to remember this, because on it you rested from (your) works and you ordained feasts for the gladdening of our souls. For you, Lord, led our fathers out of Egypt and saved (them) from the iron furnace and from the clay and the making of bricks. You redeemed them from the hands of Pharoah and those under him, and you brought them through the sea as through dry land, and you endured their character in the wilderness with all sorts of good things. You gave them the law of ten oracles clearly expressed by your voice and written by your hand. You commanded them to keep the Sabbath; you confined (them) in the sacred precinct for the sake of teaching, for exultation in the number seven. On account of this (there are) one seven and seven sevens and a seventh month and a seventh year and according to this cycle the fiftieth year is for remission. (This is) so that men may have no excuse to plead ignorance. On account of this you entrusted (them) to keep every Sabbath that no one may desire to send forth a word from his mouth in anger on the day of the Sabbath.

7.37

Fulfill the promises of the prophets and have mercy on Zion and compassion on Jerusalem, and exalt the throne of David your servant in its midst. O Master, God, accept the entreaties from the lips of your people which call upon you in truth.

7.38

We give thanks to you for all things, Master, because you have not taken your mercies and compassions from us, but in each and every generation you save, rescue, help (and) protect. For you rescued (us) even from the sword and removed (us) from hunger and nourished (us), you healed (us) from disease, and protected (us) from an evil tongue.

For all things we give thanks to you who have also given (us) an articulate voice for confessing (you) and who have also added a harmonious tongue in the manner of the plectrum as an instrument; and useful taste, appropriate touch, sight for seeing, the hearing of a sound, the ability to smell vapors, hands for works and feet for walking.

Therefore what life is sufficient and what length of ages adequate to men to give thanks? Although it is impossible to give thanks as one ought, it is right to give thanks as one can.

CHART F

The Nishmath*

...ברעב זנתנו ובשבע כלכלתנו מחרב הצלתנו ומהבר מלטתנו מחלאים רעים ורבים
דליתנו עד הנה עזרונו רחמיך ולא עזבונו חסדים על כן אברים שפלגת בנו ורוח
ונשמה שנפחת באפינו ולשון ששמתה בפינה הן הן יודו ויברכו וישבחו ויפארו
וירוממו את שמך מלכנו...

Translation

...during famine thou didst feed us, and didst sustain us in plenty; from the sword thou didst deliver us, and from pestilence didst thou rescue us, from sore and manifold diseases didst thou relieve us. Hitherto thy tender mercies have helped us, and thy lovingkindnesses have not left us. Therefore the limbs which thou hast spread forth in us, and the spirit and soul which thou hast breathed into our nostrils, and the tongue which thou hast set in our mouth, lo, they shall thank and bless and praise and glorify and extol they name, O our King.

*Text and translation in Kronholm, *Seder R. Amram*, 69f., כא.

NOTES

CHAPTER V

[1]Kohler, "The Essene Version," 418; *Origins*, 251.

[2]Baumstark, *Comparative Liturgy*, 11.

[3]Goodenough, *By Light, Light*, 339.

[4]Bousset, *Nachrichten*, 461.

[5]For a discussion of the relationship between redactions and interpolations, see J. H. Charlesworth, "Reflections on the SNTS Pseudepigrapha Seminar at Duke on the Testaments of the Twelve Patriarchs," *NTS* 23 (1977) 297-304. It is often difficult to tell the difference between the two.

[6]M. P. Brown, *The Authentic Writings of Ignatius* (Durham, NC: Duke University, 1963).

[7]1.6.10, 2.16.1, 2,20.8f, 2.21.5, 2.24.7, 2.25.10, 2.59.2, 3.19.3, *5.2.4*, 5.15.2, 5.16.5, 6.19.3, 6.30.4, *7.1.2*, *7.22.6*, *7.26.2*, 7.41.7, 8.1.1, 8.5.2,7, 8.8.5, 8.9.10, 8.11.6, 8.12.33, 8.13.10, 8.46.13, 8.48.3. The citations in italics in all the notes denote passages which are clearly the compiler's own hand. See Funk's underlining of dissimilar material in AC books 1-6 and similar material in AC 7.1-32.

[8]I.e. 4:17^{r} in Ralfs, *Septuaginta*.

[9]See 1.8.1, *2.22.12*, 2.28.6f, 4.5.4, 5.7.1, *5.15.3*, 6.10.1, 6.11.1, 6.14.1, 6.26.1, 6.30.9, *6.30.10*, *7.25.3*, 7.26.3, *7.30.2*, 7.33.2, 7.35.1,7, 7.36.1, 7.38.1, 7.41.4, 7.43.2, 7.45.3, 7.47.2, 8.5.1,7, 8.6.11, 8.9.7. The citations in italics are clearly the compiler's hand.

[10]Brightman,(*Liturgies*, xxv) cites as his example ὁ εἷς καὶ μόνος ἀληθινὸς θεός (2.6.9, 2.56.1, 5.6.7, 5.16.3).

[11]Brown, *Authentic Writings*, 50f. See *Tar.* 2, *Hero* ins.

[12]*2.26.5*, *3.3.1*, *6.14.3*, *6.15.1*, *6.16.4*, *7.26.3*, *7.30.2*, 7.33.2, 8.4.2, 8.5.6,7, 8.10.9, 8.11.4, 8.12.49, 8.18.3, 8.41.8, 8.48.3. It is obvious that in all passages where this word is found, and where we also know the compiler's source and thus can check, the word has come from the compiler. It is not clear if this word was in the Apostolic Tradition (at AC 8.4.2 and 8.18.3) or not since the Latin text is defective here. See Dix, *Apostolic Tradition*, 3, 17f.

[13]Kohler, "The Essene Version," 410. The patriarchs are spoken of as "our fathers" or "the fathers" at AC 2.14.14 (Didascalia), 2.22.12,18 (Didascalia), *7.26.3*, 7.33.1, 7.36.3. But contrast 8.12.24 which speaks of the patriarchs as "their fathers."

[14]The compiler often strings together scriptures to embellish his topics; see Chapter II.

[15] *2.14.3, 2.57.4, 3.3.2, 4.1.2, 4.5.4, 6.4.1, 6.6.4, 6.10.1, 6.14.4, 6.16.3, 6.23.3, 6.28.8*, 7.33.2, 7.34.5, 7.35.10, 7.39.2, 8.12.8,30, 8.15.4. συνείδησις is only used once where we can compare AC with the source: *2.54.1*, 7.33.2,3, 8.47.53.

[16] θυμίαμα: *2.26.8, 6.1.3*, 6.22.3, *7.30.2*, 7.33.2, 8.47.3; οἰκουμένη: 6.18.11, *6.20.5*, 6.22.4, 7.33.2.

[17] *1.6.8**, 2.43.3, *6.12.13*, 6.19.2*, 6.20.4*, 6.22.5*, 6.23.1*, 6.23.2, 6.25.2, 6.27.7, 6.28.3, 6.28.7,8, 6.30.1, 7.1.3*, 7.33.3, 8.12.25*, 8.12.30*. Those in italics are clearly from the compiler; the asterisk denotes a reference to natural law.

[18] Kohler, "The Essene Version," 411; Goodenough, *By Light, Light*, 332f.

[19] πλοῦτος: 1.8.12, 2.36.8, *4.4.2, 4.4.4, 4.6.7*, 5.5.3, 5.5.3, 7.33.3. ἀΐδιον: 5.6.7, 6.11.1, 7.33.3, 7.35.10, 7.39.3. εὐπρεπεία: 1.8.10, *3.9.4*, 7.33.3, 7.35.9. κτῆμα: 1.8.5, *2.48.2, 5.6.1*, 7.29.3, 7.33.3. ἀέναος: 7.33.3, 7.35.9, 8.12.14. εὐδιάλυτος: not listed. κάλλος: 1.3.8, *1.8.13*, 1.8.21, *5.20.8*, 7.33.3. No argument can be made either way from the vocabulary alone. At 7.35.9, however, εὐπρεπεία is used with ἀέναος as it is in 7.33.3. This may be accidental or the vocabulary in 7.33 may have influenced the compiler in 7.35.9 (we shall argue that 7.35.9 is from the compiler). This similarity does not seem to be sufficient evidence to attribute this section in 7.33.3 to the compiler.

[20] ἄτμος: 7.33.3, 7.38.4. ματαιότης: 2.61.1, *6.5.5*, 7.33.3, 7.39.3, 8.46.4. σύνολος: not listed.

[21] παλιγγενεσία: *5.7.14*, 7.33.3, 7.34.8, 7.39.4, 7.43.3, 8.6.6, 8.12.20. τρυφή may be a favorite term: *5.5.3*, 7.33.3, 7.43.4, 8.12.19. The last two passages use the word in reference to the pleasure of paradise (i.e. the Garden of Eden).

[22] For the Christian employment of the notion of rebirth, see W. C. Grese, *Corpus Hermeticum XIII and Early Christian Literature* (Leiden: Brill, 1979).

[23] See Goodenough (*By Light, Light*, 356) who follows MS a ("knowledge came before faith"). See the note in Chapter III on AC 7.33.4. MS a is alone in this reading, however. Peterson (*Miscellanea*, vol. 1, 414-17) was convinced that there is an anti-Gnostic polemic here.

[24] See J. H. Charlesworth, "Christian and Jewish Self-definition in Light of the Christian Additions to the Apocryphal Writings," *Judaism from the Maccabees to the Mid-Third Century*, ed. E. P. Sanders and A. I. Baumgarten (Philadelphia: Fortress, in press). Charlesworth notes that Christian elements often are grammatically loosely connected to their context. For example, a prepositional phrase or genitival construction may be the only Christian element.

[25] Bousset, *Nachrichten*, 455-57.

[26] Goodenough, *By Light, Light*, 325.

[27] Brightman, *Liturgies*, xxv, and see above under 7.33.

[28] *2.19.2, 2.25.7, 6.10.2, 6.11.7, 6.23.5, 6.30.10*, 7.34.6*, 7.35.10, 7.38.5*, 8.9.8*, 8.12.17*, 8.15.7, 8.37.5*, 8.37.6, 8.41.4*. The asterisk denotes where λόγικος is a special characteristic of man.

[29]Greek text in W. Cureton, *Corpus Ignatianum* (London: Rivington, 1849) 144.

[30]στρατός is found only in 7.35.3,7; φλέγω only in 5.7.15 (in Didascalia), 6.1.1 (in Didascalia), 7.35.3; νοερός is not listed; φελμουνί 7.35.1; σεραφίμ 7.35.3, 8.12.8,27; χερουβίμ 6.30.9 (in Didascalia), 7.35.3, 7.47.3, 8.12.8,27; ἐξαπτέρυγος not listed; ἐπινίκιον not listed; ἅρμα 7.35.4.

[31]*Praef. ad Dan.*

[32]S. Jellicoe, *The Septuagint and Modern Study* (Oxford: Clarendon, 1968) 84-87.

[33]ᾠδη *3.7.7*, 5.10.1, *5.20.8*, *6.22.4*, 7.35.3; ψάλλω *1.5.2*, *2.57.6*, *2.58.4*, *2.59.2*, *3.7.7*, *5.20.8*, *6.30.2*, 7.35.3,4, 8.14.1, 8.34.10.

[34]See Brightman, *Liturgies*, 50, 385.

[35]See E. Werner, "The Doxology in Synagogue and Church," 298.

[36]D. Flusser, "Sanktus und Gloria," *Abraham unser Vater. Festschrift für Otto Michel*, ed. O. Betz, M. Hengel and P. Schmidt (Leiden: Brill, 1963) 131-47.

[37]2 En 21:1 in Charles (*Apocrypha and Pseudepigrapha*, 442) also contains this reading but the *tersanctus* is absent from his B recension.

[38]*6.27.6*, *7.32.3*, 7.35.3, 8.12.8, 8.12.27.

[39]Bousset, *Nachrichten*, 437; Goodenough, *By Light, Light*, 307.

[40]Or perhaps some term (λέγω e.g.) other than ψάλλω stood in the text. See the Hebrew version.

[41]Perhaps here there originally stood προσεύχη instead of ὕμνος since this is only found in material from the compiler in AC: *1.5.2*, *2.57.6*, *3.7.7*, 7.35.6, 7.48.3.

[42]This phrase emphasizes the preeminence of the Father. See Brightman, *Liturgies*, xxv; Brown, *Authentic Writings*, 50f.

[43]χρητός not listed; φιλόδωρος 7.35.7; φλόξ 2.22.25 (in Didascalia), 7.35.7; φιμόω not listed; μετατρέπω not listed; ὑπερηφανεύω not listed, but its cognate ὑπερηφανία 7.18.1 (in Didache), ὑπερηφανός 1.3.2 (in Didascalia), 7.5.1 (in Didache), 8.2.7; καταστρώννυμι not listed.

[44]O. Michel, *Der Brief in die Hebräer* (Göttingen: Vandenhoeck und Ruprecht, 1949) 278f.

[45]To stress the uniqueness of the Father is typical of the compiler, but he does so usually with such phrases as μόνος ἀληθινὸς θεός (Brightman, *Liturgies*, xxv) or especially ἀγέννητος 7.39.2, 7.41.4, 7.42.3, 7.44.2, 7.47.2, 8.5.1, 8.6.8, 8.6.11, 8.12.6f, 8.14.3, 8.48.3; Brown, *Authentic Writings*, 53, *Hero* 6.

[46]Brightman, *Liturgies*, xxiv. The vocabulary is common for the AC: ἀόρατος 7.35.9, 8.5.1*, 8.15.7*; ἀνεξιχνίαστος 2.22.12 (in Didascalia), 7.35.19; ἀνενδεής *6.20.4*, 7.35.9, 8.5.1, 8.12.6*;

ἄτρεπτος 5.8.2 (in Didascalia) 7.35.9, 8.5.7, 8.11.4 (of people), 8.12.49 (of people), 8.18.3 (adverbially), 8.48.3 (adv.); ἀνελλιπής 7.35.9, 8.16.5; ἀκάματος 7.35.9; ἀπερίγραφος 7.35.9; ἀπρόσιτος *6.11.1* (1 Tim 6:16), 7.35.9, *7.47.2*, 8.5.1, 8.6.11, 8.15.7 (1 Tim 6:16); ἀμετανόστευτος 7.35.9; ἄναρχος *6.8.2* (of Gnostic gods), *6.10.2* (of Gnostic gods), *6.11.1*, 7.35.9, 8.5.1, 8.11.2, 8.12.6, 8.12.7, 8.37.2; ἀναλλοίωτος 7.35.9, 8.15.7; ἀμεσίτευτος 7.35.9, 8.12.7; ἀνεπιβούλευτος 7.35.9; ἀδίαχος 7.35.9; ἀτελεύτητος *5.7.7* (of Hell), 7.35.9, 7.46.15 (of time), 8.12.50 (of time), 8.37.1 (of God), 8.38.5 (of God), 8.41.4 (of God); ἀνανταγώνιστος 7.35.9. Asterisk denotes especially close parallels.

[47] Kohler, "The Essene Version," 417.

[48] Goodenough (*By Light, Light*, 308) apparently tried to eliminate this contradiction--since he claimed both passages were from the Jewish source--by translating the phrase in paragraph nine "whose work is not one of mediation." Migne (*Patrologia Graeca*, vol. 1, col. 1031) thought this only meant that God does not do anything incompletely: "Crediderim ἀμεσίτευτον ἔργον esse, quod nullis instrumentis aliunde desumptis perfectum est, ut sit idem ac ἄμεσον ἔργον, seu ut loquimur hodie, immediatum opus."

[49] Bousset, *Nachrichten*, 445.

[50] AC *2.36.2*, *2.59.3*, *5.20.19*, *7.23.3*f; also see Ps-Ignatius *Magn*. 9.

[51] See Prov 8:22.

[52] Goodenough, *By Light, Light*, 311f. Notice MS d tried to clean up the theology here. See Chapter III, on 7.36.1.

[53] Bousset, *Nachrichten*, 443; Goodenough, *By Light, Light*, 312.

[54] Kohler, "The Essene Version," 420; Bouyer, *Eucharist*, 131.

[55] Goodenough, *By Light, Light*, 312.

[56] See Chapter III, on 7.36.2.

[57] See above under *AC 7.33*.

[58] ἑβδομάς is found with the meaning of "week" in 2.16.2, 2.27.6 5.13.4, *5.20.14*f, *5.20.18*, 8.46.2, 8.47.37. No where else does it celebrate the ἑβδομάς as in 7.36.4.

[59] Translation from Birnbaum, *Daily Prayer Book*, 268.

[60] Ibid., 270.

[61] Translation from Dugmore, *Influence*, 122.

[62] The reference to the throne of David is not now found in the fifth benediction or the corresponding 17th Babylonian and 16th Palestinian benedictions of the Shemoneh Esreh, but in the 14th benediction of the Babylonian Shemoneh Esreh.

[63] This is the only place in AC where Zion is mentioned. Jerusalem is mentioned more often: *2.15.1*, 2.22.4,7,8,9,15,*17*, *2.49.3*, *2.60.1*, *5.12.6*, *6.5.7*, 6.12.1,3, 7.37.1,3, 8.2.4. David is referred to very often (see Funk's index).

[64]Greek text in M. Black, *Apocalypsis Henochi Graechi* (PVTG 3; Leiden: Brill, 1970) 19.

[65]Arndt and Gingrich, *Greek Lexicon*, 311.

[66]See *7.26.4*, 8.9.9, 8.16.4, 8.37.6, 8.38.4, 8.39.4, 8.41.5.

[67]Kohler, "The Essene Version," 421.

[68]It is interesting, however, that the Selichot prayers have lists similar to this. See, e.g., Taanith 2:4, "May he that answered Abraham our father in mount Moriah answer you and hearken to the voice of your crying this day....May he that answered our fathers at the Red Sea...Joshua in Gilgal...Samuel at Mizpeh... Elijah in Carmel...Jonah in the belly of the fish...David and his son Solomon in Jerusalem" (translation in H. Danby, *The Mishnah* [Oxford: University Press, 1933] 196). See L. I. Rabinowitz, "Selihot," *Encyclopedia Judaica*, vol. 14, cols. 1133f. For more examples, see Birnbaum, *Daily Prayer Book*, 683-86, 689-92, and Sirach 44-50, Wisdom 10-19, 4 Macc 16:20f. See also H. Thyen, *Der Stil der jüdisch-hellenistischen Homilie* (Göttingen: Vandenhoeck und Ruprecht, 1955) 11-39. However, we saw in Chapter IV that Christians also were accustomed to using such lists. Perhaps the practice of using the lists is borrowed from Judaism, but this particular list would seem to be the compiler's work.

[69]We pointed out in Chapter IV that προσεύχη was the usual translation for תפילה, but we have asserted that the clause containing προσεύχη is additional. Perhaps the source had προσεύχη instead of δέησις but the compiler preferred the latter in paragraph one and at the redundant paragraph five, more closely imitated his source.

[70]Except for παντοκράτωρ. εὐχαριστέω *2.36.6*, *4.5.1*, 6.23.3, 7.25.2, 7.25.4, 7.26.1, 7.26.2, 7.26.6, *7.27.1*, 7.27.2, 7.28.1, 7.28.2, 7.30.1, 7.38.1,4, 7.39.4, 7.43.2f, 8.1.1, 8.12.3,33,38, 8.14.2, 8.15.1. ῥύομαι not listed. ἀντιλαμβάνομαι 3.3.1, 5.3.1, 7.38.1,2,3, 8.6.5. σκεπάζω not listed.

[71]Bousset, *Nachrichten*, 447; Goodenough, *By Light, Light*, 314.

[72]Kohler, "The Essene Version," 422-24.

[73]The vocabulary here is not typical of the compiler: μαχαίρα 1.7.8, 2.6.10, 2.6.11, 2.42.5 (all in Didascalia). The compiler prefers to use the word ξίφος for sword: *5.16.9*, *6.21.2*. This term is atticistic, a tendency recognized in Ps-Ignatius (Brown, *Authentic Writings*, 62. See also AC 8.12.10, double ττ for σσ, an atticism.). λίμος *2.4.7*, 2.14.4, *4.6.4*, 7.38.3; ἐξαιρέω not listed; νόμος is too common to both the sources and compiler to be of value here; ἰάομαι *2.14.2*, 2.18.8, 2.20.3, *2.21.4*, 2.22.15, *5.7.27*, 6.28.7, 7.38.3.

[74]Perles, "Notes Critique," 101f.

[75]Birnbaum, *Daily Prayer Book*, 332. It is found in Birnbaum in the Sabbath morning service, before the Shema and the benedictions.

[76]Ibid., 334.

[77]*Magn.* 11, *Trall.* 6, *Philad.* 6.

[78]χορηγεῖς τροφήν. Cf. 8.12.6,22.

CHAPTER VI

LITERARY AND HISTORICAL QUESTIONS

The reconstructed text of the prayers effects different conclusions about their history prior to being incorporated in the AC. Scholars who have assumed the essential integrity of the text (except for some obvious Christian interpolations) used additional data in the form of redactional elements in drawing conclusions about date, provenance, milieu and original language. Now that most of the redactional material has been removed, the picture of the history of the prayers changes.

The Prayers an Oral Source or a Document?

We have in the previous chapters intentionally used the inexact terms "source" or "stratum" to describe the Jewish material of AC 7.33-38. Although every scholar has assumed that the source was written, it is impossible to be certain whether the compiler used a document or an oral source. If he used a written source, it may have been produced by a Christian who attended the synagogue and appropriated the prayers for the church, since there is some indication that Jews did not begin to write down the statutory prayers of the synagogue until the Gaonic era (c. A.D. 600-1000).[1] The Christian copyist, who had become accustomed to hearing the prayers recited in the synagogue and had come to appreciate their spiritual value, wrote down the prayers as he heard them recited. Although much of the wording would change from time to time depending upon who recited the prayers, the content of the prayers, the order, and even some of the actual phrases were fixed by this time.[2] Thus, these prayers may represent one person's recitation, or version, of the prayers in one geographical area. It is unlikely that the compiler of AC was the Christian who wrote down the prayers, since his strong anti-Judaism and his exhortations against synagogue participation would hardly have allowed him to frequent the synagogue (see below under "Date," p. 220).

But the compiler could just as well have obtained the prayers from an oral source(s). In this case, Christians (again it is not likely that the compiler was one of them) frequented the synagogue, appropriated the prayers and began to repeat them in their churches.

The compiler later incorporated into his work these prayers, which were in use in his church.

It is difficult now to discover the nature of the compiler's source (i.e. written or oral). In either case it seems reasonable to suppose that a Christian(s) prior to the compiler has contributed somewhat to the text of the prayers, whether it was the Christian who wrote down the prayers as he heard them recited in the synagogue, or the Christians who passed them on orally in their community. Evidence of any Christian redactional elements in the prayers other than the compiler's, however, is lacking. In the first place, the redactional material which we extracted from the prayers can easily be understood as the compiler's. Nothing in this material is out of place with the compiler's theological tendencies and expressions. Second, no tensions or repetitions in the reconstructed text are evident. Therefore, although one would expect *a priori* that Christians prior to the compiler contributed to the wording and content of the text, the evidence indicates either that their contribution was slight, or that one cannot now discover it. Perhaps this lack of evidence for Christian elements in the prayers can best be explained by assuming that the prayers were written down. One would expect the wording and content in a written copy of prayers to be less fluid than in a living oral tradition which was modified virtually everytime the prayers were recited.

At any rate, we should not speak of the prayers as one composition, but as compositions; we should not refer to a composer, but composers; we should not assign a date of composition, but a formative period, for the prayers are the community product of several generations of piety and worship. They were passed on orally for decades, perhaps centuries, in the synagogue, appropriated by Christians and handed down again--whether in written or oral form--for decades (see under "Date") until the compiler discovered them.

Original Language

Kohler, Bousset and Goodenough believed that Greek was the original language of the prayers. The use of the Septuagint in quoting the OT as well as the "Alexandrian or Philonic accentuation of the *Logos*...and the Wisdom" demonstrated to Kohler that the prayers had come from "Hellenic culture." The references to the Logos, however, were only in Kohler's reconstruction of the prayers where he substituted "Logos" for a reference to "Christ."[3]

Bousset and Goodenough believed that the prayers were composed in Greek using Aquila's version,[4] and later the Septuagint quotations were substituted for Aquila. Some vestiges of Aquila's version remain, however.[5] We shall analyze this view further below.

Bouyer contended that Alexandrian Judaism composed the prayers in Greek, but the author(s) had worked with Hebrew sources. He concluded this, evidently, solely by the appearance of the transliteration φελμουνί for פלמוני in the text (AC 7.35.3) in a quotation of Dan 7:13. That the composer "stumbles over expressions like Phelmoni is revealing," writes Bouyer. It shows that his knowledge of Hebrew was "rudimentary," that he worked with Hebrew sources, and that there "never was an Alexandrian Judaism, no matter how hellenized, that became really independent from Palestinian traditions."[6] Bouyer seems to have been unaware of the fact that φελμουνί appears in the Septuagint, Aquila's, and Theodotion's versions as a transliteration, and that the "composer" could have merely quoted from one of those versions, without using Hebrew sources. Indeed, in Chapter V, we argued that the compiler of AC himself had inserted the quotation based on Theodotion's version. By the compiler's time Theodotion had replaced the Septuagint for the translation of Daniel and the compiler almost exclusively quotes Daniel elsewhere from Theodotion (see above, Chapter V).

Since the Seven Benedictions, the Kedusha, and the Nishmath were originally recited in Hebrew (and are preserved in Hebrew), the Jewish prayers in AC must go back to some point to Hebrew originals. This assumption is confirmed in the prayers of AC 7.33-38 by the several verbal parallels there to the Hebrew Seven Benedictions, the Kedusha and the Nishmath (see the underlined portions of Charts C and F). For example, AC 7.38 contains the Hebrew idiom γενεὰν καὶ γενεάν (for דר ודר) which also appears in the Seven Benedictions at this point.

Additional evidence of a Semitic background for the prayers exists in AC 7.33 (see the reconstructed text, Chart E). In the first paragraph two distichs of *parallelismus membrorum*[7] appear:

> the one to whom every heart is seen as naked
> and (to whom) every hidden thought is revealed; (synonymous)
>
> to you the souls of the righteous cry out,
> upon you the hopes of the pious rely... (synonymous)

The second paragraph contains a tristich:

> the possession of wealth is not eternal,
> the beauty of comeliness is not everlasting,
> the strength of power is easily dissolved... (synthetic).[8]

In the last example, each line comprises a simple Semitic pattern: noun, construct and predicate. Poetic parallelism is not as distinct in the other Jewish prayers of AC. Only two other passages are possibly parallel:

> For there is no God except you alone,
> no holy one but you... (AC 7.35, synonymous).
>
> Fulfill the promises of the prophets
> and have mercy on Zion
> and compassion on Jerusalem
> and exalt the throne of David your servant in its midst...
> (AC 7.37, synthetic).

Parallelismus membrorum is very rare in the other prayers of AC books seven and eight. The only other example is at AC 8.15.2:[9]

> who hears those who call upon you with uprightness,
> who knows the supplications of those who are silent...
> (synonymous).

Such rarity supports the conclusion that the poetic parallelism of 7.33--and perhaps of 7.35 and 7.37--represents a Semitic original, since poetic parallelism is a Semitic construction. Of course it is possible that someone composed the prayers in Greek and produced the parallelism from imitation of the Septuagint.

Finally, the prayers bear some evidence of being translation Greek. In a recent work devoted to discovering translation Greek (from a Semitic source), R. A. Martin[10] attempted to show that certain syntactical features become numerous in translation Greek which are rare in documents originally composed in Greek, just as certain features common in composition Greek are rare in translation Greek.

He first lists six prepositions which are common in composition Greek (διά with gen. and acc., εἰς, κατά and περί with all cases, πρός with dat., ὑπό with gen.), but rarer in translations of Semitic originals. In the translations, ἐν is the most common preposition because both Hebrew and Aramaic use the preposition ב most often, and there are seldom any expressions in the Semitic languages which would normally take the other Greek prepositions as their equivalents. This evidence in the prayers of AC yields no firm conclusion (see Table I), but ἐν is the most frequent preposition (ten times) used in the prayers, with εἰς (eight times) being the second most frequent.

The second line of evidence listed by Martin is the comparison of the use of καί and δέ. He maintains that "those documents known to be a translation of Semitic sources have in every case more than two καί's copulative for every δέ...," but in composition Greek there are fewer καί's copulative than δέ's. There are considerably more καί's than δέ's in our prayers (see Table I). This statistic, then, supports our suggestion that AC 7.33-38 is based upon a Semitic source.

Martin next lists eight criteria for determining translation Greek:

1) The article is rarely separated from its substantive. The article (in Hebrew) is never separated from its substantive (Aramaic has the emphatic state), but is attached directly to it. Thus rarity of separation of the article from its substantive indicates a Semitic original.

2) The dependent genitives in translation Greek rarely preceed the word on which they depend. This relationship represents the construct state (and in Aramaic the particle די).

3) Translation Greek contains more dependent genitive personal pronouns than composition Greek. The genitive pronouns in Semitic languages are formed by attaching suffixes to the substantive.

4) Translation Greek has more genitive personal pronouns dependent upon anarthrous substantives since in the Semitic languages nouns do not usually have articles when they also have pronominal suffixes.

5) Translation Greek displays fewer attributive adjectives preceding the word they qualify, since in Hebrew and Aramaic adjectives usually follow the word they qualify.

6) There are fewer attributive adjectives employed in translation Greek, reflecting the dearth of adjectives in Hebrew and Aramaic and the frequency of the construct relationship.

7) Translation Greek has few adverbial or circumstantial participles since the Semitic languages do not use participles in this manner.

8) The dative case is infrequent in translation Greek. Because there is no dative case in the Semitic languages, this relationship is expressed with ב which is translated ἐν.[11]

Table I indicates that some of these criteria--though not all of them--are significant for the prayers of AC 7.33-38. There are no adverbial participles, adjectives rarely precede nouns, genitives almost always follow nouns and the article is rarely separated from its substantive. The latter practice contrasts sharply with the compiler's tendency to encase phrases between a noun and a substantive (i.e. a participle, see above, Chapter V).

TABLE I

Syntactical Evidence of a
Semitic Background to AC 7.33-38

Prepositions				Datives
ἐν	κατά	πρός	διά	
10	3	0	6	0
εἰς	ὑπό	περί		
8	0	0		

καί	δέ
42	3

Genitives

preceding noun: 3	following noun: 30
dependent genitive personal pronouns: 6	dependent genitive personal pronouns with anarthrous substantives: 0

Adjectives preceding noun	Attributive Adjectives
6	12

Article separate from substantive	Adverbial participle
3	0

Thus there is some evidence that the prayers have a Semitic background. First, verbal parallels exist between the prayers and their Hebrew equivalents. Secondly, several examples of a Semitic poetic form *parallelismus membrorum*--a phenomenon rare in the AC--appear, though this could be merely imitation of the Septuagint. Thirdly, Martin's syntactical evidence for a Semitic background indicates that the prayers often reflect Semitic syntax rather than that commonly employed in Greek writings.

Yet at some point the prayers must have been translated into Greek--probably by Jews since Christians would ordinarily not speak Hebrew.[12] After they were translated, the practice of oral recitation with reference to a traditional model probably continued. Thus, there may be--one would expect there to be--material in the prayers from the Greek-speaking Jewish community. It appears that the Pythagorean emphasis on the number seven as justification for the Sabbath observance is propaganda (see below) and reflects a diaspora setting where Gentiles are being converted to Judaism. There is nothing in the Hebrew prayer book parallel to this notion. If there are any other elements from the Greek-speaking Jewish community, they are now impossible to discern. One would assume, however, that the prayers are more than mere literal translations.

Tradition and Literary History of the Prayers

The state of the prayers in the AC can best be explained by postulating four stages in the history of the prayers. First, the Seven Benedictions circulated orally in Hebrew. Each person reciting the Seven Benedictions composed his prayers in a semi-impromptu manner, but with reference to the standardized model of content, order, and some expressions as Heinemann has maintained.[13] Later they were translated into Greek, whether in Palestine--even in Palestine the synagogues employed Greek, for the Jerusalem Talmud, Sota 7:1, 21b, informs us that in Caesarea there were Jews who read the Shema in Greek[14]--or in the diaspora, and continued to circulate orally, finally making their way to Syria (see below). Thirdly, the prayers were appropriated by Christians who attended the synagogue. Finally, the compiler obtained the prayers and redacted them to suit his purposes (see Table II).

As we mentioned above, Bousset and Goodenough suggested that the prayers were composed using Aquila's version and that a later editor (Christian to Bousset; mystic Jewish to Goodenough)[15] replaced the quotations from Aquila with quotations from the Septuagint,[16] but leaving behind vestiges of Aquila's version. We must emphasize, in the first place, that only one word remains that is peculiar to Aquila[17] (ὁραματισμός). It is possible that the compiler knew and used this word, since he lived and worked 250 years after Aquila completed his version of the OT. At least the word stands now in what we believe is a redactional section of AC 7.33.4 (see Chapter V above). Thus, it is unwise to accept the thesis of Bousset and Goodenough, based as it is on such meagre evidence.

Provenance

Kohler, Bousset and Goodenough refused to locate specifically the geographical origin of the prayers. They merely maintained that diaspora Judaism had produced them.[18] Bousset maintained that the statement in AC 7.33 ("and in every region of the inhabited

TABLE II

Tradition-History of the Prayers in AC 7.33-38

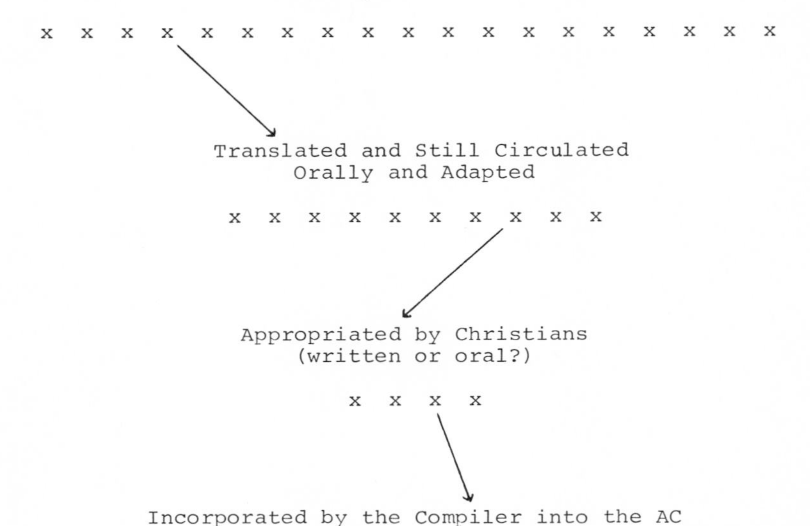

earth, incense is sent up to you through prayer and words") is strongly suggestive of diaspora Judaism.[19] A similar clause, however, appears in Mal 1:11. Although the Greek of AC 7.33 is not the same as the Septuagint of Malachi (no fragments of the other versions remain), the Malachi passage does demonstrate that a Palestinian Jew could make such a statement. Thus Bousset's assertion seems unconvincing. Bouyer assumed an Alexandrian provenance for the prayers, but offered no evidence for this assumption.[20]

Nothing in the text of the prayers serves to identify the specific geographical provenance as one would expect since the prayers were composed and at first transmitted orally. Although one would assume that the Hebrew form of the prayers originated in Palestine, external evidence exists to suggest that it was in Syria that Christians appropriated these prayers and transmitted them to the compiler of AC. Chapter II introduced us to the sources of the AC. All of the known sources but one, the Apostolic Tradition, originated in Syria, according to the consensus of opinion, and the AC itself was compiled in Syria. Although the Apostolic Tradition is a product of the Roman Hippolytus, it became popular in the East as the basis for the Egyptian Church Order in Egypt and the Testament of our Lord in Syria.[21] Thus even the Apostolic Tradition can be linked to Syria. One can conclude, then, *prima facie*, that the Jewish prayers were appropriated from Syrian synagogues since it appears that the compiler simply used sources that were readily available to him in Syria.

The relationship between Judaism and Christianity in Syria in the second, third, and fourth centuries A.D. supports this conclusion. Scholars are recognizing more and more the Jewish character of Syrian Christianity and the intimate contacts between church and synagogue in Syria. A recent article by B. D. Spinks emphasizes this point.

> East Syrian Christianity (though *not* exclusively so!) provides us with an area in which Jewish liturgy could very well have exerted an influence on the developing anaphora.[22]

R. Murray maintains that the Christianity of Adiabene[23] was merely a "breakaway movement among the Jewish community...."[24] Archaeologists have discovered in the ruins of the ancient city of Dura that, during the third century, a synagogue and a church stood in close proximity to one another.[25] Needless to say, such geographical proximity could have facilitated the interchange of ideas. Jews and Christians were apparently not separated into quarters or ghettos.

But we should also look to Western Syria as the provenance, because the interchange between Jews and Christians was continuous in that region. It was in Antioch, the center and capital of Syria, that according to Josephus, the Jews of that province were concentrated. Josephus wrote that, although Jews had spread throughout the entire empire, they were

> particularly numerous in Syria....But it was at Antioch that they specially congregated....Moreover, they were constantly attracting to their religious ceremonies multitudes of Greeks, and these they had in some measure incorporated with themselves.[26]

A bilingual city[27] with a large Jewish population,[28] Antioch proved the ideal site for the continued influence of Judaism upon Christianity. Of this city Meeks and Wilken write:

> The active influence of Judaism upon Christianity in Antioch was perennial until Christian leaders succeeded at last in driving the Jews from the city in the seventh century.[29]

Quite likely in this city, around the end of the first century, the Odes of Solomon, "the earliest Christian hymnbook"[30]--and one so influenced by Jewish thought and expression that some scholars have concluded that they were written by Jews or from a Jewish *Grundschrift*[31]--were composed. Here Ignatius, bishop of Antioch in the early second century, wrote letters to the Magnesians (8:1f) warning that living "according to Judaism" is a denial of Christian grace, and to the Philadelphians (6:1) commanding, "if anyone interpret Judaism to you do not listen to him...."[32] As Meeks and Wilken suggest, these polemical passages may be aimed at problems in Magnesia and Philadelphia, but, "almost certainly they reflect also Ignatius' experience of Judaeo-Christians in Antioch."[33] What upset Ignatius apparently was that Christians, evidently under Jewish influences, were adopting Jewish practices, not that Jewish Christians continued to practice Judaism along with their new faith.

The latter part of the second century also witnessed a close contact between Jews and Christians in Antioch. Some seventy years after Ignatius, Theophilus of Antioch (c. 180) penned his treatise to Autolycus. His exegetical method indicates that he had been thoroughly influenced by Judaism. R. M. Grant states:

> Almost everything in his exegesis can be paralleled in Jewish haggadic literature.[34]

It is even reported by Eusebius (*H.E.* 6.12.1) that a certain Christian named Domninus was converted to Judaism around A.D. 200 and that this conversion occasioned a letter from his bishop Serapion.

The evidence is less clear for the third century. To Paul of Samosata, bishop of Antioch from A.D. 260-272, was given the epithet "a Jew wearing a Christian mask."[35] Meeks and Wilken, however, are cautious about taking this accusation seriously, and conclude that all we can say for sure about Paul is that his *Christology* sounded "Jewish" to Orthodox ears.[36] G. Downey also implies that Paul's theological offense was merely his Christology.[37] Paul was also accused of practicing circumcision, but modern scholars doubt this as well.[38] Lucian of Antioch (c. 280) established a school of exegesis based, according to some scholars, upon Jewish models, and his successor, Dorotheus was learned in Hebrew.[39] Whether or not they studied with Jewish teachers is questioned,[40] though it is difficult to imagine how in the third century one could learn Hebrew anywhere else.[41] C. H. Kraeling concluded that Paul, Lucian, and Dorotheus testify "to an immediate and sympathetic contact with the Jewish scholars of the vicinity."[42] That Paul and Lucian witness to such contact, however, is not certain (though a good possibility), but Dorotheus surely does.

Finally, John Chrysostom in the fourth century, roughly contemporaneous with the compiler of AC, preached a series of eight sermons against the Jews of Antioch (c. A.D. 386). The Christians were being lured to the worship in the synagogue, and Chrysostom believed that he must attack the Judaism which seemed so attractive. Chrysostom asked, "How then can you go into a synagogue? If you make the sign of the cross on your brow, the evil power which dwells in the synagogue flees." Chrysostom maintained:

> The Jews frighten you as though you were little children and you don't even realize it. For just as coarse slaves will show ridiculous and terrifying masks to children... and make them laugh loudly; so also the Jews terrify simple Christians. How can the Jewish synagogues be considered worthy of awe when they are shameful and ridiculous, offensive, dishonored, and contemptible?

He was especially worried that the Judaizing Christians would apostacize during the upcoming feasts.

> The festivals of the wretched and miserable Jews which follow one after another in succession--Trumpets, Booths, the Fasts--are about to take place. And many who belong to us and say that they believe in our teaching, attend their festivals, and even share in their celebrations and join in their fasts.

He urged, in a later homily, "...when you see God punishing you, don't flee to your enemies the Jews...."[43] As Meeks and Wilken point out, the fierceness of his invective only indicates "a widespread Christian infatuation with Judaism."[44]

The *Sitz im Leben* in Syria, then, explains how Jewish prayers could be accepted by Christians and even incorporated into a Christian document. Someone or some group of people had an intimate enough association with Jews, probably by attending the synagogue, to discover the Seven Benedictions, and appreciate them so much that they would appropriate them for their worship, whether public or private. As we shall see below, it is doubtful that the compiler of the AC himself borrowed the prayers from Judaism, since he has a definite anti-Jewish bias. It is more likely that he inherited the prayers from previous generations. It is not necessary to agree with M. Simon that the prayers were brought to Christianity by a mass conversion of Jews.[45]

Certainly the AC itself witnesses to a Jewish influence upon the compiler's Christian community quite apart from the presence of the Jewish prayers in the work. The compiler's concern for keeping both the Sabbath and the Law was considered in Chapter V.[46] The compiler also testifies to the intimate contact between Jews and Christians in his area, though he discouraged it. He refers several times to the sin of attending the synagogue (e.g. 2.61.1, see under "Date" below). He appears to have lived in a community in Syria in which Christianity had strong ties to Judaism, but the compiler himself--and Pseudo-Ignatius if the two are the same--saw Judaism as a threat to Christianity and therefore, like Chrysostom, forbade Christians to attend the synagogue.

Thus, Syrian history supports our *prima facie* conclusion that the prayers reached their final Greek form and were appropriated by Christians in Syria. As Josephus said, however, Jews lived in practically all parts of the empire, and beyond, and we know that there was interaction with Christianity elsewhere,[47] though perhaps not to the extent of the Syrian interaction. In short, then, two lines of evidence point to, and nothing denies, a Syrian provenance for the final Greek form of the prayers. If one must be more specific than that large region, one should select Antioch as the provenance, but perhaps only because there is more information about that city than any other in Syria. Any stages between the assumed Palestinian origin of the Hebrew prayers and the Syrian setting for the final form of the prayers are now undiscoverable (see below under "Theology of the Prayers," p. 231).

Date

Chapter I outlined the main views as to the date of the composition of the prayers. Kohler affirmed that the prayers are pre-Christian--he gave no reason--and that they were appropriated by the church in the second century "when Paulinian Christianity had no share as yet in framing the constitution of the Church."[48] He gave no *terminus post quem*. Bousset maintained, on the basis of his conclusion that the composer had used Aquila's version, that the prayers must be dated after the mid-second century A.D. He gave no *terminus ad quem*, but implied that he thought the prayers were not much after the close of the second century.[49] Goodenough declared the date of the prayers to be after Philo, since the expression τὸ μὴ ὄν is, according to him, post-Philonic. The prayers were composed no later than the middle of the second century A.D., since after that period relations between Jews and Christians were "not cordial enough" for the prayers to have been appropriated by Christians.[50] Thus, he dated the prayers from A.D. 50-150. Peterson dated the prayers in the time of Hadrian, just after the Bar Cochba war (c. 135), but he gave no reason for accepting this date.[51]

These arguments will be analyzed in order: (1) We have already seen that Judaism had a pronounced influence upon Christianity, especially in Syria, during the first four centuries of the common era (see above, "Provenance"). Thus Kohler's assertion that the prayers must have been appropriated by Christians in the second century carries no validity. Further, there is no evidence for his pre-Christian dating of the prayers. (2) Bousset's conclusion that Aquila's vocabulary determines a post-135 date for the prayers is based on insufficient evidence. As we argued above the compiler may have taken prayers ante-dating Aquila, and in redacting them have used Aquila's vocabulary with which he was familiar. Bousset could only cite one word which is indubitably from Aquila. (3) Goodenough's notion that τὸ μὴ ὄν (i.e. creation from nothing) is post-Philonic may be correct--certainly he knew Philo--but it is irrelevant for dating according to Chapters IV and V above. The results of those chapters indicate that the two prayers in which this expression occurs have been so heavily edited by the compiler that very little of the original Jewish source is accessible. Furthermore, this phrase appears in the liturgy attributed to John Chrysostom (fl. at Antioch 381-97), the contemporary of the compiler of AC.[52] Although some have doubted that all of this liturgy comes from Chrysostom himself, at least the liturgy stems from the area around Antioch.[53] One would assume, then, that the phrase was a common place in West Syrian worship and not borrowed from the synagogue. (4) Goodenough's *terminus ad quem* is difficult to maintain in light of the evidence presented above on Jewish-Christian interaction during the first four centuries. No doubt scholars can point to a time when Christianity and Judaism became two separate religions--usually toward the end of the first century--with even officially hostile attitudes toward one another, as J. Parkes has admirably done in his work, *The Conflict of the Church and Synagogue*.[54] But it does not follow, therefore, that all interchange between the two religious groups ceased. Parkes is quick to recognize this when he draws attention to the several Christian scholars--Justin, Clement of Alexandria, Origen, Aphrahat, Ephraim the Syrian, and Jerome--who studied under Jewish teachers. As Parkes observes:

> But if all relations were such as a first reading of the literature which remains would suggest, it is doubtful if any Jew would have consented to teach a Christian at all.[55]

One would suppose from the polemics that there was no contact between the two groups, but then one discovers that some of the Christians must have actually been taught by Jews! Thus, relations, if not officially "cordial" did exist between Jews and Christians. If the synagogue was as accessible and as attractive to Christians in the latter second century and the third century as we know from Chrysostom's homilies that it was in the fourth century, then Christians could have appropriated the prayers at almost any time in those periods. We have no evidence to argue for probability that some Christians frequented the synagogue throughout the first three centuries, but what evidence we have presented above (under "Provenance") indicates a good possibility that such was the case.

The *Terminus ad quem*

The *terminus ad quem* should, then, be pushed back to one or two generations before the compiler, or c. A.D. 300. This date is probable because the compiler himself is not likely to have visited the synagogue or to have used prayers which he knew were Jewish. He has definite anti-Jewish feelings. In the first place, he refers to Jews as "Christ-killers" (χριστοκτόνος, 2.61.1, 6.25.1, 7.38.7). He also interpolates into the Didascalia unfavorable references to Jews and the synagogue. At 2.61.1, where the Didascalia had pronounced a ban on going to pagan temples, he adds a prohibition on entering a "synagogue of the Jews." They who do so will have no defense on the judgment day. At 2.61.3 where the Didascalia says a believer must avoid the assemblies of heretics, the compiler adds, "of the ungodly, of the heathen, of the Jews." At 5.17.1,2 he declares, "We have now no fellowship with the Jews, therefore do not keep the feast (of Passover) with them." Evidently the compiler disliked the Christian attraction for the synagogue as much as his contemporary Chrysostom did. At 6.18.3 he declares that the heretics under discussion "are more wicked than Jews and more atheistical than Gentiles," as if Jewish wickedness and Gentile atheism (=paganism?) were commonplace notions. Thus, the compiler must have inherited the prayers and must have been unaware of their origin, since he polemicized against Christians frequenting the synagogue--ironically the very practice which assisted in the compilation of his work by providing him with a source.

The *Terminus post quem*

We shall not date the original composition of the prayers of AC 7.33-38, since the prayers circulated orally at first. We shall only suggest the earliest possible date for the *form* of the Jewish stratum of the prayers. Jewish prayers were composed impromptu and orally, as Heinemann maintained (see "Original Language," above). Nevertheless, certain content, order, expression and formal characteristics became standardized. We can, then, show what stage in this process the prayers of AC 7.33-38 represents.

Other Alleged Parallels to the 7 Benedictions

Three lines of evidence suggest that the prayers are post-first century A.D. The first line of evidence is simply that the parallels in the prayers of AC to the Hebrew Seven Benedictions of the Gaonic era are much closer than the alleged parallels to the Seven in other documents. We assume that the closer the parallels to the Hebrew benedictions (as preserved in the Geniza fragments and Amram's text), the later the form of the benedictions. Since the prayers were continually developing as a living tradition until, according to Heinemann,[56] the late Amoraic period when the wording of the prayers became standardized, it follows that the closer in time one comes to this period the more similar any parallels will be.

The first of these documents with alleged parallels is the Hebrew of Sirach. 51:2 reads: "Give thanks (הודו) unto the God of praises," which is, according to Idelsohn, parallel to the third benediction, "Holy ones praise Thee every day." 51:10 reads: "Give thanks unto the Shield of Abraham," which is parallel to the first benediction, "Blessed art Thou...Shield of Abraham." 51:12 reads: "Give thanks unto the Mighty one of Jacob," which is reminiscent of the first benediction as well, "Blessed art Thou...the God of Jacob, the great, mighty, and revered God."[57] These parallels are striking, but not as complete as those in AC 7.33-38. A comparison of the two with the Hebrew Seven Benedictions results in the conclusion that the parallels in Sirach are earlier. Thus one should date the prayers after the time of Sirach (c. 190-175 B.C.).

The Psalms of Solomon also have, according to I. Levi, some parallels to the Benedictions.[58] Levi maintained that Ps 3:12 mentions the resurrection in the same terms as the second benediction:

(the sinner) falleth--verily grievous is his fall--and
riseth no more.
The destruction of the sinner is forever....

But they that fear the Lord shall rise to life eternal,
And their life (shall be) in the light of the Lord,
and shall come to an end no more.[59]

It is difficult to discern such a parallel, however. But, whether or not this speaks of the resurrection similarly to the second benediction, it does not use the same words (in Greek equivalents) as does AC 7.34: "O Quickener of the Dead." Thus the parallel in AC 7.34 is much closer. The form of the second benediction in AC is later than the form in the Psalms of Solomon (c. 40 B.C.).

Thirdly, S. Talmon[60] claims to have discovered in the Manual of Discipline (1QS 10:13-11:15) an "order of benedictions" of the Qumran sect whose themes are parallel to that of some of the Eighteen Benedictions and Sirach 51. Of these parallels only one pertains to the Seven Benedictions. There is a phrase similar to that in the first benediction ("the great, mighty הגבור and revered God, God Most High, who bestows lovingkindnesses חסדים.")[61] which reads: "on his power I shall meditate, upon his mercies I shall rely..." (בגבורתו אשוחה ועל חסדיו אשע, 1QS 10:16).[62] Although Talmon's claim is convincing, the parallel once again is vague when compared to the parallels of AC 7.33-38. This suggests that the parallels in the Dead Sea Scrolls represent an earlier stage in the history of the benedictions. Scholars date the Manual of Discipline to the late second or early first century B.C.[63] One would assume, then, that the form of the prayers in AC 7.33-38 represents a later period than the late second or early first century B.C.

This evidence indicates, therefore, that all of the other alleged parallels fall far short of the close similarity of the prayers in AC 7.33-38 to the extant forms (Palestinian and Babylonian) of the Hebrew Seven Benedictions. The alleged parallels in Sirach date from the pre-Maccabean era, and those in the Manual of Discipline and the Psalms of Solomon from the late second or first century B.C.[64] Thus if all of these alleged parallels really are parallels, a continuous chain of witnesses testify to the advanced stage of the prayers of AC 7.33-38. The parallels in AC 7. 33-38 should be at least dated, from this evidence, from the first century A.D. on. It is interesting that the rabbinic evidence corresponds with this conclusion. The earliest attributed discussion of the Seven Benedictions is among the schools of Hillel and Shammai (A.D. 10-80) in T. Beracoth 3:13.

Two differences distinguish the older parallels and the parallels of AC 7.33-38. First, the older parallels consist of a few scattered words which resemble--sometimes vaguely--a few words in the Seven Benedictions--or Eighteen--but the order of these parallels never corresponds to the Hebrew prayers. According to the Talmud (Meg 17b, Ber 28b) Simeon ha-Pakuli arranged the Eighteen in the presence of R. Gamaliel II at Jamnia in the latter part of the first century. If the Eighteen Benedictions were recited in different order before this time, it is likely that the Seven were as well. Thus the parallel of sequence or order of the benedictions between the prayers of AC and the Hebrew benedictions argues for a period after Jamnia (latter first century A.D.).

Secondly, few of the older parallels contain the formal characteristics of the Hebrew prayers. The older parallels almost never contain the introductory formula (and eulogy) ברוך אתה ''. The parallels in Sirach (in content), for instance, are introduced by the formula הודו ל "give thanks to." The usual introductory formula at Qumran was אודכה אדוני "I will give thanks to you, O Lord" (e.g. 1QS 2:31), though the formula ברוך אתה '' is rarely found also (1QS 11:15). But ברוך אתה '' would become the standard formula.[65] The prayers of AC use the Greek equivalent of this formula (εὐλόγητος εἶ κύριε) at the end of 7.33.6 (as an eulogy) and at the beginning of 7.34.1 (as an introductory formula). The Hebrew benedictions employ the formula at the beginning and end of the first benediction and at the end of the second, fourth, fifth, and sixth benedictions. It is now difficult to tell whether the formula has been edited out of AC by the compiler or whether it was absent from his source. The appearance of the formula at the beginning of AC 7.34 (=the second benediction) where it does not appear in the Hebrew text, indicates that the placement of the formula was not yet standardized at the time of the appropriation of the Jewish prayers by Christians.

The Form of the Kedusha

The second line of argument is based on the form of the Kedusha in AC 7.35.3 which suggests a post-first century A.D. date. The Kedusha[66] exists in three forms in today's synagogue liturgy: the Yotzer (the prayer before the Shema), the Amidah (the statutory prayer), and the Kedusha de Sidra (the Kedusha "after study" or after the lecture[67]). There is no consensus about which form of the Kedusha is older--each of the three has been affirmed to be the oldest[68]--but almost everyone agrees that some form of it is very old. It appears in 1 Enoch 39:12 (Similitudes) and 2 Enoch 21:1, and in early Christian sources, Rev 4:8 and 1 Clem 34:6, but with only the scripture Isa 6:3 and not Ezek 3:12. The passages are as follows:

> 1 En 39:12-14: Those who sleep not bless Thee: they stand before Thy glory and bless, praise, and extoll, saying: "Holy, holy, holy is the Lord of Spirits: He filleth the earth with spirits." And here my eyes saw all those who sleep not: they stand before Him and bless and say: "Blessed be Thou, and blessed be the name of the Lord for ever and ever.[69]
>
> 2 En 21:1: And the cherubim and seraphim standing about the throne, the six-winged and many-eyed ones do not depart, standing before the Lord's face doing his will, and cover his whole throne, singing with gentle voice before the Lord's face: "holy, holy, holy, Lord Ruler of Sabaoth, heavens and earth are full of Thy glory."[70]
>
> 1 Clem 34:6: For the Scripture says "Ten thousand times ten thousand stood by him, and thousand thousands ministered to him (Dan 7:10) and they cried Holy, Holy, Holy is the Lord of Sabaoth, the whole creation is full of his glory.[71]
>
> Rev 4:8: And the four living creatures, each of them with six wings, are full of eyes all round and within, and day and night they never cease to sing, "Holy, holy, holy is the Lord God Almighty, who was and is and is to come."[72]

All of these sources can with reasonable certainty be dated to the close of the first century A.D.[73] The source most problematic is the section of 1 Enoch known as the Similitudes, which J. T. Milik attempted to date as late as the third century.[74] Nevertheless, the main thrust of scholarly investigation of the Similitudes has been toward a late first century date.

The first occurrence of the Kedusha with the structure Isa 6:3-Ezek 3:12 is in T. Beracoth 1:9.

> R. Judah (i.e. ben Ilai, A.D. 130-160) used to respond together with him who pronounced the Benediction (עונה עם המברך): "Holy, holy, holy, is the Lord of hosts, the whole earth is full of His glory," and "Blessed be the glory of the Lord out of His place (Ezek 3:12)." All these (words) R. Judah used to say together with him who pronounced the Benediction.[76]

The structure of the Kedushas in the modern synagogal liturgy is as follows: The Yotzer, Isa 6:3-Ezek 3:12; the Amida, Isa 6:3-Ezek 3:12-Ps 146:10; de Sidra, Isa 6:3-Ezek 3:12-Exod 15:18. Finkelstein argued that the third scripture in the Kedusha of the Amida (Ps 146:10) seems out of place with the idea of sanctification, and probably found its way into the Kedusha when the Shema was inserted into it as a deceptive counter measure against the ban on saying the Shema. At any rate, many scholars believe that the scripture is a later addition.[77] Werner concluded that Exod 15:18 in the Kedusha de Sidra is a later addition as well.[78]

After the first century, the structure of the Kedusha includes both Isa 6:3 and Ezek 3:12. This leads one to conclude that the Kedusha in AC 7.35.3 which has the structure Isa 6:3-Ezek 3:12-Ps 68:18, is a post-first century product. Thus we may set the *terminus post quem* at roughly the mid-second century, or A.D. 150.

Indication of a Third Century Date

The form of the prayers could represent any time between A.D. 150 and 300, but one element in the prayers suggests that they were appropriated by Christians no earlier than the third century. Although Ps 68:18 ("the chariots of God...the Lord is among them on Sinai.") is connected with the Kedusha here, it is never associated with it in either the Jewish or Christian sources.[79] One can understand the mention of God's chariots at this point, since the chariot vision of Ezekiel 1 is a vision of God's majesty just as is Isa 6:3, but the mention of Sinai seems out of place. D. J. Halperin[80] maintains, however, that Ps 68:18 was the connecting link in a rabbinic exegetical tradition--based upon scripture lections for Pentecost--which joined the chariot vision of Ezekiel 1 to the Sinai event of Exodus 19 and 20. The Exodus section was the synagogue Torah reading for Pentecost (Shabuot) and the Ezekiel passage was the Prophetic reading. The passages were connected, Halperin assumes, by Ps 68:18 which speaks of both Sinai and chariots. It is possible, then, if Halperin's assumption is correct, that since one would associate the throne vision of Ezekiel 1 on Pentecost with Ps 68:18, one might also associate the throne vision of the Kedusha (which contains Ezek 3:12) with Ps 68:18. Halperin does not say how old he thinks this synagogal lection is, but the midrashic tradition based upon it is from the third century. That is, midrashic traditions in rabbinic literautre (The Visions of Ezekiel and Pisikta Rabbati) are reflected in Origen's *First Homily on Ezekiel*. Halperin thinks that Origen acquired these traditions while he was in Caesarea (A.D. 231-244). If this third century midrashic tradition is reflected in AC 7.35, then the final form of the prayers may be dated to approximately the middle third century or A.D. 250. One must be cautious in accepting this date, however, since one does not know precisely the date of the midrashic traditions which Halperin has used. They may go back to the second century A.D. or further. It is unlikely, however, that the traditions reach back that far since the connection of Pentecost with Exodus 19 and 20 seems to have begun in the third century (and thus Sinai could be linked with the throne vision by Psa 68:18).[81]

Milieu

The results of Chapter V are most significant for an investigation of milieu. One gets quite a different impression as to the circle in which the prayers arose when reading the prayers as they stand in the AC, than when reading the prayers as they are in the reconstructed text (Chart E).

The Essenes

In his early article in the Breslau *Monatsschrift*,[82] Kohler maintained that all of the synagogal prayers and much of the pre-Nicene liturgy had sprung from the Essene cultus. Thus he called the prayers in the AC "Christian Essene liturgy." In his subsequent publication, Kohler again explained his claim that the prayers reflected Essene thought.

> It is quite evident that these pseudo-Christian prayers are the product of a class of Hasideans, or Essenes, of Hellenic culture, as may be learned from their Scriptural quotations taken from The (*sic*) Septuagint and likewise from their Alexandrian or Philonic accentuation of the *Logos*...and the Wisdom as having formed the intermediary power with which God created the world, and particularly man.[83]

From this quotation we assume that Kohler termed any thought "Essene" if it resembled Philonic thought.

But these specific ideas, and most of the other "Philonic" elements in the prayers of AC 7.33-38 are eliminated from the reconstructed text (cf. AC 7.34.6 and the reconstruction in Chart E). The evidence of Chapter V indicates that it was the compiler who was influenced by such concepts and who introduced them into most of the prayers of AC, not only AC 7.33-38. Therefore, Kohler's basis for establishing an Essene milieu has vanished.

The Mystery

Kohler's essenism sounds similar to Goodenough's mysticism. In Chapter I we outlined Goodenough's thesis as to the milieu of the prayers. They are the liturgy used among the mystical (Philonic) Jews. Goodenough's thesis about the milieu of the prayers has not only the difficulty, like Kohler's, that much of the material in the prayers of 7.33-38 which would support it is absent from our reconstructed text, but also that he employed prayers other than 7.33-38 (mainly AC 8.12.6-27) to investigate the milieu. He maintained that 8.12.6-27 is "our best guide to the theology and philosophy of the Fragments...."[84] But we have concluded that this prayer has been so heavily edited by the compiler that only the general outline of the prayer is recoverable (i.e. praise of God as creator followed by the *tersanctus*). In addition, the investigation of Chapter IV eliminated several other prayers from consideration, since there was no good argument for Jewish authorship. A few examples will illustrate the changes which the results of Chapters IV and V necessitate.

Goodenough stated:

> Sophia in the Fragments is the daughter of God. She is "creative" (ἔντεχνος), and dispenses...the Providence of God....These statements suggest the Mystery.[85]

But we maintained above that: (1) The emphasis on God's providence is a favorite theme in AC. In every case where the word occurs in AC, where one can compare AC with its source, the word has come from the compiler. (2) The association of Wisdom with creation and providence is also a favorite theme of the compiler, and this was assumed to be redactional as well.[86]

One could read through Goodenough's handling of the prayers in his *By Light, Light* and repeat this analysis with the same results on virtually every page. His exegesis of the prayers as they stand in the AC is brilliant and penetrating, but he was mostly explaining the theology of the compiler, not the theology of the Jewish prayers.

One more example will suffice. Goodenough demonstrated rather convincingly that the author of AC 8.12.7-9 has taken an approach to God which is identical to that found in "the Mystery" (i.e. Philo): "...the thought of God in terms of the Mystery is not sporadic, but is the fundamental approach to God."[87] Thus Goodenough pointed out that like Philo, the author of this prayer denied God's spatiality,[88] and affirmed the unchangeability and invisibility of God. He then concluded: "The God of these prayers is thus the God of Philo and the Mystery."[89] We would agree with his analysis of AC 8.15.7-9. Yet the argument of Chapter IV has ruled out this prayer as coming from Judaism. Thus the Philonic elements are none other than the compiler's.

The compiler of AC, then, stood in the tradition of Theophilus of Antioch (his predecessor of some 200 years) whose similarity to Philo in theology has been pointed out by R. M. Grant.[90] The emphasis on the role of Logos and Sophia in creation as well as the notion of God as immutable and invisible are all in Theophilus. Like his predecessor, the compiler of AC was thoroughly influenced by Philo or a Philonic-type of thought. He introduced this thought throughout the AC, but especially in the prayers.[91]

The Samaritans

Baumstark[92] suggested at one point that the Samaritan liturgy should be taken into account in investigating the milieu of the prayers, since both employ Deut 4:39 (see AC 7.35.8) instead of the Shema (Deut 6:4) as the profession of the unity of God.

It is unlikely, however, that the prayers were produced in Samaritan circles. In the first place, an allusion to Deut 4:39 is also found in the Hebrew liturgy and at the same point as in the prayers of AC: in the third benediction. The underlined parts of the third benediction in Chart C point out this parallel. The scripture is not quoted, but the expansion on the scripture which is in AC 7.35.9 ("for there is no God except you alone, no holy one by you...") is alluded to in both the Babylonian ("for he alone is high and holy...") and Palestinian ("and there is no God beside you...") versions. Thus the quotation of Deut 4:39 may simply have dropped out of the Hebrew versions at a later time, or the description of God in the third benediction may have led a reciter of the Greek prayers--whether a Jew or later, a Christian--to add the scripture.

Secondly, it is improbable that these prayers sprang from Samaritanism because the Seven Benedictions are peculiarly a Jewish product. There are some prayers in the Samaritan liturgy which resemble some of the Seven Benedictions[93] but these are not in the same order and do not parallel all seven prayers.

Finally, nothing peculiar to Samaritan thought appears in the prayers. The four doctrinal pillars in Samaritanism were God, Moses (thus the Pentateuch to the exclusion of the other books), Mt. Gerizim and the judgment day.[94] The prayers never mention a holy mountain, but they do quote from OT sources other than the books of Moses (e.g. Joel 2:13, Ps 68:18, Isa 6:3). Thus it is unlikely that the prayers were composed in a Samaritan milieu.

No distinctive milieu for the prayers is evident other than merely diaspora (i.e. Syrian) Judaism. To attempt to identify what kind of diaspora Judaism produced these prayers would not be helpful in light of the nature of the evidence. Any conclusions we might reach would be much too speculative. In addition, an analysis of the theology of the prayers will show that they are not different in thought from the Hebrew prayers.

Theology of the Prayers

God

God is eternal (7.33,35), all knowing (7.33,35), omnipresent (7.35), powerful (7.34), holy (7.35) and the creator of all (7.34, 36). Yet God is also merciful (7.33), hears prayers (7.33,37) and has acted in history to give the Law (7.36) and defend the patriarchs (7.33,35,38). This same view of God is expressed in the Hebrew Seven Benedictions (and is also found in the OT and rabbinic literature): God is eternal (Ben. 2), powerful (Ben. 1, 2), holy (Ben. 3), creator (Ben. 1, 2), merciful (Ben. 1, 6), hears prayers (Ben. 5), has acted in history to defend the patriarchs (Ben. 1, 6). The attributes all-knowing and omnipresent are not explicit in the Seven Benedictions, but the fourth benediction of the Eighteen requests that God grant knowledge to man. The statement of omnipresence in AC 7.35 is not a philosophical statement (e.g. that God physically permeates the universe as the Stoics taught), but merely an affirmation of monotheism. There is no other God in existence any place else. But the notion of God as everywhere is one familiar from both the OT and rabbinic Judaism. As G. F. Moore stated,[95] the notion of omnipresence was not for the rabbis "philosophical nor primarily theological but immediately religious." The idea was that no sin can hide from God. It is also true of the statement in AC 7.35 that it is a religious statement and not a philosophical one.

Man

The prayers do not contain a complete notion of man. As one would expect in prayer, where one stands before the Eternal, man's life and this world are represented as fleeting and "easily dissolved" (7.33). Mankind is the recipient of God's mercy, for which his duty is to give thanks as best he can (7.38). This same attitude is also presented in the OT, Hebrew prayers (see the Tachanunim below) and rabbinic Judaism.[96]

Angels

The celestial retinue (seraphim, cherubim, and other angels) in AC 7.35 is no different from that in the Hebrew Kedushas. The notion of heavenly ministers is also present in the rabbinic sources. They were called cherubim, seraphim and ophanim.[97]

Eschatology

The nature of the text in AC 7.34 makes it difficult to determine precisely what stood in the source. It is evident (see Chapter V) that the compiler has edited the text heavily. Clearly, however, the prayer reflects the belief in the resurrection which is present in the second benediction, and even contains a verbal parallel at the end of the prayer, "O Quickener of the dead."

The Number Seven

This is the only element in the prayers that stands out in contrast to the Hebrew prayers and rabbinic thought. Mention is made of "the great and holy seventh day" in the Hebrew fourth benediction, but the emphasis is not on the number seven itself as it is in AC 7.36. The Pythagorean notion that number is the essence of all things and therefore various numbers hold special significance was used in propaganda by Aristobulus (fl. 50-25 B.C.)[98] and later by Philo (d. c. A.D. 50), both Alexandrians, to extol the Sabbath.[99] The Sabbath is a special day, they taught, as the Law says because of the significance of the number seven. The emphasis on the number seven in AC 7.36 also sounds like propaganda, and we would expect to find propaganda in the diaspora where Jews lived among Gentiles.[100] This section, therefore, appears to be from the diaspora community.

Thus the theology of the prayers, except for the references to the number seven, closely resembles that of the Hebrew benedictions and rabbinic Judaism. As far as we can determine, the diaspora community changed or added to the theology of the prayers only slightly.

Function of the Prayers

Peterson's assertion that AC 7.33.3 began as a private prayer instead of a synagogal prayer was mentioned in Chapter I. He was impressed with its similarity to a prayer (the Tachanun) in the modern Jewish prayer book, parts of which are quoted in the Talmud

(b. Yoma 87b, attributed to Mar Samuel, d. 254).[101] Apparently, Peterson meant to imply that all of the allegedly Jewish prayers of AC were private prayers.[102]

But it would be incorrect to assert that these prayers were not recited in the synagogue. Parts of AC 7.33 do bear slight formal similarity to the private supplicatory prayers known as Tachanunim. Heinemann[103] lists the formal characteristics of these prayers: they address God in the second person (as do the public prayers); they use the imperative (as do the public prayers); they use various divine epithets with a first-person suffix (e.g. "my God," "our Father"). Only the last characteristic differentiates private from public prayers. AC 7.33 begins with "Our eternal Father." Thus it contains the formal characteristic of the private supplicatory prayer.

AC 7.33 is also similar in content to the supplicatory prayer. It appeals to the mercy of God and confesses the inadequacies of those making the petition. See for example the Tachanun prayer in Amram's Seder (which is almost exactly like the prayer Peterson quoted):

> ...have mercy on us for we are thy servants...and worms we are. What are we? What is our life? What is our piety? What is our righteousness....Are not mighty men as nought before thee...and the wise as without knowledge....For all our works are void and emptiness, and the days of our life are vanity before thee.[104]

Yet this prayer goes on to seek God's forgiveness and to request his help in avoiding evil. These elements are absent from AC 7.33 (in both our reconstructed text and the text in AC).

These similarities do suggest that a private supplicatory prayer could have been incorporated into the first benediction, but the prayers of AC 7.33-38 were used for public synagogue worship. In the first place, the Seven Benedictions normally were for public recitation.[105] Secondly, the Kedusha could only be recited among a quorum of ten adult males and thus, was strictly for public use (b. Ber 21b).[106] Thus the prayer collection in AC 7.33-38 is probably an example of the prayers actually recited in the synagogues, as Bousset maintained.[107]

Since AC 7.33-38 represents Seven Benedictions, and not the Eighteen, these prayers were used in the Sabbath services and not in the daily ritual. Further, since the Nishmath prayer is included in these prayers (7.38, see Chapter V above), which is today only recited in the Sabbath morning service, these prayers were probably used for that service. Also the Sabbath blessing (fourth benediction) is closer to the one for the morning service in the modern prayer book of Birnbaum. Both prayers refer to the giving of the Law.[108]

Summary

The reconstructed text yields different results from the text as it stands in the AC. The compiler's source may have been oral or written, and the Greek is based upon a Hebrew source. No better suggestion for provenance than Syria can be offered. The form of the prayers is post-first century, but must have reached Christian circles by at least A.D. 300. Most significant is the different picture of milieu which the reconstruction effects. Though Goodenough's analysis of the prayers was usually insightful, he emphasized those elements which we have determined are redactional. The theology of the prayers is in the main that of the Hebrew benedictions and of rabbinic thought, and the prayers are probably an example of the Syrian synagogal Sabbath morning service in the late second to early fourth centuries A.D.

NOTES

CHAPTER VI

[1]See T. Shabb 13:4 for the ruling that the benedictions were not to be written down. Also see Avenary, "Amidah," col. 840.

[2]This statement is obvious, since this is exactly the relationship the prayers of AC 7.33-38 bears to the early Gaonic texts (i.e. Amram's and the Geniza text). See Chart C above.

[3]Kohler, "The Essene Version," 418. For Kohler's substitution of "Christ" with "Logos," see pp. 412 and 418. His statement on p. 415 at n. 37, that "the word *Palmoni*, Dan. 7.13...was no longer understood by the LXX, which translation our Essene writers follow..." is incorrect, since at this point the quotation is from Theodotion (see Chapter III, note on 7.35.3).

[4]See Chapter III on 7.33.4, and Chapter IV, pp. 141-43.

[5]Bousset, *Nachrichten*, 465-67; Goodenough, *By Light, Light*, 318.

[6]Bouyer, *Eucharist*, 121.

[7]For information on Hebrew poetry, see T. J. Conant, "Exercises in Hebrew Grammar and a Hebrew Chrestomathy," in W. Gesenius and E. Rodiger, *Hebrew Grammar* (New York: Appleton, 1860) 53-57; G. B. Gray, *The Forms of Hebrew Poetry* (London: Hodder and Stoughton, 1915) 37-83; T. H. Robinson, *The Poetry of the Old Testament* (London: Duckworth, 1947); R. K. Harrison, *Introduction to the Old Testament* (Grand Rapids: Eerdmans, 1969) 965-75.

[8]The phrase "the beauty of comeliness" may itself be a semitic construct as also the phrase in the next line, "the strength of power."

[9]See Chapter V. This same section appears also in 7.33.

[10]R. A. Martin, *Syntactical Evidence of Semitic Sources in Greek Documents* (SCS 3; Missoula, MT: SBL, 1974).

[11]Ibid., 23-36.

[12]R. A. Kraft has maintained a similar conclusion about apocalyptic works: "Who translated (the apocalypses) from Semitic into Greek?...I suspect that a good deal of the translation work... was done by and for Jews...." See his "The Multiform Jewish Heritage of Early Christianity," in *Christianity, Judaism and Other Greco-Roman Cults*, ed. J. Neusner (Leiden: Brill, 1975) pt. 3, 194.

[13]Heinemann, *Prayer in the Talmud*, 43.

[14]See S. Lieberman, *Greek in Jewish Palestine* (New York: Jewish Theological Seminary, 1942) 29-67.

[15]Bousset, *Nachrichten*, 465f; Goodenough, *By Light, Light*, 318.

[16]Several quotations remain in the reconstructed text; see especially 7.35.

[17]See above, Chapter IV on 7.33.4.

[18]Kohler, "The Essene Version," 418. Kohler did say they had come from "Essenes, of Hellenic culture, as may be learned from The (*sic*) Septuagint and likewise from their Alexandrian or Philonic accentuation of the *Logos*...." Does he mean that the prayers were produced in Alexandria? Goodenough, *By Light, Light*, 357: "The analysis of the Fragments has led us back...to Judaism, to Hellenistic Judaism, and specifically to the Mystery...." Bousset, *Nachrichten*, 487: "In den vorliegenden Gebeten präsentiert sich ein Judentum im Gewand griechischer Sprache, tief beruhrt von hellenistischer Geiste, das Z.T....eine Fortentwicklung über Philo hinaus zeigt und im Besitz einer griechischer Liturgie ist." Bousset claimed that the prayers exhibit "nachchristlichen hellenistischen Diasporajudentum..." (489).

[19]Bousset, *Nachrichten*, 464.

[20]Bouyer (*Eucharist*, 120) evidently thought that Goodenough claimed an Alexandrian provenance for the prayers: "The fantastic hypothesis of this remarkable scholar...is that these texts would have been composed by Alexandrian Jews who cast their Judaism in the form of a 'mystery religion'...." Bouyer rejected Goodenough's hypothesis of a mystery liturgy, but must have accepted his supposed Alexandrian provenance, for on the next page he speaks of Alexandria as the home of the prayers. Yet, Goodenough never mentioned Alexandria specifically as the place of composition for the prayers.

[21]See above, Chapter II.

[22]B. D. Spinks, "The Jewish Liturgical Sources for the Sanctus," *The Heythrop Journal* 21 (1980) 178.

[23]In Persia, but Syriac speaking.

[24]R. Murray, *Symbols of Church and Kingdom. A Study in Early Syriac Tradition* (Cambridge: University Press, 1975) 8. See also J. Neusner, *Aphrahat and Judaism* (Leiden: Brill, 1971) about the most famous Christian resident of Adiabene. Neusner states on p. 4 that the relationship between the Christian and Jewish communities of Adiabene was "vigorous, intimate, and competitive." Aphrahat wrote several treatises answering the Jewish critique of Christianity in the mid-fourth century A.D. See also H. Lietzmann, *The Founding of the Church Universal*, trans. B. L. Woolf (New York: Scribner's, 1938) 352, on Aphrahat's knowledge of rabbinic learning.

[25]M. Rostovtzeff, *Dura-Europos and its Art* (Oxford: Clarendon, 1938) 100-34; p. 41 has a plan of the city showing the locations of the church and synagogue.

[26]*War* 7.44-45, trans. H. St. J. Thackeray, *Josephus* (LCL; Cambridge: Harvard, 1961).

[27]Lietzmann (*Founding of the Church*, 340f) notes that both Greek and Syriac were spoken in Antioch.

[28]C. H. Kraeling ("The Jewish Community at Antioch," *JBL* 51 [1932] 136) estimated the population at 45,000 at the time of Augustus out of a total of 300,000 residents, and 65,000 at the time of John Chrysostom (fourth century) out of a total of 500,000 residents. Meeks and Wilken (*Jews and Christians*, 8), however, make the numbers much lower--22,000 Jews out of 150,000 inhabitants. Yet Meeks and Wilken agree with Kraeling that the Jewish population must have equaled at least twelve percent of the total. Proportionately, then, there was a large Jewish population in Antioch. For rabbinical information about the Jews of Antioch, see S. Krauss, "Antioche," *REJ* 45 (1902) 26-49. See also G. Downey's volume, *A History of Antioch in Syria* (Princeton: Princeton University, 1961) esp. 272-316, 337-41.

[29]Meeks and Wilken, *Jews and Christians*, 18.

[30]J. H. Charlesworth, *The Odes of Solomon* (Oxford: Clarendon, 1973) p. VII. See also his *The Pseudepigrapha and Modern Research* (Missoula, MT: Scholars Press, 1976) 190: "The original language, Syriac, and the affinities with the Dead Sea Scrolls, the Johannine literature, and Ignatius of Antioch indicate that the Odes may have been composed in or near Syrian Antioch."

[31]A. Menzies, "The Odes of Solomon," *Interpreter* 7 (1910) 7-22; A. Harnack and J. Flemming, *Ein Jüdisch-christliches Psalmbuch aus dem ersten Jahrhundert* (TU; Leipzig: Hinrichs'sche, 1910) Bd. 35, Ht. 4.

[32]The translation of Ignatius is from Lake, *The Apostolic Fathers*. See the excellent summary of Ignatius's anti-Jewish polemic in Meeks and Wilken (*Jews and Christians*, 19f) to which we are indebted here. See also the important article by C. K. Barrett, "Jews and Judaizers in the Epistles of Ignatius," *Jews, Greeks and Christians. Essays in Honor of William David Davies*, ed. R. Hammerton-Kelly and R. Scroggs (Leiden: Brill, 1976) 220-44.

[33]Meeks and Wilken, *Jews and Christians*, 19f.

[34]Grant, *After the New Testament* (Philadelphia: Fortress, 1967) 136.

[35]Said by Chrysostom in *Expo. in Psalms* 109.2. See Meeks and Wilken, *Jews and Christians*, 23, 47 n. 120.

[36]Ibid., 24.

[37]Downey, *History*, 312f.

[38]Philasterius, *De Haer. Liber* 64. See Kraeling, "The Jewish Community," 155.

[39]Ibid.; Eusebius *H.E.* 7.32.2.

[40]R. M. Grant believes they did; see "Early Antiochene Anaphora," 93. Meeks and Wilken affirm that one could suppose that they did, but there is no evidence for it; see *Jews and Christians*, 22.

[41]Origen and Jerome studied Hebrew with the rabbis. N.R.M. de Lange (*Origen and the Jews* [Cambridge: University Press, 1976] 22) doubts that Origen knew Hebrew well enough to read it, however.

[42]Kraeling, "The Jewish Community," 155.

[43]*Hom.* 8:7, 1:3, 1:1, 8:8, trans. Meeks and Wilken, *Jews and Christians*, 118, 92, 86, 123.

[44]Ibid., 31.

[45]Simon, *Verus Israel*, 436.

[46]See above, Chapter V on AC 7.33, 36.

[47]See A. L. Williams (*Adversus Judaeos* [Cambridge: University Press, 1935]) who gives a detailed account of Christian polemic against Jews in various parts of the empire. Obviously, one would not need to polemicize what was not a threat and thus we should assume that Judaism competed with and interacted with Christianity in these areas. See also Simon's monumental work, *Verus Israel*; R. L. Wilken, *Judaism and the Early Christian Mind* (New Haven: Yale University, 1971); idem, "Insignissima Religio, Certe Licita? Christianity and Judaism in the Fourth and Fifth Centuries," *The Impact of the Church Upon Its Culture*, ed. J. C. Brauer (Chicago: University of Chicago, 1968) 39-66; idem, "Melito, the Jewish Community at Sardis, and the Sacrifice of Isaac," *Theological Studies* 37 (1976) 53-69, who argues that the Jewish view of the Akedat influenced Christian thinking at Sardis (in Lydia) at the time of Melito; A. M. Hulen, "The Dialogues with the Jews as Sources for the Early Jewish argument against Christianity," *JBL* 51 (1932) 58-70, who maintained that the Jews leveled a "powerful counter-argument" to the early Christian apologists; M. Wiles, "The Old Testament in Controversy with the Jews," *Scottish Journal of Theology* 8 (1955) 113-26, who discusses various scriptures (especially Messianic passages) whose interpretation was disputed.

[48]Kohler, *Origins*, 257, 259; idem, "Didascalia," 593, and "The Essene Version," 418.

[49]Bousset, *Nachrichten*, 465.

[50]Goodenough, *By Light, Light*, 357.

[51]Peterson, *Miscellanea*, vol. 1, 414, 417.

[52]Brightman, *Liturgies*, 369:28, 384:27.

[53]Brightman (ibid., xciif) points out that some have doubted that all of this liturgy is from Chrysostom because the earliest MS of the liturgy attributes only three prayers to Chrysostom. But Brightman notes that the MS seems to open abruptly and suggests that the omission of Chrysostom's name at the beginning (in the title) of the work is accidental.

[54]J. Parkes, *The Conflict of the Church and the Synagogue* (New York: Temple, 1969) 91. See also M. H. Shepherd, Jr. ("The Occasion of the Initial Break Between Judaism and Christianity," in *Harry Austryn Wolfson Jubilee Volume* [Jerusalem: American Academy for Jewish Research, 1965] 703-17) who believes that the initial break occurred in A.D. 40-41, however. The work of W. D. Davies (*The Setting of the Sermon on the Mount*, 256-315)--who suggests that the Sermon on the Mount "was fashioned under" the impact of Jamnia, as a counterpart to it, to present the way of the "New Israel"--is also informative.

[55]Parkes, *Conflict*, 117f.

[56]Heinemann, *Prayer in the Talmud*, 51f.

[57]Translation from Idelsohn, *Jewish Liturgy*, 21. Hebrew text in F. Vattioni, *Ecclesiastico* (Naples: Istituto Orientale di Napoli, 1968).

[58]I. Levi, "Les Dix-Huits Benedictions et les Psaumes de Solomon," *REJ* 32 (1896) 161-78.

[59]Translation in Charles, *Apocrypha and Pseudepigrapha*, 635.

[60]S. Talmon, "Machzor habirath shel cath midbar Yehudah," *Tarbiz* 29 (1959-60) 15.

[61]See Chart C above for the Hebrew text and translation of the first benediction.

[62]The Hebrew text is from Talmon's article ("Machzor habirath," 15).

[63]See G. Vermes, *The Dead Sea Scrolls* (Cleveland: Collins-World, 1977) 45f. F. M. Cross dates the script of 1QS to 100-75 B.C. See his *Scrolls from Qumran Cave I* (London: Clowes, 1974) 4.

[64]A. Marmorstein believed that he had found on a papyrus fragment a Greek translation of the Hebrew which represents the form of the Eighteen Benedictions at the beginning of the common era. The dating of this "form" of the Eighteen is problematic, however, since H. I. Bell and T. C. Skeat date the papyrus fragment of this prayer to the fourth century A.D. The prayer is as follows:

> Sanctify, sustain, gather, establish, glorify, confirm, pasture, raise up (?), enlighten, pacify, administer, perfect--the people which Thou hast established...keep us...heal us...cast us not away...remit whatever we have done amiss...receive from us these psalmodies....

But the similarities are vague and such resemblances as there are with the Seven only consist of one word: "Raise up"=the second benediction, "who quickens the dead." "Receive from us these psalmodies"=the fifth benediction "accept...your people Israel and their prayer." If Marmorstein has correctly identified this as a Jewish prayer, however, and if he has correctly dated the form of the benedictions to the early first century A.D., then our prayers in AC are later; at least they would post-date the latter part of the first century A.D. See A. Marmorstein, "The Oldest Form of the Eighteen Benedictions," *JQR* n.s. 34 (1943) 137-59; H. I. Bell and T. C. Skeat, *Fragments of an Unknown Gospel and Other Early Christian Papyri* (London: Trustees, 1935) 56. Bell and Skeat, the editors of the papyrus, thought it was a Christian prayer.

[65]Heinemann, *Prayer in the Talmud*, 39f.

[66]See the note in Chapter III on 7.35.3.

[67]See the article "Kedusha" in *Encyclopedia Judaica*, vol. 10, cols. 875-77.

[68]Kohler, "The Essene Version," 396f; Finkelstein, "La Kedouscha," 3; L. Ginzberg, "Notes sur la Kedousda et les benedictions du Chema," *REJ* 98 (1934) 77; E. Werner, "The Doxology in

Synagogue and Church," 293-99; Price, "Jewish Morning Prayers," 153-68; and Spinks, "The Jewish Liturgical Sources," 171, all favor the Yotzer as the oldest Kedusha. Elbogen, *Jüdische Gottesdienst*, 6f; Baumstark, "Trishagion und Qeduscha," 18-23; and D. Flusser, *Abraham Unser Vater*, 129-52, argued for the Kedusha de Sidra as the oldest. Heinemann (*Prayer in the Talmud*, 232) defended the antiquity of both the Kedusha of the Yotzer and the Amida.

[69] Translation from Charles, *Apocrypha and Pseudepigrapha*, vol. 2, 211.

[70] Translation by N. Forbes in ibid., 442.

[71] Translation from Lake, *The Apostolic Fathers*, 67.

[72] Translation from the RSV.

[73] See Charlesworth, *Pseudepigrapha and Modern Research*, 98 (1 Enoch) and 104 (2 Enoch). Clement of course lived in Rome and wrote not later than A.D. 100 (Lake, *Apostolic Fathers*, 5) and the NT Apocalypse is usually dated to the end of the first century (e.g. P. Feine, J. Behm and W. G. Kummel, *Introduction to the New Testament*, trans. A. J. Mattill, Jr. [Nashville: Abingdon, 1966] 329).

[74] J. T. Milik (*The Books of Enoch* [Oxford:Clarendon, 1976] 91, 96) says the Similitudes are Christian and were composed c. A.D. 270.

[75] See Charlesworth's report on the SNTS seminar at Tübingen which was held in 1977. The sessions which discussed the Enoch literature reached a consensus about the date of the Similitudes: "...no one agreed with Milik's late date for the Parables; these date from the early or later part of the first century A.D." See J. H. Charlesworth, "The SNTS Pseudepigrapha Seminars at Tubingen and Paris on the Books of Enoch," *NTS* 25 (1979) 315-23, esp. 322.

[76] Translation from A. L. Williams, *Tractate Berakoth* (London: Society for Promoting Christian Knowledge, 1921) 9. Hebrew text in M. S. Zuckermandel, *Tosephta* (Trier: Lintz'schen, 1882).

[77] Finkelstein, "La Kedouscha," 2; Liber, "Structure and History of the Tefillah," 341; Werner, "Doxology in Synagogue and Church," 299; but Idelsohn stated that all three responses go back to the second temple (*Jewish Liturgy*, 98).

[78] Werner, "Doxology in Synagogue and Church," 299.

[79] Ps 68:18 is never connected with Isa 6:3.in the early literature so far as we can tell from the citations in J. Allenbach et al., *Biblia Patristica* (Paris: Editions de centre National de la Recherche Scientifique, 1975). The verse is seldom quoted in Christian literature. In rabbinic literature it usually is quoted in reference to God's activity on Sinai (PR 21:7-10, 47:2, Ex R on 20:1), or to decide how many are in God's army (Gen R on 32:16, Ex R on 23:20, Lev R on 24:2, Sifre on Num 6:26, Num R on 2:2) or to point out that in wartime God acts alone but in peacetime he has a large retinue, i.e. 20,000 (Ex R on 22:1, Sifre Num on 12:5).

[80] D. J. Halperin, "Origen and Judaism: Some remarks on Shared Exegetical Traditions" (Paper read at the 1980 session of the SBL and kindly loaned to me). For the modern readings on Pentecost, see A. C. Chiel, *Guide to Sidrot and Haftarot* (New York: KTAV, 1967) 331-35. The modern reading does not have Ps 68:18.

[81] L. Jacobs ("Shavuot," *Encyclopedia Judaica*, vol. 14, cols. 1320f) notes that though connecting Pentecost with the giving of the Law on Sinai (Exodus 19, 20) may have been earlier, the first clear references to this notion are from the third century (Pes 68b). J. C. Rylaarsdam ("Feast of Weeks," *Interpreter's Dictionary of the Bible*, vol. 4, 828) claims that the reading of Exodus 19, 20 on Pentecost began c. A.D. 200.

[82] Kohler, "Ueber die Ursprünge," 443-50, 497.

[83] Kohler, "The Essene Version," 418.

[84] Goodenough, *By Light, Light*, 348.

[85] Ibid., 343.

[86] See above, Chapter V.

[87] Goodenough, *By Light, Light*, 340.

[88] See the note on 8.15.7 in Chapter III, above p. 111.

[89] Goodenough, *By Light, Light*, 336-40.

[90] Grant, *After the New Testament*, 137f, 145-51; and idem, *Theophilus of Antioch Ad Autolycum*, xv-xvii (the text and translation).

[91] The implication of this conclusion for the thesis of Goodenough is significant. Although we have not proven and would not maintain that a mystical Judaism did not exist, the denial that a separate liturgy served this part of Judaism weakens Goodenough's argument that mystical Judaism was an organized cultus with its own prayers.

[92] Baumstark, *Comparative Liturgy*, 12.

[93] See J. Bowman, *Samaritan Documents Relating to their History, Religion and Life* (Pittsburgh: Pickwick, 1977).

[94] See J. MacDonald, *The Theology of the Samaritans* (London: SCM, 1964) 49; J. A. Montgomery, *The Samaritans* (Philadelphia: Winston, 1907) 347; J. Bowman, *The Samaritan Problem*, trans. A. M. Johnson (Pittsburgh: Pickwick, 1975) 157.

[95] See G. F. Moore, *Judaism* (Cambridge: Harvard, 1932) 371. For the rabbinic idea of God, see 357-400.

[96] Ibid., 390-96 (Ps 145:89) for the notion of God's mercy. For life as fleeting, see Aboth 3:1: man comes from a fetid drop and goes to the worms.

[97] Moore, *Judaism*, 401-13. See Ezekiel 1, Hagigah 12b.

[98] The date is from S. Sandmel, *Judaism and Christian Beginnings* (New York: Oxford, 1978) 265.

[99]See the note in Chapter III on 7.36.4.

[100]See the section on propaganda in E. Schürer, *The Literature of the Jewish People* (New York: Schocken, 1972) 262-320. One of the purposes of propaganda was to show that Judaism was as culturally advanced as any other nation or religion. Thus a defense of Sabbath observance by a Pythagorean notion of number in AC 7.36.

[101]Peterson, *Miscellanea*, vol. 1, 413f. See Elbogen, *Jüdische Gottesdienst*, 91.

[102]Peterson wrote: "Es handelt sich in ihr um eine Sammlung von privaten jüdischen Morgen-Gebeten, nicht aber, wie man vorschnell behauptet hat, um Synagogale, also öffentlich Gebete" (*Miscellanea*, 414). This may be polemic against Bousset who had maintained that these were synagogal prayers. See below.

[103]Heinemann, *Prayer in the Talmud*, 190. See S. B. Freehof, "The Origin of the Tahanun," *HUCA* 2 (1925) 339f.

[104]Translation in Hedegard, *Seder*, 128f.

[105]Heinemann, e.g., called them the "statutory Prayers of the synagogue" (*Prayer in the Talmud*, 218).

[106]See Idelsohn, *Jewish Liturgy*, 94.

[107]Bousset, *Nachrichten*, 489.

[108]Birnbaum, *Daily Prayer Book*, 354. For the other Sabbath blessings, see 268 (evening) and 454 (afternoon). Amram's seder has only one Sabbath blessing.

SELECT BIBLIOGRAPHY

Texts and Translations

Arnim, I. *Stoicorum Veterum Fragmenta*. Lipsiae: Teubneri, 1921.

Bell, H. I. and Skeat, T. C. *Fragments of an Unknown Gospel and Other Early Christian Papyri*. London: Trustees, 1935.

Birnbaum, P. *Daily Prayer Book*. New York: Hebrew Publishing, 1977.

Brightman, F. E. *Liturgies, Eastern and Western*. Oxford: Clarendon, 1896.

Bunsen, C.K.J. *Analecta Ante-Nicaena*. Aalen: Scientia, 1968 (first published in 1854).

Charles, R. H. *Apocrypha and Pseudepigrapha of the Old Testament*. Oxford: Clarendon, 1976.

Charlesworth, J. H. *The Odes of Solomon*. Oxford: Clarendon, 1973.

Colson, F. H. *Philo*. LCL; Cambridge: Harvard, 1965-68.

Connolly, R. H. *Didascalia Apostolorum*. Oxford: Clarendon, 1929.

Danby, H. *The Mishnah*. Oxford: University Press, 1933.

Darnell, D. R. "Hellenistic Synagogal Prayers," *Pseudepigrapha of the Old Testament*, volume II. Ed. J. H. Charlesworth. Garden City, NY: Doubleday, in press.

Dix, G. *The Treatise of the Apostolic Tradition*. London: SPCK, 1937.

Easton, B. S. *The Apostolic Tradition of Hippolytus*. New York: MacMillan, 1934.

Epstein, I., ed. *The Babylonian Talmud*. London: Soncino, 1935-52.

Funk, F. X. *Didascalia et Constitutiones Apostolorum*. Paderborn: Schoeningh, 1905.

Grant, R. M. *Theophilus of Antioch Ad Autolycum*. Oxford: Clarendon, 1970.

Hedegard, D. *Seder R. Amram Gaon, Part I*. Motala: Broderna, 1951.

Hennecke, E.; Schneemelcher, W.; and Wilson, R. McL. *New Testament Apocrypha*. Philadelphia: Westminster, 1976.

Kronholm, T. *Seder R. Amram Gaon, Part II*. Lund: Gleerup, 1974.

Lake, K. *The Apostolic Fathers*. LCL; Cambridge: Harvard, 1970.

Lightfoot, J. B. *The Apostolic Fathers*. London: MacMillan, 1889.

Lohse, E. *Die Texte aus Qumran: Hebräisch und Deutsch.* München: Kosel, 1964.

Migne, J.-P. *Patrologiae: Series Graeca.* Paris: Garnier, 1886.

Milik, J. T. *The Books of Enoch.* Oxford: Clarendon, 1976.

Moberg, A. *Book of the Himyarites.* Lund: Gleerup, 1924.

Ralfs, A. *Septuaginta.* Stuttgart: Würthembergische, 1935.

Roberts, A.; Donaldson, J.; and Coxe, A. C., eds. *The Ante-Nicene Fathers.* Grand Rapids, MI: Eerdmans, 1975. Volume 7.

Schechter, S. "Geniza Specimens," *JQR* O.S. 10 (1898) 656.

Thackeray, H. St. J. *Josephus.* LCL; Cambridge: Harvard, 1961.

Williams, A. L. *Tractate Berakoth.* London: SPCK, 1921.

Reference Works, Lexical and Grammatical Aids

Altaner, B. *Patrology,* trans. H. C. Graef. New York: Herder and Herder, 1960.

Brown, F.; Driver, S. R.; and Briggs, C. A. *A Hebrew and English Lexicon.* Oxford: Clarendon, 1968.

Cross, F. L. and Livingstone, E. A., eds. *The Oxford Dictionary of the Christian Church.* London: Oxford, 1974.

Hatch, E. and Redpath, H. A. *A Concordance to the Septuagint and Other Greek Versions of the Old Testament.* Graz, Austria: Akademische, 1954.

Jastrow, M. *A Dictionary of the Targumim, the Talmud Babli and Yerushalmi, and the Midrashic Literature.* New York: Judaica, 1975.

Kittel, G., et al., eds. *Theological Dictionary of the New Testament.* Grand Rapids, MI: Eerdmans, 1974.

Lampe, G.W.H. *A Patristic Greek Lexicon.* Oxford: Clarendon, 1961.

Liddell, H. G.; Scott, R.; Jones, H. S.; and McKenzie, R. *A Greek-English Lexicon.* Oxford: Clarendon, 1968.

Quasten, J. *Patrology.* Utrect-Antwerp: Spectrum, 1950-53.

Reider, J. and Turner, N. *An Index to Aquila.* Leiden: Brill, 1966.

Smyth, H. W. *A Greek Grammar for Colleges.* New York: American, 1920.

Monographs and Articles

Arnold, E. V. *Roman Stoicism.* Cambridge: University Press, 1911.

Audet, J.-P. *La Didache: Instructions des Apotres.* Etudes Biblique; Paris: Gabalda, 1958.

Avenary, H. "Amidah," *Encyclopedia Judaica*, ed. C. Roth and G. Wigoder. Jerusalem: MacMillan, 1971. Vol. 2, cols. 840f.

Barrett, C. K., "Jews and Judaizers in the Epistles of Ignatius," *Jews, Greeks and Christians. Essays in Honor of William David Davies*, ed. R. Hammerton-Kelly and R. Scroggs. Leiden: Brill, 1976, pp. 220-44.

Baumstark, A. and Botte, B. *Comparative Liturgy*, trans. F. L. Cross. Westminster, MD: Newman, 1958.

Baumstark, A. "Trishagion und Qeduscha," *Jahrbuch für Liturgiewissenschaft* 3 (1923) 18-32.

________. "Zur Herkunft der monotheistischen Bekenntnisformeln im Koran," *Oriens Christianus* 37 (1953) 6-22.

Bickermann, E. J. "The Civic Prayer for Jerusalem," *HTR* 55 (1962) 163-85.

Botte, B. "Liturgie chrétienne et liturgie juive," *Cahier Sioniens* 3 (1949) 215-23.

Brown, M. P. *The Authentic Writings of Ignatius*. Durham, NC: Duke, 1963.

Bousset, W. "Eine jüdische Gebetssammlung im siebenten Buch der apostolischen Konstitutionen," *Nachrichten von der Königlichen Gesellschaft der Wissenschaften zu Göttingen: Philologisch-historische Klasse* (1915) 438-85.

Bouyer, L. *Eucharistie*. Tournai, Belgium: Desclée, 1966. English trans. E. U. Quinn. Notre Dame: Notre Dame, 1968.

Burkitt, F. C. "The Didascalia," *JTS* 31 (1930) 258-65.

Charlesworth, J. H. "Christian and Jewish Self-Definition in Light of the Christian Additions to the Apocryphal Writings," *Judaism from the Maccabees to the Mid-Third Century*, ed. E. P. Sanders and A. I. Baumgarten. Philadelphia: Fortress, 1980.

________. *The Pseudepigrapha and Modern Research*. Missoula, MT: Scholars Press, 1976.

Connolly, R. H. *The So-Called Egyptian Church Order and Derived Documents*. Cambridge: University Press, 1916.

Cresswell, R. H. *The Liturgy of the Eighth Book of the Apostolic Constitutions*. London: SPCK, 1906.

Daniélou, J. *Theology of Jewish Christianity*, trans. J. A. Baker. London: Longman and Todd, 1964.

Davies, W. D. *The Setting of the Sermon on the Mount*. Cambridge: University Press, 1966.

Dugmore, C. W. *The Influence of the Synagogue upon the Divine Office*. London: Humphrey Milford, 1944.

Elbogen, I. *Der jüdische Gottesdienst in seiner geschichtlichen Entwicklung*. Frankfurt: Kauffmann, 1931.

Finkelstein, L. "The Development of the Amidah," *REJ* N.S. 16 (1925/26) 1-43, 127-70.

________. "La Kedouscha et les Benedictions du Schema," *REJ* 93 (1932) 1-26.

Funk, F. X. *Apostolischen Konstitutionen*. Frankfurt: Minerva, 1970.

Galtier, P. "La date de la Didascalie des Apôtres," *Aux Origines du Sacrement de Penitence*. Rome: Universitatis Gregorianae, 1951.

Gavin, F. *The Jewish Antecedents of the Christian Sacraments*. New York: KTAV, 1969.

Goodenough, E. R. *By Light, Light*. New Haven: Yale, 1935.

Grant, F. C. "The Modern Study of the Jewish Liturgy," *ZAW* 65 (1953) 59-77.

Grant, R. M. *After the New Testament*. Philadelphia: Fortress, 1967.

________. "Early Antiochene Anaphora," *Anglican Theological Review* 30 (1948) 91-94.

Gray, G. B. *The Forms of Hebrew Poetry*. London: Hodder and Stoughton, 1915.

Hardy, E. R. "Kedusha and Sanctus," *Studia Liturgica* 6 (1969) 183-88.

Harnack, A. *Geschichte Altchristliche Literature*. Leipzig: Hinrichs, 1904.

Heinemann, J. *Prayer in the Talmud*, trans. R. S. Sarason. Berlin: Gruyter, 1977.

Hirsch, E. G. "Shemoneh Esreh," *Jewish Encyclopedia*, ed. I. Singer. New York: Funk and Wagnals, 1903. Vol. 11, p. 276.

Hoffman, L. A. *The Canonization of the Synagogue Service*. Notre Dame: University of Notre Dame, 1979.

Hulen, A. M. "The Dialogues with the Jews as Sources for the Early Jewish Argument Against Christianity," *JBL* 51 (1932) 58-70.

Idlesohn, A. Z. *Jewish Liturgy*. New York: Henry Holt, 1932.

Kohler, K. "Didascalia," *Jewish Encyclopedia*, ed. I. Singer. New York: Funk and Wagnals, 1903. Vol. 4, pp. 592-94.

________. "The Essene Version of the Seven Benedictions as Preserved in the vii Book of the Apostolic Constitutions," *HUCA* 1 (1924) 410-25.

________. "Essenes," *Jewish Encyclopedia*, ed. I. Singer. New York: Funk and Wagnals, 1903. Vol. 5, pp. 224f.

________. *The Origins of the Synagogue and the Church*. New York: MacMillan, 1927.

Kohler, K. "Ueber die Ursprünge und Grundformen der synagogalen Liturgie," *MGWJ* 37 (1893) 441-51, 489-97.

Kraeling, C. H. "The Jewish Community at Antioch," *JBL* 51 (1932) 130-60.

Kraft, R. A. *Barnabas and the Didache*. Toronto: Nelson, 1965.

Krauss, S. "Antioche," *REJ* 45 (1902) 26-49.

Leclercq, H. "Constitutions Apostoliques," *Dictionaire D'Archeologie Chrêtienne et De Liturgie*, ed. F. Cabrol and H. Leclercq. Paris: Letouzey, 1914. T. 3, pt. 2, cols. 2735f.

Levi, I. "Lex Dix-Huits Bénédictions et les Psaumes de Solomon," *REJ* 32 (1896) 161-78.

Liber, M. "Structure and History of the Tefillah," *JQR* N.S. 40 (1959) 331-57.

Lieberman, S. *Greek in Jewish Palestine*. New York: Jewish Theological Seminary, 1942.

Lietzman, H. *The Founding of the Church Universal*, trans. B. L. Woolf. New York: Scribner's, 1938.

________. *Mass and the Lord's Supper*, trans. D.H.G. Reeve. Leiden: Brill, 1953.

Ligier, L. "The Origins of the Eucharistic Prayer: From the Last Supper to the Eucharist," *Studia Liturgica* 9 (1973) 161-85.

Loeb, I. "Les dix-huit Bénédictions," *REJ* 19 (1889) 17-40.

Lütkemann, L. and Ralfs, A. "Hexaplarische Randnoten zu Isaias 1-16," *Nachrichten der Königlichen Gesellschaft der Wissenschaften zu Göttingen. Philologisch-historische Klasse* (1915) 259-61.

MacLean, A. J. *The Ancient Church Orders*. Cambridge: University Press, 1910.

Marmorstein, A. "The Oldest Form of the Eighteen Benedictions," *JQR* N.S. 34 (1943) 137-59.

Martin, R. A. *Syntactical Evidence of Semitic Sources in Greek Documents*. SCS 3. Missoula, MT: University of Montana, 1974.

Maxwell, W. D. *An Outline of Christian Worship*. Oxford/London: Milford, 1936.

Meeks, W. A. and Wilken, R. L. *Jews and Christians in Antioch in the First Four Centuries of the Common Era*. Missoula, MT: Scholars Press, 1978.

Milgrom, A. E. *Jewish Worship*. Philadelphia: Jewish Publication Society of America, 1971.

Moore, G. F. *Judaism in the First Centuries of the Christian Era, the Age of the Tannaim*. Cambridge: Harvard, 1946.

Murray, R. *Symbols of Church and Kingdom. A Study in Early Syriac Tradition*. Cambridge: University Press, 1975.

Neusner, J. *Aphrahat and Judaism*. Leiden: Brill, 1971.

Oesterley, W.O.E. *The Jewish Background of the Christian Liturgy*. Oxford: Clarendon, 1925.

O'Leary, L. *The Apostolical Constitutions*. London: SPCK, 1906.

Parkes, J. *The Conflict of the Church and the Synagogue*. New York: Temple, 1969.

Perles, F. "Notes Critique sur Le Text de la Liturgie Juive," *REJ* 80 (1925) 101f.

Peterson, E. "Henoch im jüdischen Gebet und in judischer Kunst," *Miscellanea Liturgica in Honorem L. C. Mohlberg*. Roma: Liturgiche, 1948. Vol. 1, pp. 413-17.

Price, C. P. "Jewish Morning Prayers and Early Christian Anaphoras," *Anglican Theological Review* 43 (1961) 153-68.

Probst, F. *Liturgie der drei ersten christliche Jahrhunderte*. Darmstadt: Wissenschaftliche, 1968; first printed, 1870.

Rabinowitz, L. I. "Seliḥot," *Encyclopedia Judaica*, ed. C. Roth and G. Wigoder. Jerusalem: MacMillan, 1971. Vol. 14, cols. 1133f.

Rankin, O. S. "The Extent of the Influence of the Synagogue Service upon Christian Worship," *JJS* 1 (1948) 27-32.

Richardson, C. C. "The Date and Setting of the Apostolic Tradition of Hippolytus," *Anglican Theological Review* 30 (1948) 38-44.

Rostovtzeff, M. *Dura-Europos and its Art*. Oxford: Clarendon, 1938.

Sandmel, S. *Judaism and Christian Beginnings*. New York: Oxford, 1978.

Schirmann, J. "Hebrew Liturgical Poetry and Christian Hymnology," *JQR* 44 (1953/54) 130-41.

Schürer, E. *History of the Jewish People*. Edinburgh: Clark, 1924.

Shepherd, M. H., Jr. "The Occasion of the Initial Break Between Judaism and Christianity," *Harry Austryn Wolfson Jubilee Volume*. Jerusalem: American Academy for Jewish Research, 1965.

Simon, M. *Verus Israel*. Paris: Boccard, 1948.

Skutsch, F. "Ein neuer Zeuge der altchristlichen Liturgie," *Archiv für Religionswissenschaft* 13 (1910) 291-305.

Spanier, A. "Die erst Benedicktion des Achtzehngebetes," *MGWJ* 81 (1937) 71-76.

Spinks, B. D. "The Jewish Liturgical Sources for the Sanctus," *The Heythrop Journal* 21 (1980) 168-79.

Srawley, J. H. *The Early History of the Liturgy*. Cambridge: University Press, 1947.

Turner, C. H. "A Fragment of an Unknown Latin Version of the Apostolic Constitutions," *JTS* 13 (1911/12) 492-510.

________. "A Primitive Edition of the Apostolic Constitutions and Canons," *JTS* 15 (1913/14) 53-65.

________. "Notes on the Apostolic Constitutions. The Compiler an Arian," *JTS* 16 (1914/15) 54-61.

________. "Notes on the Apostolic Constitutions," *JTS* 31 (1929/30) 128-41.

Volkes, F. E. "The Didache-Still Debated," *The Church Quarterly* 3 (1979) 57-62.

Warren, F. E. *The Liturgy and Ritual of the Ante-Nicene Church.* London: SPCK, 1912.

Werner, E. "The Doxology in Synagogue and Church, a Liturgico-Musical Study," *HUCA* 19 (1945/46) 276-328.

________. *The Sacred Bridge*. London: Dobson, 1959.

Wendland, P. "Zwei angeblich christliche liturgische Gebete," *Nachrichten der Königlichen Gesellschaft zu Göttingen. Philologisch-historische Klasse* (1910) 330-34.

Wiles, M. "The Old Testament in Controversy with the Jews," *Scottish Journal of Theology* 8 (1955) 113-26.

Wilken, R. L. "Insignissima Religio, Certe Licita? Christianity and Judaism in the Fourth and Fifth Centuries," *The Impact of the Church Upon Its Culture*, ed. J. C. Brauer. Chicago: University of Chicago Press, 1968.

________. *Judaism and the Early Christian Mind.* New Haven: Yale University Press, 1971.

________. "Melito, the Jewish Community at Sardis, and the Sacrifice of Isaac," *Theological Studies* 37 (1976) 53-69.

Williams, A. L. *Adversus Judaeos*. Cambridge: University Press, 1935.

Wolfson, H. A. *Philo*. Cambridge: Harvard, 1948.

Zeller, E. *Stoics, Epicureans and Sceptics*, trans. O. J. Reichel. New York: Russel, 1962.